Core Cultural Concepts is the first series on key concepts in cultural studies to be used for cultural studies students. It aims to provide readers with concise, accessible critical guides to the central concepts in the study of culture.

Class

Andrew Milner

SAGE Publications
London • Thousand Oaks • New Delhi

First published 1999

SAGE Publications Ltd
6 Bonhill Street
London EC2A 4PU

SAGE Publications Inc
2455 Teller Road
Thousand Oaks, California 91320

SAGE Publications India Pvt Ltd
32, M-Block Market
Greater Kailash – I
New Delhi 110 048

British Library Cataloguing in Publication data

A catalogue record for this book is available from
the British Library.

ISBN 0 7619-5244-6
ISBN 0 7619-5245-4 (pbk)

Library of Congress catalog card number 99–70888

Typeset by Photoprint, Torquay, Devon
Printed in Great Britain by Biddles Ltd, Guildford, Surrey

For David, James and Robert,
Ciarán and Liam

Contents

Acknowledgements

Once again, I am indebted to my partner, Verity Burgmann, and to our three sons, David, James and Robert, for emotional and personal support. I am indebted to friends and colleagues in the Centre for Comparative Literature and Cultural Studies and in the Department of Anthropology and Sociology at Monash University, and in the Centre for Research in Philosophy and Literature at Warwick University, as also to staff at both the Monash University Library and the Warwick University Library. Comparisons are always invidious, I know, but special thanks are due to Chris Chamberlain, Amanda Macdonald, David Roberts, Gail Ward and Chris Worth at Monash, Andrew Benjamin, Fred Inglis and Heather Jones at Warwick. I am grateful to Chris Rojek and Robert Rojek for the patience with which they helped along various stages of the project. For making our time at Warwick so very pleasant thanks are due to my father, John Milner, and to Ann Dudgeon, Sheila Jones, Andrew Keogh, Richard Milner, Joyce and Phil Morton, Clive Dixon and Kathy Prendiville. None of these should be held in any way responsible for the argument that follows. Acknowledgement is also due to Faber and Faber for permission to quote from T.S. Eliot's 'Gerontion', as published in *The Complete Poems and Plays of T.S. Eliot*, Faber and Faber, London, 1969, p.38.

1

The Strange Death of Class

The English word 'class' derives from the Latin *classis*. At its most obvious and uncontroversial, the term is used to refer to a particular group or category identifiable within a system of classification. Very commonly, of course, it refers to that special system of classification applied by schools to their students. Such usages have been present in the English language since the seventeenth century (Williams, 1976, p. 51). In a more fully sociological sense, however, the word can also be used to denote a social group, conceived as located within a hierarchical order of unequal such groups, the identity and membership of which is primarily determined by 'economic' considerations such as occupation, income and wealth. Class in this sense of the term – 'social class' – is a much more recent usage, dating only from the time of the Industrial Revolution in the late eighteenth and early nineteenth centuries. The novelty in the later usage consists, not so much in the recognition of the simple fact of social inequality, for this had long been designated by other, older terms – rank and order, estate and degree – as in the new sense of its social constructedness. As Raymond Williams explains:

> The essential history of the introduction of **class** . . . relates to the increasing consciousness that social position is made rather than

> merely inherited. All the older words . . . belong to a society in which
> position was determined by birth . . . What was changing conscious-
> ness was . . . the new sense of a . . . particular *social system*[1] which
> actually created social divisions, including new kinds of division.
> (Williams, 1976, p. 52)

The point should be obvious: whilst such supposedly inherited
distinctions as those between lord and peasant, master and slave,
were in principle representable and often actually represented
as in some sense 'natural', the acquisition of wealth or income
through the marketplace is almost impossible to imagine thus.

This new sense of the mutability of social structures, on the
one hand, and of the capacity for mobility of individuals within
these structures, on the other, has constituted an important part
of what it meant to be 'conscious' of 'class' over the last two
centuries. Such class consciousness has been widespread
throughout the so-called 'advanced capitalist' societies of
Europe, North America, East Asia and Australasia: for many
liberals, it has bespoken conservatism's uncompromising awareness of its own right to privilege; for many socialists, working-
class consciousness has been precisely what was needed to
begin the movement toward a truly 'classless' society. Class
consciousness of one kind or another also made for intellectual
debate and discussion about the social meaning of class, a
debate which has tended to centre on three relatively distinct
intellectual formations: Marxism, sociology and, more recently,
Cultural Studies. The sociologist, Anthony Giddens, once distinguished four different levels of 'class consciousness', running
from mere 'class awareness' (which on his account isn't strictly
a form of consciousness at all) through 'class identity' and
'conflict consciousness' to 'revolutionary class consciousness',
in the fully Marxist sense of the term (Giddens, 1981, pp. 111–
113). For sociology, class consciousness is an object of study, a
phenomenon present in or absent from the individuals or groups
it surveys. The discipline makes no claims of its own to any
status as itself a form of such consciousness. Marxism, by contrast, often asserted exactly this claim: that it was working-class
consciousness 'raised' to the level of theory. But the assertion
became progressively less plausible as the twentieth century

wore on, so much so that 'late Marxism' (Jameson, 1990) often preferred to imagine itself as an alternative 'critical' sociology, the dark shadow of the sociological mainstream it dismissed as 'bourgeois' or 'traditional' (Horkheimer, 1972, p. 244). Cultural Studies, however, was an altogether different matter. For, if ever there was an academic discipline the intellectual origins of which were marked by class consciousness, then it was surely Cultural Studies.

Class and the Origins of Cultural Studies

What now goes under the rubric of Cultural Studies began life, during the late 1950s and early 1960s, as an immanent critique of the older discipline of English Literature. English Studies then still occupied a very peculiar place in British life, as the primary location of a public intellectual discourse about the prior history, current condition and future prospects for the moral development of English society as a whole.[2] The most influential proponents of this version of the discipline had been F.R. Leavis, Q.D. Leavis and their 'Leavisite' collaborators around the journal *Scrutiny*. For the Leavisites, English Literature was as much about 'culture' as 'literature' in any narrow technical sense of the term. In the late 1940s, F.R. Leavis had sketched out the prospectus for an ideal university 'English School', arguing for the central cultural significance of what he termed the 'literary mind' (Leavis, 1948, p. 55). In this account, the true values of a national culture were seen as sustained by and through its literary language: 'By "culture"', he argued, 'I mean the use of such a language' (Leavis, 1948, p. 145). The proper object of literary studies was thus to develop, not so much a particular kind of technical academic knowledge, as a particular kind of person able to use a particular kind of language. 'In any period', he wrote, 'it is upon a very small minority that the discerning appreciation of art and literature depends.' This minority

> constitute the consciousness of the race (or a branch of it) at a given time. For such capacity does not belong merely to an aesthetic realm: it implies responsiveness to theory as well as to art, to science

and philosophy in so far as these may affect the sense of the human situation and the nature of life. (Leavis, 1948, pp. 143–144)

In short, Leavis hoped to create a discipline that would assess the cultural value of whole communities and whole civilizations. Such grand claims led by an almost inescapable logic to a view of the English School as 'a centre of consciousness (and conscience) for our civilization' (Leavis, 1962, p. 30).

The occasion for this latter remark is interesting: that of a very public controversy between Leavis and the novelist, C.P. Snow. In his 1959 Rede Lecture, Snow had argued for the existence of two cultures, the one 'scientific', the other 'literary', and for these to be brought into a more creative interaction with each other. Leavis published his initial reply to Snow in 1962, but returned to the theme 10 years later in a second essay, 'Luddites? or There is Only One Culture'. Here, he argued that neither of Snow's two 'cultures' properly deserved the term: 'there is only *one* culture', he wrote; 'to talk of two . . . is to use an essential term with obviously disqualifying irresponsibility' (Leavis, 1972, p. 88). For Leavis, culture was neither literary, in the sense that Snow had used the term, nor scientific. Rather, it was 'knowledge of basic human need that is transmitted by . . . "cultural tradition" ' (Leavis, 1972, p. 92) and such knowledge is the collaborative creation of a whole community, a 'third realm' neither private nor public. Thus understood, culture is necessarily singular: 'We have no other; there is only one, and there can be no substitute. Those who talk of two and of joining them would present us impressively with the sum of two nothings'. That sum, he elaborated, 'is the void the modern world tackles with drugs, sex and alcohol' (Leavis, 1972, p. 93). Neither Leavis's cultural pessimism nor his stress on the singularity and internal unity of culture was in itself at all idiosyncratic. Rather, they derived from the central history of the concept of 'culture', as it had proceeded from Romanticism onwards. Deliberately defined in opposition to merely mechanical 'civilization', culture had almost invariably been understood as unitary in character and often as positively organic. Ironically, it would require the creation of an academic discipline specifically devoted to the study of 'culture' to call into question this unitary sense of the term's meaning.

John Stratton and Ien Ang have recently observed that the 'mythic history' of British Cultural Studies proceeds by way of three founding fathers, 'Richard Hoggart, Raymond Williams and, though himself young enough to be a son, Stuart Hall' (Stratton and Ang, 1996, p. 368). For Stratton and Ang such histories remain suspect as instances of the '(white) Great Man (*sic*) theory of (colonial, patriarchal) history'. I confess to an enduring susceptibility to histories, even mythic ones, unpostmodern though they undoubtedly are. But my history would be significantly different from the one Stratton and Ang define in order to disown. A more plausible, albeit less economical, genealogy would begin with the Leavises, proceed to Williams and Hoggart, but also to the historian, E.P. Thompson, and move on to Hall only at the beginning of episode three. Written thus, the history of British Cultural Studies commences, not with Williams, but rather with the Leavises' appalled fascination with 'mass civilization' and the 'herd instinct', especially as it registered in Q.D. Leavis's *Fiction and the Reading Public* (Leavis, 1948, pp. 141–171; Leavis, 1979, p. 151). Thompson, Williams and Hoggart had all trained as undergraduates in English Literature, Thompson and Williams at Leavis's own university, Cambridge, Hoggart at Leeds. All three were led from a recognition of the significance of class cultures towards a practical 'deconstruction' of the unitary concept of culture deployed in Leavisite English: for Hoggart, the values and practices of working-class life had created a 'class culture' much richer than the 'kind of classless culture' marketed by the mass media (Hoggart, 1958, p. 343); for Williams, 'working-class culture' was itself a 'remarkable creative achievement' (Williams, 1963, p. 313); for Thompson, the culture of the early labour movement was both 'heroic' and distinguished by its 'intelligence and moral passion' (Thompson, 1963, p. 832). Borrowing Giddens's terms, we could say that Hoggart had described and endorsed a form of working-class 'identity', Williams a form of working-class 'conflict consciousness', and Thompson 'revolutionary class consciousness' itself.[3] All three were a world away from the Leavises' scarcely concealed contempt for mass civilization.

Hitherto, English Literature had focused its attention on one particular kind of culture, 'high' literature, and had mis-represented it as the inner truth of all culture. Henceforth, Cultural Studies would be concerned, in principle at least, with all kinds of culture. We shall examine Hoggart, Williams and Thompson for their respective notions of class in Chapter 4 below. For the moment, however, let us note only the general shape of their achievement. In *Culture and Society*, Williams had identified four different kinds of meaning attaching to the word 'culture', those referring to: an individual habit of mind; the intellectual development of a whole society; the arts; and the whole way of life of a social group (Williams, 1963, p. 16). When Williams, Hoggart and Thompson first broached the subject matter of what would eventually become Cultural Studies, they began in effect to shift attention from the third to the fourth sense of the term, in short, from culture as the term was commonly used in the humanities to culture as in the social sciences. Where English Literature had defined literature as a timeless, 'aesthetic' category, Cultural Studies would come to see cultural value as socially constructed. From its inception, then, the new discipline sought to explain the interplay of cultural texts, cultural identity and social inequality. And much more than is now commonly recognized, all of this revolved around the central question of social class.

Identity Politics and Cultural Studies

When Cultural Studies first began to institutionalize itself as an academic discipline, it still retained much of the initial focus on class. This was particularly evident, for example, in the early work of the Centre for Contemporary Cultural Studies at Birmingham University, especially in the first years of Stuart Hall's Directorship. If much of the Centre's interest fell on youth cultures, then these were nonetheless typically imagined as class-specific rather than cross-class formations. The paradigmatic

instance is provided by the essays collected in *Resista
through Rituals* (Hall and Jefferson, 1976). The interest in the
cultural politics of class became progressively 'decentred', however: substantively, by an increasing preoccupation with the
cultural effects of other kinds of cultural difference – gender,
race, ethnicity, sexuality; theoretically, by the growing influence
of post-structuralism and postmodernism. The substantive issue
was itself the highly politicized effect of highly political movements, the 'new social movements' as Alain Touraine dubbed
them (Touraine, 1981, pp. 9–10). A self-consciously politicized
discipline, Cultural Studies would always have been predisposed to engage with the new politics of a new movement. But
the questions these movements sought to address were also
concerned precisely with differences in cultural identity, such as
seemed peculiarly appropriate to Cultural Studies. Here, then,
was a new research agenda for a new discipline, holding out the
prospect of almost indefinite extension. The discipline's initial
response was to 'add on' the differences – of gender and race
in particular – to the existing discourse about class. Witness,
for example, the Birmingham Centre's first encounters with
feminism (Women's Studies Group, 1978). Theoretically, such
addition produced Marxist-feminism (cf. Barrett, 1988), practically, a sense that new social movement radicalism could and
should be combined with older forms of working-class radicalism. With hindsight, however, this moment of simultaneous
engagement with class and gender, class and race, appears both
brief in duration and transitional in character. The collapse of
the 1974–79 Labour Government, the defeat of the 1984–85
miners' strike, the sheer scale of Thatcherism's triumph over the
labour movement, all seemed to attest to the necessity for both
a cultural theory and a practical politics that would go beyond
class.

From popular feminist movies to successful gay newspapers,
there is no doubting the very real achievement of the new social
movements, certainly in the United States and in Australia, but
even to some extent in Britain. They have effected a quite
unprecedented 'decentring' of traditional (white, straight, male,
middle-class) cultural authority. In practice, however, this has

been the direct effect of a combination of the hopes and aspirations of the more financially 'empowered' segments of the new social movements with the logics of the market and the commodity aesthetics they enjoin. The new subcultures of difference were typically initiated by political movements of an often quasi-socialistic character, but sustained only by an effective monetary demand for commodifiable counter-cultural texts. It seems likely, then, that identity politics will eventually be better understood as an effect of, rather than an alternative to, postmodern late capitalism. The resultant redistributions of cultural advantage have unsurprisingly turned out to be less than equitable: in the market for gay lifestyles, black consciousness or sisterhood, as in other markets, one only gets what one pays for. In the words of a prominent British gay activist: 'Consumerism is the new gay zeitgeist . . . Too bad if you're poor. If you haven't got the lifestyle, you aren't a proper gay . . . The gay community is being hijacked by the gay market' (Tatchell, 1996, p. 13). There is no gainsaying either the general accuracy of this observation nor the sense of outrage it seeks to express. But hijacking cannot be the right word for a process that has been almost entirely endogenous to the new social movements themselves. For most of their short histories, these movements have contained an overwhelming preponderance of intellectually trained personnel amongst their activists. Typically, they have been organized, not by some random sample of those they claim to represent, but by professional intellectuals whose class position has in fact been systematically unrepresentative. These are 'middle-class' movements, as I will provisionally but clumsily designate them (we shall have cause to question the utility of the term in later chapters). It is barely surprising that they should have become increasingly attracted to individualist and consumerist solutions to discrimination, as distinct from more collective forms of structural change.

These political interests have registered very forcefully, both in Cultural Studies itself and in cultural theory more generally, primarily by way of the turn toward post-structuralism and postmodernism. I use the term post-structuralism here as a kind of theoretical shorthand to denote the combination of Derridean deconstruction, Foucauldian genealogy and Lacanian psycho-analysis which gained intellectual currency throughout much of the Anglophone world during the late 1970s and early 1980s, and which in many respects still continues to 'frame' theoretical debate across the humanities. The term 'postmodernism' is also intended as shorthand, to denote the predominant motifs in post-Second World War, 'late capitalist' culture, especially insofar as these have taken on a distinctly pluralist, populist and televisual character.[4] When cultural theory embraced the new postmodern pluralism, and its characteristic play of 'difference', it opened up a theoretical space within which some at least of the culturally marginalized could assert their own cultural specificities. The results have become familiar, in Cultural Studies and in many of the more traditional humanities disciplines: radical feminism, queer theory, postcolonial theory, black studies, and so on. But in theory, as in practice, some differences are more equal than others. As Stefan Collini has noted, in a discussion directly aimed at Cultural Studies: 'In the frequently incanted quartet of race, class, gender and sexual orientation, there is no doubt that class has been the least fashionable . . . despite the fact that all the evidence suggests that class remains the single most powerful determinant of life-chances' (Collini, 1994, p. 3). In theory, as in practice, too bad if you're poor. With the benefit of hindsight, it has become increasingly clear that the 'silent revolution' of the new social movements (Inglehart, 1977) and the 'postmodern turn' in cultural theory have proven surprisingly compatible with the dominant neo-liberal and utilitarian politico-economic logics of the last two decades of the century. As Judith Williamson once remarked, of the ways in which capitalist mass marketing itself constructs consumption as difference: 'the ideology of difference is not, in fact, different from the ideologies that imprison us all' (Williamson, 1986, p. 116).

Theory and Evidence

The most straightforward explanation for this growing lack of theoretical interest in class difference would be that class has ceased to be of central empirical significance to our culture. This view has been argued by such avowedly 'postmodern' cultural theorists as Jean-François Lyotard and Jean Baudrillard, with much subsequent effect in and on Cultural Studies. For Lyotard, 'the social foundation of the principle of division', that is, 'class struggle', has 'blurred to the point of losing all . . . radicality' (Lyotard, 1984, p. 13). For Baudrillard, the 'hyperreality' of contemporary media society buries the social, so that the '*social . . . does not exist anymore*'. And with the social, so too go socialism, social class and the proletariat:

> The history of the social will never have had time to lead to revolution: it will have been outstripped by signs of the social and of revolution . . . the concept of class will have dissolved . . . into some parodic, extended double, like 'the mass of workers' or simply into a retrospective simulation of the proletariat. (Baudrillard, 1983, pp. 82, 85–86)

Analogously postmodern arguments have also surfaced in recent sociological theory. Zygmunt Bauman has concluded that the entire conceptual repertoire of mainstream sociology, class included, seems devoted 'to the study and the service of unfreedom' and hence irreparably 'modern' in character. Comparing the concepts of social class and 'social movement', he argues for the theoretical superiority of the latter, on the grounds that 'it is fully its own creation; it generates its own subject; it constitutes itself into a social agent' (Bauman, 1992, pp. 54–55). Agnes Heller and Ferenc Fehér insist that 'today's politics . . . cannot be understood in modernist-class categories' (Heller and Fehér, 1988, p. 3). Giddens himself, once a leading exponent of sociological 'class analysis', now Director of the London School of Economics (and, in effect, the Vice-Chancellor for the Social Sciences), appears to believe that class is a less significant 'marker[s] of social differentiation' than '[L]ifestyle and taste' (Giddens, 1994, p. 143). These are all social theorists in the grand fashion, rather than empirical sociologists. But the argument finds some resonance even amongst the more empirically minded: Ray Pahl, for example, has described the concept of class as 'ceasing to do any useful work'; Holton and Turner regard it as tied to the 'tired comparison between conflict and consensus' (Pahl, 1989, p. 710; Holton and Turner, 1994, p. 803).

At least at the levels of class awareness, class identity and class consciousness, all this is simply unsupported by evidence. Quite the contrary, the class character of British culture seems as undeniable as ever. Marshall, Newby, Rose and Vogler's nationwide survey of 1,770 respondents, conducted during 1984, that is, a good five years into Thatcherism, found that well over 90 per cent of their sample were able to place themselves as either 'working class' or 'middle class'; that almost 73 per cent felt class to be 'an inevitable feature of modern society'; and that conflict consciousness was widespread amongst manual working-class voters (Marshall et al., 1988, pp. 143, 247–248). Their conclusions are very clear:

> Social class is to the fore among conceptions of collective identity. It is still the case that important differences in shared beliefs and values are structured more obviously by class than by other sources of social cleavage . . . Social class still structures voting intentions . . . and does so no less today than in the recent past . . . there has been no secular decline in the tendency for collective identities and collective action to develop on a class basis. (Marshall et al., 1988, pp. 267–268)

Nor is there anything especially unusual about Britain in this respect. Comparing survey data from three different countries in three different continents, the American sociologist, Erik Olin Wright, found clear evidence for an 'overall linkage between class location and class consciousness', with Sweden the most ideologically polarized, Japan the least and the United States somewhere in between (Wright, 1997, pp. 417, 428). A comparable study of a fourth country in a fourth continent detected similar patterns of ideological polarization between the same class locations, albeit with significantly more 'pro-capitalist' responses right across the sample (Emmison, 1991, p. 255).[5]

There are differences in the levels of cultural salience that attach to social class in different national cultures: class consciousness appears unusually high in Britain and Sweden, for example, unusually low in Australia and Japan. But the available sociological evidence clearly shows class position to be a primary determinant of cultural behaviour, attitudes and life-style, irrespective of this general level of 'awareness' of class. Indeed, empirical sociological research is so invariant in its findings on this subject as to call into question the further point of continued speculation about the supposed 'death of class'. As Clegg and Emmison succinctly observe, being 'for' or 'against' class 'is tantamount to being for or against the atmosphere' (Clegg and Emmison, 1991, p. 37). In general, however, recent theoretical debates have been almost entirely immune to empiri-cal considerations of this kind. Indeed, the single most remark-able aspect of the postmodern reaction against class has been its aggressively 'theoreticist' character: in short, and not to put too fine a point on it, the decentring of class amongst cultural and social theorists has been most readily effected precisely to the degree that their discussions have been 'data-free', to bor-row John Goldthorpe's telling phrase (Goldthorpe, 1990, p. 431). Unusually amongst social theorists, Scott Lash and Roy Boyne have recognized the 'excessive' quality of this postmodernist antipathy to class. The neglect of class stratification, they con-clude, seems both 'politically reprehensible in times of increased unemployment and social inequality, and . . . intellectually unjustifiable in the absence of an empirically informed theoretical demonstration that the working classes do not still remain a highly important force for social change' (Lash, 1990, p. 116).[6] For Goldthorpe, as for many other empirical sociologists, this intellectual indefensibility brings the matter to an end: free from entanglement with 'philosophy of history' or 'critical theory', sociological class analysis remains happily secure in its 'promis-ing future' (Goldthorpe and Marshall, 1992, p. 393). But neither Cultural Studies nor grand social theory seem at all likely to disappear from the academic curriculum, nor would it be altogether desirable for either so to do: empirical sociology needs at least some 'theory', if only as a source of testable hypotheses. For those who would persist with either or both, the precise shape of this data-freedom and of the theoretical concepts that inform it still needs to be understood. This, then, is our immediate problem: to explore the theoretical meaning and significance of the concept of class for each of our three major intellectual formations, by turn: Marxism, sociology and Cultural Studies.

Notes

1 Italics used for emphasis within quotations are always as in the original.

2 This is to repeat something of Anderson's argument that Britain alone of the major European countries produced neither a classical sociology nor an indigenous national Marxism. He concludes that: 'The displaced home of the totality was . . . literary criticism . . . Driven out of any obvious habitats, the notion found refuge in the least expected of studies' (Anderson, 1992, pp. 96–97). Totalizing thought is now much less fashionable than when this essay was written. But the empirical power of the observation still holds: a role normally taken by sociology or by Marxism had in England been performed by English Studies.

3 Given their subsequent political and intellectual development, it might seem strange to describe Williams and Thompson thus: by the late 1970s, the terms would need to be reversed. But in the early 1960s it was still Thompson who was the revolutionary.

4 Felperin identifies two main versions of post-structuralism, the 'textualist' and the 'contextualist', which he associates respectively with Derrida and Foucault (Felperin, 1985, pp. 71–72). Easthope points to two roughly parallel currents within British post-structuralism (Easthope, 1988, p. 153). Hawthorn describes the term postmodernism as referring variously to the non-realist and non-traditional 'high' art of the post-Second World War period; to art which radically accentuates certain key modernist characteristics; and to aspects of a more generally 'late capitalist' culture (Hawthorn, 1992, p. 110). I am concerned here mainly with the first and third usages. Much of the substance of the debate about late capitalist culture concerns both its 'aesthetic populism' and its distinctly televisual qualities (Jameson, 1991, pp. 2, 76).

5 Wright's data tested for the distribution of 'procapitalist' or 'proworker' attitudes across 12 different 'class locations'. They were drawn from random samples of 1,498 respondents across the United States, 1,145 respondents across Sweden and 823 respondents in the Tokyo region surveyed between 1980 and 1987 (Wright, 1997, p. 75). The Australian data were drawn from a nationwide sample of 1,195 respondents surveyed during 1986. By international standards, class appeared unusually insignificant as a basis for subjective cultural identity in Australia: only amongst capitalists, expert managers and experts did more than half of the respondents even think of themselves as belonging to a social class (the percentages were 100, 52 and 52 respectively) (Emmison, 1991, p. 264). But if 'social class' *per se* seemed relatively insignificant, 'occupation' was nonetheless the single most important source of social identity, more important than nationality, gender, religion or ethnicity (Emmison and Western, 1991, p. 290). Occupation may not be entirely identical to class, but it is normally

considered to be at the core of class relations. The strong showing of occupation, as compared to class, seems to indicate the discursive non-availability of class as a category in this allegedly 'classless society', rather than a positive preference for non-class over class identities. Moreover, the survey found strong empirical correlations between class location, certain political attitudes (towards trade unionism, government intervention and private enterprise) and voting intentions (Western et al., 1991, pp. 335–336).

6 Lash and Boyne's remarks are directed at Habermasian critical theory as well as at French post-structuralism. Unlike Giddens, who rejects the notion of the postmodern, but not the substance of postmodernism (Giddens and Ahmed, 1997, pp. 18–19), Habermas remains clearly antipathetic to the latter. For reasons of economy, I have chosen not to discuss Habermas here. But it is surely deeply symptomatic of the 'postmodern' turn in our intellectual culture that a self-defined 'Marxist', like Habermas, should be so persuaded of the essential archaism of class politics (Habermas, 1979, p. 33; Habermas, 1981, p. 33).

2

Marxist Theories
of Class

For obvious politico-historical reasons, associated above all
with the collapse of Communism in Eastern Europe, Marx has
become a distinctly unfashionable thinker of late. Even Derrida's
mournings (Derrida, 1994) have failed to prevent the progressive
elimination of Marx's legacy from much of the academic curriculum, not least from the once staunchly 'Marxist' area of Cultural
Studies. Giddens now regards this legacy as close to definitively
superseded: Marxism has been pronounced dead before, only to
rise phoenix-like from its ashes, he concedes, but 'the position
. . . today quite plainly *is* different . . . The difference is the
failure of socialism' (Giddens, 1995, p. xiii). This failure extends
beyond Soviet Communism, he argues, to embrace Western
welfare socialism and much else besides: 'welfare socialism
has become conservative and Communism is no more . . . There
is no Third Way . . . and with this realization the history of
socialism as the avant-garde of political theory comes to a close'
(Giddens, 1994, pp. 68–69). It is possible that these remarks will
eventually reveal more about the internal demoralization of
the British intellectual Left than about the fate of Marxism: in
the same year that Giddens announced the failure of socialism,
the *Russian* Communist Party polled 15.5 million votes, or 22.3

per cent of the total, in free and fair parliamentary elections
(Lester, 1997, p. 35). But, whatever its present or future prospects, there can be no doubting Marxism's previous influence on
twentieth-century thought and action, the founding moment of
British Cultural Studies not excluded. For that reason alone,
any adequate account of the concept of class will require some
discussion of Marx and Marxism. For both reasons, then, for
its own sake and for its subsequent impact on Cultural Studies,
we begin with an exploration of the general contours of this
Marxian legacy.

Marx on Class

More than that of any other social theorist, Marx's name is
apparently inextricably connected to the concept of class. Yet
he displayed relatively little interest in formal definitions of
class categories, of the kind that have exercised contemporary
British sociologists like Goldthorpe or Runciman (Goldthorpe
and Hope, 1974; Goldthorpe and Heath, 1992; Runciman, 1972,
1974). The Australian sociologist, R.W. Connell, once sought to
distinguish 'stratification theory', which is essentially 'dimensional', that is, it sets out to locate people in different strata
measured according to various 'dimensions' of inequality, from
'class analysis', which is typically 'generative', that is, it sets out
to identify those fundamental transformations in the social
structure which generate corollary transformations in the class
system (Connell, 1983, pp. 85–90, 92–96). In these terms, much
of Goldthorpe's work is stratification theory rather than class
analysis. For Connell, the primary instance of generative theory,
by contrast, is that provided by Marx himself. This distinction
between dimensional and generative logics seems helpful, but
there is no obvious reason to equate these with, respectively,
stratification theory and class analysis. Whatever may be true of
Runciman, whom Connell cited as a leading 'stratificationist'
(Connell, 1983, p. 85), there is no denying Goldthorpe's commitment to a kind of 'class analysis' that is nonetheless not especially
generative. Such analysis may be of only marginal relevance

to the type of historical sociology that interests Connell (cf. Connell and Irving, 1992), but it has far-reaching implications both for Goldthorpe's view of contemporary British society and for his practical political opinions. I prefer to disentangle these two sets of distinctions, then, between the dimensional and the generative, and between stratification theory and class analysis, so as to acknowledge the debt owed Marx both by Connell and by Goldthorpe. For, in truth, Marx's approach was at once dimensional and generative: the generative component has a certain analytical primacy (hence, the tardiness of his attempt to define class, postponed until the very last unfinished chapter of *Capital*); but the dimensional component remains in play nonetheless (hence, the attempt itself).

As Connell notes, the generative component in Marx devolves upon a theory of 'modes of production' (Connell, 1983, p. 95). For Marx, human societies were classifiable, in a kind of comparative historical sociology, according to the predominant structural characteristics of their modes of production, that is, very loosely, their 'economic' systems. The term 'economic' needs to be understood, however, as meaning not the market in particular, but the many and varied ways in which socially organized human labour is applied to the world so as to produce value. For Marx, it is the mode of production of any given society that 'generates' its characteristic forms of class inequality. In the 1859 'Preface' to *A Contribution to the Critique of Political Economy*, he defined mode of production as the dynamic combination of two main components: firstly, the 'relations of production', that is, the economic relations between groups of people, which are primarily forms of class structure; and secondly, the 'productive forces', that is, the forms of available productive technique, including technology and raw materials (Marx, 1975a, p. 425). Here Marx also identified four major modes of production, 'Asiatic, ancient, feudal and modern' (Marx, 1975a, p. 426), although it is clear that these are not necessarily inclusive categories. This notion of a succession of modes of production, each with its own characteristic relations of production, allowed Marx to historicize and therefore relativize the economic categories, such as wages and profit, typically taken as timeless in mainstream economic theory. Formally, class is near-universal for Marx: in all hitherto existing societies, wherever there is a surplus of production over the simple survival needs of the society, there will be a division of labour between, at the very least, one exploited and productive class and one exploiting and non-productive class. Hence the famous opening lines to *The Communist Manifesto*:

> The history of all hitherto existing society is the history of class struggles. Freeman and slave, patrician and plebeian, lord and serf, guild-master and journeyman, in a word, oppressor and oppressed, stood in constant opposition to one another . . . (Marx and Engels, 1967, p. 79)

But irrespective of this formal near-universality,[1] each particular mode of production generates quite different sets of relations between exploiting and exploited classes: between slaves and slave-owners in the ancient mode of production; between serfs and lords in the feudal; 'proletarians' and 'bourgeoisie' in the modern capitalist.

There is, in Marx's view, some necessary 'fit' between productive forces and relations of production, a relationship often conceived by many subsequent Marxists as one of technological determinism, where the forces causally determine the relations. There is some warrant for this reading: clearly, Marx sees the productive forces as establishing the material preconditions for the existence of appropriate relations of production. But, equally clearly, the development of the productive forces is to some extent dependent on the development of the relations of production, if only at the point where these latter become 'fetters' on the former. This last notion is crucial to Marx's theory of social change, his explanation as to how one mode of production can eventually generate the conditions of transformation into another. Again, the argument is nicely put in the 1859 'Preface':

> At a certain stage of development, the material productive forces of society come into conflict with the existing relations of production . . . From forms of development of the productive forces these relations turn into fetters. Then begins an era of social revolution . . . No social order is ever destroyed before all the productive forces for which it is sufficient have been developed, and new superior

relations of production never replace older ones before the material conditions for their existence have matured within the framework of the old society. (Marx, 1975a, pp. 425–426)

This seems to me a perfectly defensible and plausible set of propositions, not certainly as some kind of absolute 'truth', but as the better of the currently available theoretical alternatives, in explaining the transition from feudalism to capitalism, for example, or that from antiquity to feudalism.[2]

If this is Marx's general 'theory of history', in Cohen's phrase (Cohen, 1978), its main empirical reference point remains the modern bourgeois mode of production and the capitalist relations that accompany it. The central point here is that capitalism alone of all hitherto existing modes of production is essentially a system of commodity production, that is, production for the market. In pre-capitalist class societies, the exploitation of producers by non-producers had been effected through one or another form of direct politico-juridical coercion: slave-owners legally owned their slaves; and feudal lords had legal title to control, though not to own, the lands to which their serfs were legally tied. Both slaves and serfs could be compelled by force to work for their masters, so that surplus was extracted ultimately through the threat or actuality of direct coercion. The novelty of capitalism, for Marx as for many other nineteenth-century socialists, consisted in the creation of a system of exploitation in which the relations of production were contractual rather than imperative. The exploited class, the 'proletariat', in Marx's phrase, is a class of formally free labourers, whose labour-power is sold to their employers in exchange for wages. Like most nineteenth-century economists, Marx subscribed to a 'labour theory of value', in which the relative value of commodities was held to be determined by the amount of labour-power necessary to produce them. Since labour-power is itself a commodity, its value is equivalent to the amount of labour socially necessary to (re)produce it. Marx is clear that in a competitive labour market the workers will be paid the full exchange value of their labour-power. The system remains exploitative, nonetheless, because labour alone of all commodities is productive of value and because workers actually produce considerably more value than the amount necessary for the reproduction of their own labour. As Marx has it:

> the value of labour-power, and the value which that labour-power creates in the labour-process, are two entirely different magnitudes; and this difference of the two values was what the capitalist had in view, when he was purchasing the labour-power . . . What really influenced him was the specific use-value which this commodity possesses of being *a source not only of value, but of more value than it has itself*. (Marx, 1970, p. 193)

Capitalist relations of production thus generate a very particular class structure, according to Marx, in which the owners of capital buy labour-power from propertyless wage-earners, who are themselves obliged to sell it on the labour market in return for wages. This is simultaneously a relationship of formal equality and substantive inequality.

The central social actors in Marx's account of capitalism are these two main social classes: the capitalist class, or the 'bourgeoisie', on the one hand; the working class, or 'proletariat', on the other. In *The Communist Manifesto*, Marx and Engels had announced with great éclat that:

> Our epoch, the epoch of the bourgeoisie, possesses . . . this distinctive feature: it has simplified the class antagonisms. Society as a whole is more and more splitting up into two great hostile camps, into two great classes directly facing each other: Bourgeoisie and Proletariat. (Marx and Engels, 1967, p. 80)

Elsewhere, however, their accounts were often much more nuanced. The unfinished last chapter of *Capital*, which Marx was writing at the time of his death, famously identifies the 'three big classes of modern society' as wage-earners, capitalists and landowners, 'whose respective sources of income are wages, profit and ground-rent'. Moreover, he proceeds to note the existence of other 'middle and intermediate strata' which 'obliterate lines of demarcation everywhere' (Marx, 1974, p. 885). In more occasional works, such as 'The eighteenth Brumaire of Louis Bonaparte', written in 1852, he often deploys multi-class models with great flexibility, so as to analyse contemporary political events. Here, for example, he argues that the 'Legitimists', supporters of the Bourbon claimants to the French throne, represented big landed property; their rivals, the 'Orleanists', represented big capital; the French 'social-democrats', the urban 'petty bourgeoisie', or self-employed; and Bonaparte himself, by turn, the 'lumpenproletariat', that is, the semi-criminal 'refuse of all classes', and later the class of small peasant proprietors (Marx, 1973a, pp. 173–177; 197–198, 238–245). Empirically, Marx found little difficulty in recognizing both that there were many more than two classes and that, in any case, social classes would sometimes be internally divided into what he termed class 'fractions' (Marx, 1973b, p. 259). But, as he observed himself, 'this is immaterial for our analysis' (Marx, 1974, p. 885). Theoretically, Marx continued to adhere to a view of the capitalist mode of production as tending, over time, toward an empirical approximation of the two-class model originally outlined in the *Manifesto*. Hence his insistence, as late as the last chapter of *Capital*, that 'the continued tendency and law of development of the capitalist mode of production' is to separate labour from the means of production, and to concentrate and centralize those means, 'thereby transforming labour into wage-labour and the means of production into capital' (Marx, 1974, p. 885). If ever all labour is so separated from the means of production, if ever all means of production are so transformed into capital, then there will indeed be only two great classes, the proletariat and bourgeoisie.

Why did Marx anticipate this tendency toward a dichotomous class structure? The reasons are interesting and tell us much about his sense of the generative logic of capital. He argued that the central structural dynamic of the capitalist mode of production, organized as it is around competition, would be one of accumulation, where each individual firm will be under continuous pressure to accumulate so as to compete successfully with its rivals. Hence the extraordinarily dynamic qualities of modern industrial capitalism: 'The bourgeoisie', wrote Marx and Engels, 'cannot exist without constantly revolutionizing the instruments of production, and thereby the relations of production, and with them the whole relations of society' (Marx and Engels, 1967, p. 83). But from this very dynamism comes the source of crisis, both a long-run tendency towards a falling rate of profit and short-run tendencies towards over-production. The former arises as the social-systemic effect of the individual capitalist's predisposition to substitute capital for labour, through such devices as mechanization and automation. For any one firm this is an entirely rational move, which should enable it to out-compete its rivals. But for the system as a whole, the effect is to increase the proportion of what Marx terms 'constant capital' (machinery, plant, etc.) to 'variable capital' (in short, labour-power) within the production process and therefore, since labour is the source of value, to produce a fall in the overall rate of profit. As Marx has it: 'The progressive tendency of the general rate of profit to fall is . . . *an expression peculiar to the capitalist mode of production* of the progressive development of the social productivity of labour' (Marx, 1974, p. 213). The crises of over-production are explained more simply as a direct effect of the lack of regulation in capitalist economies. In all previous economic systems production had been directly for use, thereby in effect precluding the possibility of over-production, if not of under-production. But under capitalism production takes place, not for direct consumption, but for sale on markets the behaviour of which can never be entirely predictable. The result will be periodic crises of over-production and a consequent 'vicious circle' (Marx, 1974, p. 255) of boom and slump. The problem is both fundamental and ineluctable in a market economy, Marx concludes: 'the capitalist mode of production . . . comes to a standstill at a point fixed by the production and realisation of profit . . . not the satisfaction of requirements' (Marx, 1974, p. 258).

The effects on the class structure of capitalism's primary competitive dynamic, combined with this subsequent cycle of boom and slump, overlaid on a general tendency for the rate of profit to fall, are essentially fourfold. In the first place, Marx believed that the initial accumulative dynamic would tend to eliminate such pre-capitalist classes as feudal lords and serfs or, where they existed, slave-owners and slaves. Because of the greater efficiency of capitalism, capitalistic production will tend to out-compete non-capitalist forms of economic organization. Secondly, the long-run dynamic within the capitalist system will be to eliminate the 'middle and intermediate strata', the petty bourgeoisie, the peasantry and so on, all of which will be progressively out-competed by the bourgeoisie, and hence reduced to the condition of wage labour. Thirdly, Marx predicted that the periodic crises within the capitalist economy would tend to result in a greater concentration of capital in fewer hands – in short, an ever-expanding proletariat and an ever more concentrated and centralized bourgeoisie – since in each crisis the smaller, less efficient capitalists will be bankrupted. 'One capitalist', he observes, 'always kills many' (Marx, 1970, p. 763). Finally, he anticipated a progressive pauperization of the working class itself, as the pressures of a declining rate of profit feed through into wages. A sub-theme here is that of the growth of an 'industrial reserve army' of labourers, unemployed during slumps but available for employment in booms. 'The first word . . .', writes Marx,

> is the creation of a relative surplus-population, or industrial reserve army. Its last word is the misery of constantly extending strata of the active army of labour, and the dead weight of pauperism . . . Accumulation of wealth at one pole is, therefore, at the same time accumulation of misery, agony of toil, slavery, ignorance, brutality, mental degradation, at the opposite pole . . . (Marx, 1970, pp. 644–645)

Some of Marx's theses seem to have been borne out by subsequent events: capital has become increasingly concentrated; the class of employees has grown in proportionate strength (at least insofar as we continue to include 'white-collar' workers in their ranks); the self-employed class declined correspondingly, right through from the late nineteenth century until the mid-1970s (although not thereafter); and there is some evidence for a long-run decline in profitability. Some have proven false: there is little evidence of any general pauperization in Western capitalist societies, at any rate not since the Second World War; nor of a tendency to ever greater crises of over-production, again at least not since the Second World War. That a number of elements in the argument require modification and amendment is barely surprising: these were attempts at scientific prediction rather than prophecy. But, as a general analysis and critique of the developmental tendencies within capitalist civilization, it remains surprisingly plausible.

Marx's notion of a progressive simplication of the class structure is central to his account of the future transition to socialism. The novel element here, by comparison with the general theory of social change, is contained in the thesis that capitalism is the last and highest stage of class society, that capitalist relations of production are or will soon become a fetter on further development, and that the organized working class will overthrow capitalism so as to establish a post-capitalist, classless society. Marx and Engels famously announce the eventual demise of capitalism in the closing lines to the first part of *The Communist Manifesto*:

> The advance of industry, whose involuntary promoter is the bour-geoisie, replaces the isolation of the labourers, due to competition, by their revolutionary combination, due to association . . . What the bourgeoisie . . . produces, above all, is its own grave-diggers. Its fall and the victory of the proletariat are equally inevitable. (Marx and Engels, 1967, pp. 93–94)

Less resounding no doubt, but equally assured nonetheless, is Marx's own prediction in *Capital* that:

> The monopoly of capital becomes a fetter upon the mode of produc-tion . . . Centralisation of the means of production and socialisation of labour at last reach a point where they become incompatible with their capitalist integument . . . The knell of capitalist private property sounds. The expropriators are expropriated. (Marx, 1970, p. 763)

Or so Marx hoped. The slippage here, from a set of testable hypotheses about probable future changes in the shape of the class structure to what was in fact a relatively untestable prophecy of social revolution, is almost immediately apparent to us, conscious as we necessarily are of the non-appearance of Marx's revolution.[3] But there is more than a simple leap of faith at work here. The crucial missing component from our account of Marx's theory of revolution is his notion of class conscious-ness and of the connections between social structure and social belief. There are two major questions at issue here, one pertain-ing specifically to the working class itself, the other more generally to all social classes in all modes of production.

The first of these is the whole matter of what Marx meant by 'alienation', a notion first explored in the 'Economic and philosophical manuscripts of 1844'. Here, Marx established a conceptual dichotomy between actually existing alienated labour, in which labour-power is transformed into a commodity and the worker reduced to a mere thing, and an ideal of non-alienated labour incorporated in the notion of 'species-being'. By the latter term he meant the humanness of humanity, as constituted by our capacity for conscious, collective, creative production: 'Conscious life activity directly distinguishes man from animal life activity. Only because of that is he a species-being . . . Only because of that is his activity free activity.' But alienated or 'estranged' labour 'reverses the relationship', Marx continues, 'so that man . . . makes his life activity, his *being* [*Wesen*], a mere means for his *existence*' (Marx, 1975b, p. 328). Estranged labour is thus in some quite fundamental sense a denial of human nature. If the working class, alone of all hitherto existing exploited classes, is so radically alienated from its own essential human nature, then it has a uniquely powerful incentive to overthrow the system of commodity production. As Marx would later write: 'the class of the proletariat . . . is . . . in its abasement the *indignation* at that abasement, an indignation to which it is necessarily driven by the contradiction between its human *nature* and its condition of life' (Marx, 1975c, p. 36). Many subsequent Marxists found all of this hopelessly romantic and so consigned it to the pre-history of Marx's ideas. But even as late as Volume I of *Capital*, there is a clear echo of this notion in the concept of 'commodity fetishism', that is, the process by which human relations in a market economy assume 'the fantastic form of a relation between things' (Marx, 1970, p. 72). For Marx, modern civilization is founded essentially on commodified, alienated labour, as distinct from the kind of free, unalienated labour in which innate humanity finds its authentic expression.

The most important idea in Marx, insofar as class consciousness is concerned, is not that of alienation, however, but that of ideology. In its most general form, his theory of ideology maintains simply that: 'Life is not determined by consciousness, but consciousness by life' (Marx and Engels, 1970, p. 47). The notion is elaborated, in Marx's own very succinct formulation, in the 1859 'Preface':

> The totality of . . . relations of production constitutes the economic structure of society, the real foundation, on which arises a legal and political superstructure and to which correspond definite forms of social consciousness. The mode of production of material life conditions the general process of social, political and intellectual life. (Marx, 1975a, p. 425)

These general propositions, in turn, give way to two much more specific theses: that the ideas of the ruling class are the ruling ideas; and that different classes tend to produce different forms of class consciousness. The first is argued in *The German Ideology* itself: 'The ideas of the ruling class are in every epoch the ruling ideas: i.e. the class which is the ruling *material* force of society, is at the same time its ruling *intellectual* force' (Marx and Engels, 1970, p. 64). Culturally dominant ideas thus become, for Marx, the ideal expression of the dominant material relations, produced in the interests of the ruling class, and by that class's own specialist ideologists. The second proposition, that different classes produce their own rival forms of consciousness, is also hinted at in *The German Ideology*. For, although ruling ideas may be dominant, they are not thereby uncontested. Rather, rival classes produce rival ideas in the struggle for social leadership, and historically these become increasingly more abstract and universal in form: 'For each new class . . . is compelled . . . to represent its interest as the common interest of all the members of society . . . it has to give its ideas the form of universality, and represent them as the only rational, universally valid ones' (Marx and Engels, 1970, pp. 65–66). Like the class struggle itself, this struggle for intellectual and cultural mastery will come to an end only in the future classless society to be ushered into being by the proletarian revolution. The latter version of the theory of ideology becomes much more central in Marx's concrete analyses of actual class conflict. In 'The eighteenth Brumaire', for example, he postulates a clear distinction between the objective fact of class position and the subjective fact of a deliberately aware class consciousness. Discussing the French peasantry, he argues that:

> In so far as millions of families live under economic conditions of existence that separate their mode of life, their interests and their cultural formation from those of the other classes and bring them into conflict with those classes, they form a class. In so far as these small peasant proprietors are merely connected on a local basis, and the identity of their interests fails to produce a feeling of community, national links, or a political organization, they do not form a class. (Marx, 1973a, p. 239)

Class has both an objective and a subjective dimension, then, and a class is only truly itself insofar as it becomes conscious of itself. Marx had earlier sought to theorize this through the distinction between class position as 'common situation' and the unity in struggle of a 'class for itself', or, as later Marxists would reformulate this, between class 'for itself' and 'in itself' (Marx, 1976, p. 211). For Marx, the French peasantry could only ever be a class in itself, an aggregate of 'isomorphous magnitudes', much like 'a sack of potatoes' (Marx, 1973a, p. 239), he unkindly observed. The only modern classes able truly to act for themselves are those capable of independent political and industrial organization in their own interests, in short, the bourgeoisie and the proletariat, capitalists and workers. 'Of all the classes . . .,' wrote Marx and Engels, 'the proletariat alone is a really revolutionary class . . . The proletarian movement is the self-conscious, independent movement of the immense majority' (Marx and Engels, 1967, pp. 91–92). There is no necessary incompatibility between the two arguments: crucially, both insist that consciousness (therefore by implication culture) is also always ideology, that is, that it is conditioned by material reality. Taken to extremes, however, they tend to become so: if the ruling ideas are so powerful as to dominate all other ideas, then there can be no oppositional working-class consciousness, no possibility of a proletariat 'for itself'; conversely, if every class were to develop its own distinctive class consciousness, then there would be no real 'ruling ideas'. Marx himself seemed to have had little difficulty in holding to both arguments, treating the ruling ideas as dominant, but also seeing working-class life-experience as repeatedly giving birth to rival oppositional consciousnesses. Such oppositional consciousnesses would only become fully oppositional, that is, revolutionary, he assumed, at moments of extreme crisis, when the ruling ideas would in fact cease to rule.

Marxism after Marx: Socialism, Communism, Western Marxism

Both themes were widely canvassed in the political debates of the international socialist movement, the so-called Second International, during the last quarter of the nineteenth century and the first of the twentieth.[4] One of the central matters at issue between the International's leading German theorists – Karl Kautsky, Eduard Bernstein and Rosa Luxemburg – was precisely this question of whether or not socialist consciousness could develop spontaneously out of working-class life experience, especially that of industrial conflict. Luxemburg tended towards a kind of 'class practice' Marxism, which predicted precisely such spontaneous development, Kautsky and Bernstein towards a kind of 'ruling ideas' Marxism, which held that the workers had to be led to socialism through the politico-ideological interventions of a socialist political party (Luxemburg, 1986; Kautsky, 1996). In 1902, the Kautskyist position in these debates received reinforcement and radical refurbishment from the International's Eastern front, in the shape of a pamphlet *What Is To Be Done?* published in Geneva by the exiled Russian Marxist, Vladimir Lenin. Much more determinedly than either Kautsky or Bernstein, Lenin insisted that revolutionary-socialist consciousness would have to be imported into the proletariat from external, party-political sources: 'Class political consciousness', he wrote, 'can be brought to the worker *only from without* . . . from outside the economic struggle, outside the sphere of the relations between the workers ' (Lenin, 1970, p. 123). Left to themselves, he observed, workers are 'able to work out merely trade-union consciousness' (Lenin, 1970, p. 80). Nor was this simply a matter of relatively 'higher' and 'lower' levels of the selfsame proletarian consciousness: quite the contrary. Lenin argued, in the most curious of inversions, that trade-union consciousness is itself ultimately a vehicle for *bourgeois* ideology. Any 'belittling of the Socialist ideology,' he writes, '*any withdrawing* from it, means by the same token the strengthening of the bourgeois ideology . . . the spontaneous development of the labour movement leads precisely to its subordination to the bourgeois ideology' (Lenin, 1970, pp. 89–90). Given all that we know from empirical sociology about the practical bourgeois aversion to almost all things trade-unionist, this seems inherently improbable. Lenin anticipates the reader's objection, but insists, nonetheless, that working-class consciousness does indeed tend spontaneously only towards bourgeois ideology. This is so, he explains, in strangely 'idealist' terms, because of the enormous power of the ruling ideas themselves: bourgeois ideology is 'far older in origin . . . more completely developed, and . . . possesses *immeasurably* greater means for being spread' (Lenin, 1970, pp. 90–91).

What, then, is the source of socialist consciousness, if not working-class life-experience? Lenin's answer is twofold. In the first place, he stresses the importance of Marxist theory: 'There can be no revolutionary movement', runs the much-quoted aphorism, 'without a revolutionary theory' (Lenin, 1970, p. 75). But Lenin knew as well as the next bourgeois intellectual that such theory was no more a sociologically immaculate conception than is trade unionism. In the second place, he quite deliberately and explicitly identifies the source of socialist theory in 'the educated representatives of the propertied classes – the intelligentsia' (Lenin, 1970, p. 80). He even goes so far as to admit that Marx and Engels, the 'founders of modern scientific Socialism . . . themselves belonged by social status to the bourgeois intelligentsia' (Lenin, 1970, p. 80). Indeed, they did. But what had provided many other Marxists with the occasion for embarrassment provides Lenin with the rationale for a political party 'of a *different kind*', an 'organization of revolutionaries . . . people whose profession consists of revolutionary activity' (Lenin, 1970, p. 156). Professions, we should remind

ourselves, are typically middle-class organizations, distinguishable in theory and in practice from the more proletarian
trade unions by the extent of their pretension to scientific and
technical expertise, that is, 'theory'. To summarize: working-
class people spontaneously generate bourgeois ideology; proletarian consciousness, by contrast, is the creation of bourgeois
intellectuals. This is 'ruling ideas' Marxism with a vengeance,
its central propositions as apparently contrary to logic as to
evidence.

Lenin himself appears to have had second thoughts about
What Is To Be Done? (Cliff, 1975, pp. 175–176). The International,
for which he had held the Russian franchise, fell apart in August
1914, ruined by its own incapacity to resist the various European nationalisms and militarisms. As it turned out, neither
working-class spontaneity nor socialist political correctness was
able to prevent the march to war. With the International went
Lenin's illusions in Kautsky, Kautsky's in Germany, and also
much of Marx's own intellectual and political legacy. The Marxisms that arose thereafter owed far less to Marx than was commonly admitted by their respective champions and detractors.
At the risk of oversimplification, we can identify two major
such traditions: Communist Marxism on the one hand; 'Western
Marxism' on the other. Very schematically, we may characterize
Communism in terms of its simultaneous defence of: firstly,
the major theoretical tenets of pre-1914 Socialist orthodoxy
(Marxism as a science, the base/superstructure model, history
as progress); and secondly, the actually existing 'socialism'
brought into being in Russia in 1917 by Lenin and the Bolsheviks.
This was the kind of Marxism adhered to by the Communist
parties, but also very often by 'left-wing' activists within the
Social Democratic and Labour parties. 'Western Marxism', by
contrast, came to combine a strongly 'idealist' version of high
theory, the key concepts of which (consciousness, will, agency,
hegemony, totality) were all essentially anti-materialist, with an
increasingly critical political stance *vis-à-vis* the Soviet Union.
The term was first coined by Merleau-Ponty to distinguish the
kind of critical, humanist Marxism that developed in Western

Europe by way of reaction against 'eastern' Communist Marxism (Merleau-Ponty, 1974), its obvious exemplars including Gramsci, Lukács, Korsch, the Frankfurt School and Sartre, but not in this usage Althusser's 'structural Marxism'. Perry Anderson later expanded the term to include the latter, adding that the entire tradition shared 'one fundamental emblem: a common and latent *pessimism*', which derived from 'the failure of proletarian revolutions in the advanced zones of European capitalism after the First World War' (Anderson, 1976, pp. 88, 92).

On the latter point, Anderson was mistaken: to the contrary, Western Marxism was born out of a moment of near-messianic optimism in the immediate aftermath of the Bolshevik Revolution. Whatever its ultimate focus on the depoliticizing consequences of reification, bourgeois hegemony, the culture industries, and so on, the original emphasis fell on the imminently revolutionary potential of proletarian class consciousness, counter-hegemony and revolutionary will. If Western Marxism eventually survived only by virtue of its institutional location within the Western university system, its original home, nonetheless, had been on the 'infantile' left wing of organized Communism (Lenin, 1975b). All of this is self-evidently apparent in Lukács's *History and Class Consciousness*, the founding text for the entire tradition, clearly intended as a theorization of, rather than a heresy from, Bolshevism. Even more suggestive, however, is Gramsci's much-cited article on 'The revolution against *Capital*', published in *Avanti!* in December 1917, as a salute to the Bolshevik Revolution. 'This is the revolution against Karl Marx's *Capital*', he wrote:

. . . The Bolsheviks reject Karl Marx . . . These people are not 'Marxists' . . . [Their] thought sees as the dominant factor in history, not raw economic facts, but man, men in societies, men in relation to one another, reaching agreements with one another, developing through these contacts . . . a collective, social will; men coming to understand economic facts, judging them and adapting them to their will until this becomes the driving force of the economy and moulds objective reality, which lives and moves and comes to resemble a current of volcanic lava that can be channelled wherever and in whatever way men's will determines. (Gramsci, 1977, pp. 34–35)

No doubt, Gramsci is generally right in this assessment: the Bolshevik Revolution had indeed been a revolution against Marx and against 'classical' Marxism. Where Marx himself had conceived a dialectic between being and consciousness, Lenin formulated the binary opposition between ruling ideas and revolutionary theory, ideology and science. Gramsci, however, elides the obvious 'scientism' in Lenin's thought, translating revolutionary theory as social will. Here, then, in embryo is the broad outline of subsequent Western Marxist polemics against Communist Marxism. For our purposes, however, what also remains significant is their common understanding of revolution as a triumph of practice over determinism, consciousness over being, the ideal over the material. I now want to consider Lukács's *History and Class Consciousness* and Sartre's *Critique of Dialectical Reason* as later instances of 'class practice' Marxism; Marcuse's *One Dimensional Man* and Althusser's theory of ideology (Althusser, 1971) as instances of 'ruling ideas' Marxism; and Gramsci's own theory of hegemony as occupying a position in some ways straddling the two.

Class Practice Marxism: Lukács and Sartre

Lukács's *Geschichte und Klassenbewusstsein* was published in German in 1923, its first French translation in 1960, the English *History and Class Consciousness* as late as 1971. It was the work of a relatively young man, only recently a participant in the Hungarian Revolution of 1919, still a committed revolutionary, and often impatient with the apparent conservatism of a developing Communist orthodoxy. Here, the stress on agency and consciousness served to underwrite a leftist rejection of the political fatalism apparently implicit in more orthodox economic determinisms. In general, Communist Marxism tended to theorize the relationships between culture and society through one or another version of the base/superstructure model. For the young Lukács, by contrast, the emphasis fell on the imminently revolutionary potential of proletarian class consciousness and revolutionary will. For Lukács:

> History is at its least automatic when it is the consciousness of the proletariat that is at issue . . . Any transformation can only come about as the product of the – free – action of the proletariat itself. (Lukács, 1971, pp. 208–209)

As the identical subject and object of history, 'simultaneously the subject and object of its own knowledge' (Lukács, 1971, p. 20), the proletariat was, for Lukács, the bearer of a form of class consciousness that could render the historical process itself, no less, virtually transparent. In Marx, as in Hegel, the revolutionary principle is the dialectic rather than materialism, Lukács argued: 'the concept of totality, the subordination of every part to the whole unity of history and thought' (Lukács, 1971, pp. 27–28). Thus the idea of totality provides a positive pole against which to develop his central critical concept, that of 'reification'. Here Lukács expands upon the discussion of commodity fetishism in Volume I of *Capital*, reading it by way of his own familiarity with both Hegel and Weber, so as to develop what is, in effect, a textual reconstruction of Marx's theory of alienation. By reification he means the process by which human relations come to be understood as relations between things, an important instance of which is commodity fetishism itself. Lukács so radically generalizes the notion, however, that capitalism becomes a veritable system of reification: human reality is necessarily 'detotalized' under capitalism, both by commodity fetishism and by the various reified forms of consciousness, including science itself (Lukács, 1971, pp. 6–7).

For Lukács, reified thought can be overcome only by the proletariat's coming to consciousness of itself as the identical subject and object of history. However, for Lukács, as for Lenin, such class consciousness is by no means coextensive with the empirical consciousness of real working-class people. Quite the contrary. 'By relating consciousness to the whole of society', he writes:

> it becomes possible to infer the thoughts and feelings which men would have in a particular situation if they were *able* to assess both it and the interests arising from it in their impact on immediate action and on the whole structure of society . . . class consciousness consists in fact of the appropriate and rational reactions 'imputed' [zugerechnet] to a particular typical position in the process of

production. This consciousness is, therefore, neither the sum nor the
average of what is thought or felt by the single individuals who make
up the class. (Lukács, 1971, p. 51)

There is a striking similarity between this notion of an 'imputed'
class consciousness and that of the 'ideal type' developed by
Lukács's one-time mentor, the sociologist Max Weber, and still
widely used today in sociological investigations into class consciousness.[5] There is a crucial difference, nonetheless, and one
that takes on a very directly political relevance: where Weber
had held that an ideal type 'cannot be found empirically anywhere in reality' (Weber, 1949, p. 90), Lukács insisted, to the
contrary, that 'imputed' class consciousness can become actualized in the empirical consciousness of a working class organized
and led by the revolutionary Communist Party. The party, he
writes, 'is the historical embodiment and the active incarnation
of class consciousness . . . the incarnation of the ethics of the
fighting proletariat'; its 'moral strength' is 'fed by the trust of the
spontaneously revolutionary masses . . . nourished by the feeling
that the party is the objectification of the workers' own will
(obscure though this may be to themselves)' (Lukács, 1971,
p. 42).

It is difficult to avoid the speculation that this notion – that of
a party which can know the workers' will better than the
workers do themselves – opened the way for Lukács's journey
from Leninism to Stalinism. We need not deny the logical
possibility that a political party, or a group of individuals or
even one individual, might at some moment achieve a truly
representative consciousness of the kind Lukács postulates.
Both Lukács himself and his disciple, Lucien Goldmann, later
made interesting, albeit controversial, use of the notion of
an actualized ideal-typical consciousness, the *'maximum of
potential consciousness'* (Goldmann, 1969, p. 103), in their work
on the sociology of art and literature. In the special circum-
stance of acute social polarization and widespread quasi-
insurrectionary class conflict, such as Lukács had experienced
during the immediate aftermath of the First World War, there
is a plausible case to be made for the temporary empirical
adequacy of this model of the relationship between a political

party and a social class. But to imagine such symbiosis as enduring or even as at all durable seems quite unwarranted. Clearly, empirical proletarian consciousness, party-political consciousness and revolutionary consciousness are normally likely to prove non-coincidental, however we may prefer to define the latter. Obliged to choose between the empirical consciousness of real workers and the maximum possible consciousness supposedly embodied in the party, Lukács was quite clear as to where his final loyalties lay: 'because the party aspires to the highest point that is objectively and revolutionarily attainable . . . it is sometimes forced to adopt a stance opposed to that of the masses; it must show them the way by rejecting their immediate wishes' (Lukács, 1971, pp. 328–329). This makes good dialectical sense, no doubt, but only on the condition of a willing suspension of disbelief on the subject of party-political institutions. Everything we know about the empirical record of Socialist, Communist, Social-Democratic and Labour parties, whether in or out of power, suggests to the contrary, however, that these are social institutions subject to much the same pressures as any other: governed by Michels's iron law of oligarchy, but also by Gouldner's iron law of democracy (Michels, 1959, pp. 377–393; Gouldner, 1976, p. 384); by turn opportunist or principled, incompetent or inspired, ignorant or enlightened, incorruptible or dishonest; and therefore quite unsuited to the role allocated them by Lukács.

Sartre's *Critique de la raison dialectique* is a much more recent work than *History and Class Consciousness*: the first volume was published in French in 1960, in English translation in 1976. But, like Lukács, Sartre sees Marxism's central theoretical object as precisely the free, conscious action of the working class: dialectical reason, he insists, is above all else 'the logic of freedom' (Sartre, 1976, p. 69). Unlike Lukács, however, he distinguishes between 'totality', as passive holism, and what he terms 'totalization', that is, totality as project, totality as 'a *developing* activity' (Sartre, 1976, p. 46). For dialectical reason to be true, it must be able to show that human history can be understood as a multiplicity of such projects or totalizations. The aim of the *Critique* is thus to demonstrate that the different practices which can be found and located at a given moment of the historical temporalization finally appear as partially totalizing and as connected and merged in their very oppositions and diversities by an intelligible totalization from which there is no appeal. (Sartre, 1976, p. 817)

So Sartre sets out to show how need, scarcity, alienation, can each be rendered intelligible as projects, formed through a subject–object dialectic between humanity and scarce matter, wherever the latter takes precedence over the former. The 'practico-inert' is the term he coins to describe the absorption of free practice into inert matter, the 'equivalence between alienated *praxis* and worked inertia' (Sartre, 1976, p. 67). And the peculiar significance of the working class is 'that the organized *praxis* of a militant group originates in the very heart of the practico-inert' (Sartre, 1976, p. 316).

In the last chapter of Book 1 and the first six chapters of Book 2,[6] of the first volume, Sartre maps out a set of analytical categories designed to render group behaviour intelligible as *praxis* or totalization. Famously, the two most important of these are the 'series' on the one hand, the 'fused group' on the other. By the series, Sartre means a type of collectivity in which scarce matter forms an interior bond of 'alterity', or otherness, that is, where people interiorize the passivity of matter into their own practice: the example he starts from is that of a bus queue in the Place Saint-Germain (Sartre, 1976, pp. 256–269). By the fused group, he means a type of collectivity in which the project of freedom forms its interior bond, where people consciously aim to overcome passivity and scarcity: the opening example is that of the storming of the Bastille in 1789 (Sartre, 1976, pp. 351–363). Marx's class 'in itself' would only ever be a series, his class 'for itself' of necessity a fused group. Lukács had envisaged the movement from the one to the other as a kind of transcendence, a qualitative transformation in which in-itselfness is radically superseded by for-itselfness, at least amongst the party militants. Sartre, by contrast, acknowledges no such discontinuity between the two conditions: 'the group is always marked by the series,' he writes, '. . . it becomes its reality in the milieu of freedom, . . . and a series is determined, even in its totally inorganic practico-inert layers, by the sovereign self-production of the group' (Sartre, 1976 p. 679). Once the antithesis between alienated series and fused group has been established, Sartre proceeds to an account of three sub-types of group – by turn, the surviving or pledged group, the organization, and the institution – each of which represents, by comparison with its predecessor in the sequence, a further degeneration from fusedness towards seriality. For Sartre, the working class can be analysed, in terms of these categories, as simultaneously 'an institutionalized organizational group . . ., either a fused or a pledged group . . . and . . . a seriality which is still inert . . . but . . . profoundly affected by the negative unity of the pledged groupings' (Sartre, 1976 p. 683); or, as his editor succinctly summarizes the argument, as 'Institution, Fused Group and Series' (Sartre, 1976, p. 678).

The central focus for Sartre's account of class practice falls on the interrelationships between the trade union as an 'institutionalized apparatus', the various ensembles of 'direct-action groups' and the collective as defined by the practico-inert (that is, the class in itself) (Sartre, 1976, p. 685). Interestingly, the workers' party figures in this analysis only by way of an analogical extension from the trade union.[7] Unlike Lukács, Sartre refuses to assign any a priori theoretical superiority to the socialist party, whether it be understood as an institutionalized apparatus (as Sartre himself clearly viewed it) or as a combat group (as the young Lukács might have preferred):

> The working class is neither pure combativity, nor pure passive dispersal nor a pure institutionalized apparatus. It is a complex, moving relation between different practical forms each of which completely recapitulates it, and whose true bond with one another is totalization (as a movement which each induces in the others and which is reflected by each to the others). (Sartre, 1976, p. 690)

Class practice thus acquires a distinctly open and plural character: it develops 'in the unity of pluridimensional reciprocities between heterogeneous structures each of which contains the others' (Sartre, 1976, p. 707). This openness is at once both a gesture towards the potential for non-party militancy and an anticipation of its likely failure (as also that of institutionalized party or union organizations). For if 'class is *praxis* and inertia, dispersal of alterity and common field' (Sartre, 1976, p. 701), then neither Leninist organization nor Luxemburgist spontaneity will ever provide any rock-solid guarantee for the triumph of the one over the other. All that remains is a set of formal alternative possibilities, each intelligible to dialectical reason, but none predetermined to actualization.

But Sartre's is a Western Marxism in its not-so-latently pessimistic later stage of development, very different in tone and tenor from the revolutionary optimism of *History and Class Consciousness*. If all possibilities remain formally open, then the weight of the analysis clearly falls, nonetheless, on the processes of degeneration from fusedness through institutionality into seriality. Nowhere is this more apparent than in Sartre's references to the fate of the Russian Revolution. Institutions are marked by the emergence of sovereignty, 'the absolute practical power of the dialectical organism' (Sartre, 1976, p. 578); and, with it, eventually the emergence of the sovereign leader, 'the institution *of one man* as a mediation between institutions' (Sartre, 1976, p. 618). Where Lukács had imagined the revolutionary party as the ultimate site of freedom, Sartre would insist that 'the first moment in the construction of socialist society . . . could only be the indissoluble aggregation of bureaucracy, of Terror and of the cult of personality' (Sartre, 1976, p. 662). Readily conceding that in the Soviet Union 'the Party and the State were Stalin', he adds that this was so, not contingently, not as a result of bad luck or mismanagement or historical backwardness, but because the very idea of the 'dictatorship of the proletariat (as a real exercise of power through the totalization of the working class) . . . is absurd . . . a bastard compromise between the active, sovereign group and passive seriality' (Sartre, 1976, p. 662). If there is hope that this first stage might nearly be over or that future socialist revolutions might occur in more propitious circumstances, Sartre remains adamant that terror and the cult of personality are expressions 'of the necessity that a common action . . . should practically reflect upon itself so as constantly to control and unify itself In the untranscendable form of an individual unit' (Sartre, 1976, p. 662).

There is a certain realism, no doubt, to this hardnosed recognition that class practice determines its own alienation from itself. But the subsequent fate of the erstwhile Soviet Union suggests a whole range of alternative hypotheses, not least that Stalinism might have developed, not so much as a kind of degenerative institutionalization of working-class self-activity, akin to trade union officialdom in the West, but as the embryonic form of a new form of non-proletarian class dominance.

Ruling Ideas Marxism: Marcuse, Althusser and Post-Althusserianism

For the young Lukács, writing at the beginning of Hobsbawm's 'Age of Catastrophe' (Hobsbawm, 1995, p. 6), class practice had promised a fusion of party and class which would finally dispel both reification and alienation; for Sartre, writing with benefit of hindsight in the immediate aftermath of that catastrophe, it meant only an ontological denial of determinism, stripped of all but the most abstract promise of any substantive class freedom. Hobsbawm's 'Golden Age' would lead later Western Marxists to deny even this abstract possibility. Chronologically speaking, Marcuse was Sartre's predecessor rather than his successor, seven years his senior in fact. But where Sartre remained a determinedly European thinker, Marcuse's long Californian exile had led him to confront the inner workings of the United States itself, the paradigmatic instance of post-war late-capitalist society. Where Sartre's *Critique* remained preoccupied with the problems of Stalinism, revolution and class struggle[8] – precisely the central questions for inter-war Marxism – Marcuse's *One Dimensional Man* is self-evidently immersed in the new problems of post-war affluence and relative social stability. Marcuse had been one of a group of non-Communist Marxist intellectuals working at the Institut für Sozialforschung at the University of Frankfurt, the so-called 'Frankfurt School', who were forced into exile in the United States – where the Institut was temporarily re-established at Columbia University – during the Nazi period. Although many of the School's more prominent figures, notably Adorno and Horkheimer, had eventually returned to the post-war Bundesrepublik, Marcuse himself remained in America, teaching at Brandeis and later at San Diego. In both its native German and émigré American manifestations, the School seemed to provide the American New Left with a Western Marxist alternative to the theoretical vulgarities of Stalinized Communism. First published only four years after Sartre's *Critique*, *One Dimensional Man* rapidly acquired cult status amongst 1960s student radicals, both in the United States and elsewhere.

For Adorno and Horkheimer, modern capitalism had become a fully rationalized system of domination, its continued social stability powerfully underwritten by the technologies of the mass media, or 'the culture industries', as they termed them. Where the older 'authentic' arts had involved a necessary confrontation with established traditional styles, the new mass media, they argued, were centred around the practice of imitation. 'In the culture industry,' they wrote, 'imitation finally becomes absolute. Having ceased to be anything but style, it reveals the latter's secret: obedience to social hierarchy' (Adorno and Horkheimer, 1979, p. 131). The central function of popular entertainment is thus that of effective and successful ideological manipulation in the interests of big business. The proletariat, which had seemed to the young Lukács a prospective identical subject and object of history, was thereby reconceptualized as a passive 'mass', the object of systematic manipulation by the culture industries. Much of this was taken over into American intellectual radicalism by way of Marcuse. For Marcuse, as for Adorno and Horkheimer, 'technological society' was above all 'a system of domination' (Marcuse, 1972, p. 14). For Marcuse, as for Adorno and Horkheimer, a combination of mass affluence and mass media had delivered the working class into the arms of the bourgeoisie:

> If the worker and his boss enjoy the same television programme and visit the same resort places . . . then this assimilation indicates not the disappearance of classes, but the extent to which the needs and satisfactions that serve the preservation of the Establishment are shared by the underlying population. (Marcuse, 1972, p. 21)

The working class in one-dimensional society had thus become 'a prop of the established way of life', whose triumph over the bourgeoisie could only ever 'prolong this way in a different setting' (Marcuse, 1972, p. 197). For Marcuse, as for Adorno and Horkheimer, Marx's dialectic was thereby reduced to a theory bereft of practice: 'Dialectical theory', he concludes, 'defines the historical possibilities . . . but their realization can only be in the practice which responds to the theory, and, at present, the practice gives no such response' (Marcuse, 1972, p. 197). But where Adorno and Horkheimer had been driven thence toward an almost unmitigated 'Cultural Pessimism' (the German word is *Kulturpessimismus*), Marcuse still clung to the hope that others might prove better qualified than the proletariat to serve as the midwife of history. In the book's closing pages, he looks to 'the substratum of the outcasts and outsiders', located 'underneath the conservative popular base', for the chance that 'the historical extremes may meet again: the most advanced consciousness of humanity, and its most exploited force' (Marcuse, 1972, pp. 199–200). His actual hopes were invested in the poor black ghettos, with people 'of other races and other colours, the unemployed and the unemployable' (Marcuse, 1972, p. 200), but with a little poetic licence student radicals were soon also able to imagine themselves thus.

If Marcuse had found himself reluctantly obliged to deny the working class that capacity for collective social agency long assigned it by Marxism, then Althusser would deny the entire human species virtually all capacity for any kind of agency. In their earlier studies, *For Marx* (Althusser, 1969) and the co-authored *Reading Capital* (Althusser and Balibar, 1970), Althusser and his co-workers had re-read Marxism as if it were a structuralism, so that the Lukácsian and Sartrean prioritization of agency and *praxis* was altogether subsumed into a general theory of structural determination. To the more generally 'Western' sense of Marxism as a kind of humanist critique of capitalism – whether it be 'critical theory', 'dialectical reason' or 'socialist humanism' – Althusser had countered a strong reaffirmation of the notion of Marxism as science, sharply distinguished from, and counterposed to, ideology, both by its own defining 'knowledge function' and by the 'epistemological break' from which it had been founded. This Marxist science was characterized above all, according to Althusser, by a new mode of explanation, in which 'structural causality' was substituted for both 'mechanical' and 'expressive' models of causation (Althusser and Balibar, 1970: 186–187). Here Althusser reformulated Marx's analytical distinction between the mode of production, the legal and political superstructure, and the forms of consciousness, as a theory of three relatively distinct 'levels' within the social formation: the economic, the political and the ideological. In this formulation, the political and the ideological are neither superstructural effects of the material base, as in orthodox Communism, nor expressions of the truth of the social whole, as in Marxist humanism, but instead relatively autonomous structures, each with its own specific effectivity, situated within a structure of structures, each level of which is subject to '*determination of the elements of a structure . . . by the effectivity of that structure . . .* [and] *determination of a subordinate structure by a dominant structure*' (Althusser and Balibar, 1970, p. 186). History is thus a 'process without a subject' (Althusser, 1972, p. 185), individual human beings merely the 'supports' of 'functions' within a 'structure' (Althusser and Balibar, 1970, p. 180).

The more radical implications of this structuralist reworking of Marx are at their most apparent at two connected points: in the theory of ideology and in the theory of class. Althusser's own explicit theorization of ideology is contained in the much-quoted essay 'Ideology and ideological state apparatuses', included in the *Lenin and Philosophy* collection, which first appeared in English in 1971. As in the earlier work, Marx's forms of consciousness are here represented as relatively autonomous structures of 'ideology'. Against the common Marxist view of ideology as Hegel's 'Spirit' (*Geist*) stood on its head – determined by rather than determining Being, but still Spirit nonetheless – Althusser insisted that ideology was itself material, that it was necessarily embedded in institutions: 'an ideology always exists in an apparatus, and its practice, or practices' (Althusser, 1971, p. 166). Where most Marxists, Marx included, had tended to reserve the term 'state' to refer to explicitly 'political' or 'repressive' institutions, Althusser expanded its embrace to include the 'Ideological State Apparatuses', acronymically the 'ISAs': the religious ISA, the educational ISA, the family ISA, the legal ISA, the political ISA, the trade union ISA, the communications ISA and the cultural ISA (Althusser, 1971, p. 143). The fundamental rationale for this move was that each of the various ISAs, whether or not a legally public institution, performed the same function as the '(Repressive) State Apparatus', that is, to secure '*the reproduction of the relations of production*' (Althusser, 1971, p. 148).

Dismissing Marx's own theory of ideology, by turn, as 'not Marxist', 'positivist' and 'historicist', Althusser proceeded to insist that, no matter how varied the history of particular ideologies, ideology in general '*is eternal*': it always represents 'the imaginary relationship of individuals to their real conditions of existence' (Althusser, 1971, pp. 158, 160–162). If ideology is indeed thus, then there can be no prospect for any definitive transcendence of ideology such as Lukács had imagined available to the working class as identical subject and object of history. For Althusser, as for structuralism more generally, subjects are only ever the effects of ideology. Indeed, this is how ideology works, this is what ideology does: '*all ideology has the function . . . of "constituting" concrete individuals as subjects*' (Althusser, 1971, p. 171). We only become individual subjects, then, by virtue of the functioning of ideology; all else is mere biological nature. Moreover, Althusser formulates this proposition in the most radically structuralist of terms: ideology '*hails or interpellates*' concrete individuals, much as a policeman hails, 'Hey, you there!' (Althusser, 1971, pp. 173–174). It was precisely this Althusserian theory of ideology that provided British Cultural Studies with its initial introduction to structuralist and post-structuralist thematics: as Easthope observes, in Britain post-structuralism was much more indebted to Althusserianism than were its intellectual counterparts in France and the United States (Easthope, 1988, pp. 21–22, 161–164). To cite an obvious example, Terry Eagleton's *Criticism and Ideology* set out to elaborate 'a Marxist theory of literature' centred on the twin concepts of 'mode of production' and 'ideology'; and a structuralist 'science of the text', taking as its theoretical object the way literature 'produces' ideology (Eagleton, 1976, pp. 44–63, 64–101). Even more influentially, Stuart Hall's various overviews of the current state of the theoretical art in Cultural Studies clearly affirmed the radical superiority of structuralist notions of ideology over supposedly 'culturalist' conceptions of experience (Hall, 1978; Hall, 1980a).[9] His successor at the Open University, Tony Bennett, still persists in the view that higher education can usefully be understood as an ideological state apparatus (Bennett, 1998, p. 35; cf. Bennett, 1992).

For all the frequency with which he would on occasion invoke the 'class struggle', Althusser's own contribution to class theory was relatively modest.[10] Other Althusserians were not so reticent, however. It is to their work, and especially that devoted to the subject of the 'new middle class' that we now turn. By far the most immediately influential of the Althusserian class theorists was Nicos Poulantzas, whose *Classes in Contemporary Capitalism* can still serve as a representative instance of the argument. Just as the individual subject had been for Althusser an effect of ideology, so too for Poulantzas social classes were not collective subjects, as in Lukács or Goldmann, but rather 'the effects of the structure within the social division of labour' (Poulantzas, 1975, p. 14). Just as the social formation had been constituted for Althusser from out of three relatively autonomous levels, the economic, the political and the ideological, so too for Poulantzas 'structural class determination involves economic, political and ideological class struggle' (Poulantzas, 1975, p. 16). In practice, this stress on the political and ideological constitution of class led to the characteristic hypercomplexity of post-Althusserian class schemata. So Poulantzas distinguished between 'the structural determination of class', or class 'place', on the one hand, and 'class position' on the other, where the latter term refers to the kind of political alignment formed 'in the conjuncture'. Both are marked by ideology, politics and economics (Poulantzas, 1975, pp. 14–15). Class determination operates at the level not only of social classes, but also of class fractions, class strata and what

Poulantzas terms 'categories', that is, groups defined primarily by their politico-ideological location – the examples he cites are the state bureaucracy and the intelligentsia (Poulantzas, 1975, p. 23). Class position, by contrast, operates through concepts of strategy, as in Poulantzas's distinction between the 'power bloc' and the 'people', respectively alliances between dominant and dominated classes and fractions (Poulantzas, 1975, p. 24). Analytically, this Poulantzan apparatus could allow for an almost indefinite expansion of the number of class places and class positions; practically, however, its most important effect was the discovery of the 'new petty bourgeoisie'. This is the term Poulantzas uses to refer to the employed 'middle class', that is, the stratum of 'white-collar', non-manual workers. Despite their relatively unambiguous status as employees, Poulantzas chose to define this layer, not as part of the working class, but as the twentieth-century equivalent to Marx's self-employed petty bourgeoisie.

This is so for reasons that are at once economic, political and ideological: economically, Poulantzas insisted, somewhat implausibly, that this stratum doesn't actually produce surplus value; politically, that it exercises a supervisory role in relation to the working class (which is sometimes true empirically and sometimes not); and ideologically, that it is separated from the working class by virtue of the distinction between mental and manual labour (Poulantzas, 1975, pp. 222–223, 228–229, 233–235). The latter point is especially important: for Poulantzas, the new petty bourgeoisie can be considered a distinctive social class precisely because of the way in which it 'is located by the extended division between mental and manual labour . . . in the reproduction of capitalist political and ideological relations' (Poulantzas, 1975, p. 252). The rapid development and growth of this class of salaried employees is perhaps the single best example of a long-run trend in the evolution of advanced capitalist societies clearly unanticipated either by Marx himself or by most early Marxists. Marx's own prediction that the intermediate strata would be progressively eliminated, whilst by no means entirely irrelevant to the self-employed classes, seems quite inapplicable to this new middle stratum. For mainstream

sociology, its arrival had held out the more or less immediate
prospect of 'embourgeoisement'. But the initial Marxist or quasi-
Marxist response, at least in France, had been to hail its
appearance as that of a 'new working class', as for example
in Serge Mallett or the early Alain Touraine (Mallett, 1975;
Touraine, 1966). So when Poulantzas first broached the matter
of the new petty bourgeoisie, in a document intended for
distribution to the Confédération Française Démocratique de
Travail (CFDT) – ironically, the labour organization most
directly representative of precisely this layer of employees – he
had specifically singled out for attack Touraine's work on the
subject (Poulantzas, 1973, pp. 28n, 35).

As Erik Olin Wright soon noted, the full effect of Poulantzas's
insistently Althusserian rigour would be to consign something
like 70 per cent of the American workforce to the ranks of
the petty bourgeoisie (Wright, 1979, p. 55). No doubt, from the
standpoint of an austerely post-Marxist post-structuralism, to
make this observation 'is not necessarily to make a criticism'
(Frow, 1995, p. 122n). But for any Marxist even remotely committed to the idea of a socialist politics, the notion that the
socialist tradition's preferred social agent, the working class,
should have been reduced to such a small minority, even in its
preferred type of society, the most advanced of capitalisms,
presented almost insuperable problems. Hence, a whole range
of attempts by various post-Poulantzan class theorists to come
up with a more restricted definition of the new middle class.
These run from, at the most restricted end of the range, Carchedi's
relatively tight definition of the new middle class as those who
perform the global function of capital, but without owning the
means of production (essentially managers and supervisors);
through the Ehrenreichs' 'Professional-Managerial Class'; to, at
the least restricted end, Wright's and Callinicos's shared sense of
the new middle class as a compound of two main 'contradictory
class locations' occupied by managers and supervisors on
the one hand, semi-autonomous credentialled employees on the
other (Carchedi, 1977, p. 89; Ehrenreich and Ehrenreich, 1979,
p. 12; Wright, 1979, p. 63; Callinicos, 1983, p. 103). Each of these
writers went some way towards recognizing the existence of a

new class or classes previously unacknowledged in Marxist theory; each inherited a characteristically post-Althusserian pre-occupation with taxonomic classification almost for its own sake; and each was driven to define class position in essentially politico-ideological terms (if only to avoid the 'economistic' conclusion that much of the new middle class was actually a new working class). Callinicos alone had the judgement to concede that the new middle class is 'not a *class* in the sense that the bourgeoisie and the proletariat are a class . . . it is a collection of heterogeneous social layers who have in common an ambiguous and intermediate position' (Callinicos, 1983, pp. 103–104). But this insight sits uneasily beside his strong sense of the cultural specificity of the new middle class. Neither a post-Althusserian sense of the importance of the politico-ideological instance nor a more classically Marxist understanding of the relations of production seems at all adequate to the explanation of a culture as socially distinct as that described in Callinicos's borrowings from Raphael Samuel (Callinicos, 1983, pp. 107–108; cf. Samuel, 1982). For some more adequate explanation we might have to look beyond Marxism altogether.

The Turn to Gramsci

At one level, the shift from class practice Marxism to ruling ideas Marxism bespeaks no more than the recognition of a simple empirical datum, the non-appearance of socialist revolution in the West. These extreme reformulations of Marx's ruling ideas thesis, whether Marcusean or Althusserian, were able to generate very clear explanations for the proletariat's failure to consign capitalism to the dustbin of history: in short, some version or another of the proposition that it had been ideologically duped. But the solution posed its own problems, two in particular. Epistemologically, it raised the question of the theorist's qualification to reach this conclusion: in short, who speaks thus? who pronounces judgement on the labour movement in this fashion? Politically, it raised the question as to whether any social order conceived in this way, that is, as something close to an ideologically self-sealing homeostatic system, could ever be overthrown by any oppositional social force. The answer to the first question should be readily apparent. Not only Marcuse and Althusser, but also Lukács and Sartre occupy much the same speaking position as Lenin, that of the would-be professional revolutionary, perhaps in his day job as professional academic. For all the subsequent doubts about subsequent Communisms – and Marcuse at least was unimpeachably anti-Communist (Marcuse, 1971) – Western Marxism in all its many variants remained predicated on the shared assumption that a socialist revolution would indeed be a 'revolution against *Capital*', a matter of consciousness brought 'from without', rather than being experienced from within. The contrast between this and Marx remains striking: neither Lenin nor any of our twentieth-century Marxists could ever have sincerely proclaimed, as Marx and Engels had, that they 'do not set up any sectarian principles of their own, by which to shape and mould the proletarian movement' (Marx and Engels, 1967, p. 95). I doubt we can make much sense of this difference between classical Marxism and its successors until we begin to acknowledge the cultural specificity of the intelligentsia, considered as a relatively distinct social class. As to the second problem, the political inefficacy of such exaggerated accounts of the power of ruling ideologies soon became apparent even to many on the New Left, whether erstwhile Marcuseans or repentant post-Althusserians.

In Britain, at least, these considerations came to inform something of what Tony Bennett would later describe as the 'turn to Gramsci' (Bennett, 1986). Like Lukács, Gramsci had been a Communist activist during the 'revolutionary' period immediately following the First World War:[11] he co-edited *L'Ordine Nuovu*, the journal of the Turin factory councils, in the 'Red Years' of 1919–20 (Spriano, 1975; Williams, 1975); elected to parliament in 1924, he had led the Italian Communist Party until its suppression and his own arrest late in 1926. The *Quaderni del carcere* were written between 1929 and 1935, from a Fascist prison in the most difficult of circumstances, and first appeared in English translation in a very limited selection in 1957, in a much more extensive collection in 1971, the same year as the first English translation of *History and Class Consciousness* (Gramsci, 1957; Gramsci, 1971). The *Quaderni* would eventually inspire almost universal admiration on the Western Left: as the then editor of the British *New Left Review* observed in 1977, 'no Marxist thinker after the classical epoch is so . . . respected in the West' (Anderson, 1977, p. 5). Nowhere was this admiration more widespread nor more enthusiastic than in academic Cultural Studies: Gramsci's concept of hegemony seemed to Raymond Williams 'one of the major turning points' in cultural theory (Williams, 1977, p. 108); for Stuart Hall, it had 'played a seminal role in Cultural Studies' (Hall, 1980b, p. 35). Here, then, was the possibility of a mid-way position, somewhere between class practice Marxism and ruling ideas Marxism, where working-class consciousness could be analysed as neither necessarily virtuously heroic nor necessarily hopelessly duped.

Distinguishing between 'political society' on the one hand and 'civil society' on the other, Gramsci had concluded that: 'State = political society + civil society, in other words hegemony protected by the armour of coercion' (Gramsci, 1971, p. 263). The term 'hegemony' here denoted those processes by which a system of values and beliefs supportive of the existing ruling class permeates the whole of society. Hegemony is thus a value consensus, very often embodied in common sense, but constructed, nonetheless, in the interests of the dominant class. Every state, Gramsci argued, 'is ethical in as much as one of its most important functions is to raise the great mass of the population to a particular cultural and moral level . . . which corresponds . . . to the interests of the ruling class'. The schools, the courts and 'a multitude of other so-called private initiatives and activities' together constitute 'the apparatus of the political and cultural hegemony of the ruling classes' (Gramsci, 1971, p. 258). Initially, the British reception of Gramsci was refracted through Althusserianism, so that this distinction between civil and political society appeared little more than a prototypical formulation of that between ideological and repressive state apparatuses. But, where Althusser theorized his ISAs as structural determinants of the subordinate subject's subordinacy,

Gramsci had viewed the creation and maintenance of hegemony as crucially a matter of practical 'intellectual and moral leadership'. Distinguishing between 'domination' and 'leadership', he had insisted that:

> A social group can, and indeed must, already exercise 'leadership' before winning governmental power . . .; it subsequently becomes dominant when it exercises power, but even if it holds it firmly in its grasp, it must continue to 'lead' as well. (Gramsci, 1971, pp. 57–58)

As Williams recognized, this was something rather different from Althusserianism (Williams, 1977, pp. 109–110). For Gramsci, hegemony is materially produced by the practice of conscious agents and so may be countered by alternative, counter-hegemonic, practices: where ideology as structure is essentially a matter for textual decoding or 'symptomatic reading', hegemony as culture is a matter for political and moral contestation. Hegemony is thus never in principle either uncontested or absolute, but is only ever an unstable equilibrium, ultimately open to challenge by alternative social forces.

The practical functioning of Gramsci's 'apparatus of hegemony' is essentially the work of the intellectuals, whom he nicely characterized as 'the dominant group's "deputies" exercising the subaltern functions of social hegemony and political government' (Gramsci, 1971, p. 12). As is well known, Gramsci distinguished between 'organic' and 'traditional' intellectuals. Organic intellectuals were of the kind which each major social class creates for itself, so as to 'give it homogeneity and an awareness of its own function', and were thus necessarily affiliated to these other classes (Gramsci, 1971, p. 5). Traditional intellectuals, by contrast, were those ecclesiastics, administrators, scholars, scientists, theorists and philosophers who 'experience through an "*esprit de corps*" their uninterrupted historical continuity and their special qualification' and 'thus put themselves forward as autonomous and independent of the dominant social group' (Gramsci, 1971, p. 7). In Gramsci's view, this autonomy is essentially illusory, and is in any case less characteristic of historically more recent kinds of secular intellectual than of the older ecclesiastical intelligentsia (Gramsci, 1971, p. 8). In both respects subsequent developments appear to have belied his expectations: the rapid expansion of the modern university system and the coincidental decline in the power and prestige of organized religion have combined to secure for the secular traditional intelligentsia an autonomy at least as assured as that of ecclesiastics; moreover, the entire traditional intelligentsia (in contradistinction to the 'organic' intellectuals either of the bourgeoisie or of the working class) now exercises a degree of institutional and discursive autonomy sufficient to constitute it as a distinctive social group, if not exactly a social class in the strictly Marxist sense of the term.

For Gramsci himself, however, the central problem remained that of the creation of a layer of organic working-class intellectuals capable of leading their class in the battle for counter-hegemony. As he had written in the closing pages of 'The modern prince': 'one has to . . . stimulate the formation of homogeneous, compact social blocs, which will give birth to their own intellectuals . . . their own vanguard – who in turn will react upon those blocs in order to develop them' (Gramsci, 1971, p. 205). This is a recognizably quasi-Leninist formulation, but with two characteristically Gramscian inflections: firstly, the stress on pedagogy as distinct from organization ('to develop them'); and secondly, the much more 'organic' conception of the relationship between party and class (the vanguard is 'their own'). The latter question bears directly on the matter of Gramsci's subsequent impact on Western intellectual radicalism, especially the New Left. For, insofar as the relationship between radical intellectuals and the social movements for which they claim to speak is indeed organic, then it becomes possible to imagine that relationship as requiring no party-political mediation of the kind prescribed by both Lenin and Gramsci. There can be no doubt that Gramsci did subscribe to a more generally Communist conception of the vanguard party: the modern prince was, in fact, the party itself (Gramsci, 1971, p. 147). Moreover, for Gramsci, as for Lenin, the party was essentially an organization of intellectuals: 'A human mass does not . . . become independent in its own right without . . . organising itself; and there is no organisation without intellectuals, that is without organisers and leaders' (Gramsci, 1971, p. 334). Simultaneously, however, he also insisted that the development of these organic intellectuals 'is tied to a dialectic between intellectuals and masses'. Thus:

> every leap forward towards a new breadth and complexity of the intellectual stratum is tied to an analogous movement on the part of the mass of the 'simple', who raise themselves to the higher levels of culture and at the same time extend their circle of influence towards the stratum of specialised intellectuals, producing outstanding individuals and groups of greater or less importance . . . The parties recruit individuals out of the working mass, and the selection is made on practical and theoretical criteria at the same time. The relation between theory and practice becomes even closer the more the conception is vitally and radically innovatory and opposed to old ways of thinking. (Gramsci, 1971, pp. 334–335)

The model is that of Gramsci's own career: the scion of an impoverished lower middle-class family, educated at a traditional university, recruited thence into the Socialist Party, and transformed into an organic intellectual during the Turin factory councils movement. Stripped of its close identification with expressly Communist organizational forms, this was a model which could speak powerfully to New Left intellectuals, especially to those working in Cultural Studies, whose business was in any case the academic study of 'hegemony'. We shall return to this matter of the peculiar appropriations and reappropriations of Gramsci by British Cultural Studies in Chapter 4.

After the Fall: Post-Marxism or Late Marxism?

Given that Western Marxism had developed in part as a reaction against Communist Marxism, but also often in tacit sympathy with leftist critiques of Western social democracy, one might have expected it to enjoy a certain immunity to the protracted crisis of the Communist and non-Communist Left during the 1980s and 1990s. But, if anything, the internal crises of Western Marxist theory pre- rather than postdate those within both Eastern Communism and Western socialism. The key developments here are registered most clearly in Laclau and Mouffe's 'post-Marxist' (Laclau and Mouffe, 1985, p. 4) theory of radical-democratic politics. As early as 1977, Laclau had drawn the plausible inference from Althusserianism that ideological 'elements' can have no necessary class connotation and that, at the concrete level of the social formation, the dominant contradiction is that between the 'people' and the 'power-bloc', rather than between classes (Laclau, 1977, pp. 99, 108). In their later collaborations, Laclau and Mouffe would go further: to argue that, insofar as there is any relation between social position and cultural identity, this can only be an effect of discourse, that is, in more conventionally Gramscian terms, an effect of the struggle for hegemony. To the classical Marxist notion of 'objective interests' they counterposed a 'contradictory plurality'; to that of the 'unity and homogeneity of class subjects', a 'set of precariously integrated positions which . . . cannot be referred to any necessary point of future unification' (Laclau and Mouffe, 1985, pp. 84–85). 'The logic of hegemony', they concluded, is 'a logic of articulation and contingency', which 'has come to determine the very identity of the hegemonic subjects' (Laclau and Mouffe, 1985, p. 85). Their account thereby precluded the possibility, not merely of any necessary connection between working-class interests and socialist politics, but of any determinate connection between any class position and any discursive or ideological construct. As Hall observed, on this model 'there is no reason why anything is or isn't potentially articulable with anything . . . critique of reductionism has apparently resulted in the notion of society as a totally open discursive field' (Grossberg, 1996, p. 146).

The political implications of the analysis were spelt out very clearly. The project of radical democracy cannot be derived from the supposedly essential identity of the working class, they argued, but will need to be built by a plurality of different groups between which there are no 'necessary links' (Laclau and Mouffe, 1985, p. 178). This will in turn require 'the construction of a new "common sense", which would change the identity of the different groups so that the demands of each group are articulated equivalentially with those of the others' (ibid., p. 183). The central self-imposed obstacle in the way of any such counter-hegemony thus turns out to be '*classism*', that is, 'the idea that the working class represents the privileged agent in which the fundamental impulse of social change resides' (ibid., p. 177). There is still a place both for socialism and for the labour movement in the 'democratic revolution', they conceded, but this will not be derived from any necessary antagonism inherent in the form of the wage-labour/capital relation. Quite the contrary: 'Only if the worker *resists* the extraction of his or her surplus-value by the capitalist does the relation become antagonistic . . . The pattern and intensity of the antagonism depend, therefore . . . on the way in which the social agent is constituted *outside the relations of production*' (Laclau and Mouffe, 1987, p. 103). There are thus 'no apriori privileged places in the anti-capitalist struggle' (Laclau and Mouffe, 1987, p. 104). Whether this new sense of the determining power of the discursive (though that is not how Laclau and Mouffe would have put it) should be considered 'post-Marxist' or simply non-Marxist (Geras, 1987, p. 44), there is no denying its appeal to many ex-Marxist scholars, not least those working in Cultural Studies. Much of the appeal undoubtedly arose from the more loosely 'postmodern' character of their work, in which post-Marxism figured alongside post-structuralism, postcolonialism, post-humanism, and so on, as part of a more general *fin-de-siècle* post-Enlightenment sensibility. In this sense, 'post-Marxism' clearly extends well beyond Laclau and Mouffe and their more immediate circles. As Wright has recently noted, being post-Marxist 'is fashionable these days' (Wright, 1994, p. 8). But the reception was by no means universally sympathetic, either for Laclau and Mouffe's own work or for post-Marxism more generally.

Laclau and Mouffe's thesis of the disconnectedness of social position and cultural identity can itself be read in three ways: as an ontological proposition concerning the necessary disarticulation of being and consciousness; as a historical proposition concerning the contemporary postmodern condition; or as part of a wider epistemological critique of Marxism's pretensions to scientificity. A counter-argument for the continuing relevance of Marxist theories of class could be prosecuted at any of these three levels. A principled defence of 'political' Marxism would almost certainly take issue, at the very least, with the first two propositions: such is the case presented very forcefully by Ellen Meiksins Wood, for example, in *The Retreat from Class*. A more 'postmodern' Marxism might dispute the argument from ontology, whilst nonetheless conceding something of its contemporary empirical force: this is the procedure adopted by Fredric Jameson in his various writings on postmodernism and late capitalism. Finally, a more conventionally 'sociological' Marxism, such as that espoused by Wright in the United States or John Westergaard in Britain, might simply settle for an epistemological defence of the empirical adequacy of Marxist theories of class. Let us consider each in turn very briefly.

Wood's *The Retreat from Class* was explicitly directed at Laclau and Mouffe's post-Marxism, arguing that it had neither historical nor ontological warrant. Likening their work to the 'True Socialism' criticized by Marx and Engels in *The German Ideology*, she argued that this 'new "true" socialism' (or 'NTS') had developed more or less contemporaneously with the Anglo-American New Right, as a reaction to much the same cause, the militant labour unrest of the 1970s and early 1980s (Wood, 1986, pp. 1, 10). The 'theoretical expulsion of the working class from . . . the socialist project' cannot have been a response to empirical trends in late capitalism, she observed, since it arose precisely 'at the very moment when workers in several European countries were exhibiting a new militancy, and . . . in Britain it has reached new heights whenever militant workers have dominated the political scene' (Wood, 1986, p. 10). She speculates freely as to the likely explanations for this 'irony', noting the possibility that the NTS might be 'the ideological representation of a specific social interest in its own right' (Wood, 1986, p. 186). But her own interest lay primarily in a defence of Marx's materialist ontology against the discursive turn in post-structuralist post-Marxism. Marxism had been right to insist that production is essential to human existence, she concludes; right to insist that political movements are grounded in social interests; right too to insist that the socialist political project is more securely grounded in working-class politics than elsewhere:

> there is such a thing as a working class, people who by virtue of their situation in the relations of production and exploitation share certain fundamental interests, and . . . these class interests coincide with the essential objective of socialism, the abolition of class, and . . . the classless administration of production by the direct producers themselves. (Wood, 1986, p. 189)

From this admirably succinct restatement of Marxist materialism, Wood proceeds to a resounding reaffirmation of the traditionally socialist view that 'tremendous goals' can be achieved, if only our 'particular struggles for emancipation' can be unified, not by the 'phantoms of "discourse"', but by 'the politics of *class*' (Wood, 1986, p. 200). Although Wood is Canadian, the immediate occasion for much of her political optimism seems to have been the 1984–85 British miners' strike: as she pointedly explains, the book was written during the strike and its conclusion completed only very shortly thereafter (Wood, 1986, p. 180). With the benefit of hindsight, however, Wood's conclusions seem distinctly ingenuous. For all their heroism (this surely is an appropriate term for a strike that lasted more than 12 months), the coalminers were engaged in an almost entirely defensive struggle, at a time and on a terrain chosen by their class enemies, and they went down to a terrible defeat. As Alex Callinicos, as hardnosed a Marxist as they come, observed in an early review of Wood: 'the intellectual shift to the right is largely a consequence of the collapse of working-class militancy . . . the NUM's defeat . . . gave the NTS a huge shot in the arm' (Callinicos, 1987, pp. 111–112). Wood's appeal to 'the historical record' (Wood, 1986, p. 186) thus turns out to be a double-edged sword, which could just as easily claim her or the NTS as its victim. The defeat and demoralization that followed, both for the mining communities and for the British labour movement as a whole, suggest less sanguine readings of these events than that anticipated by Wood.

Jameson, by contrast, is much less certain of the immediate empirical prospects either for class struggle or for socialist politics. If Wood's Marxism was a restatement under more or less contemporary conditions of something like classical Marxism, then Jameson's is much more self-consciously aware of itself as a kind of 'late Marxism', a term he borrows from the German to describe Adorno's critical theory (Jameson, 1990, p. 11). For Jameson, Adorno has a peculiar relevance and appropriateness to postmodern late capitalism, precisely insofar as more activist forms of socialist commitment seem increasingly unavailable (Jameson, 1990, p. 249). This is Marxism understood as a great refusal, both of the increasingly 'totalized' global system itself and of the postmodernist ideologies that legitimize that system, perversely enough through a rejection of the very notion of totality. There is much that is admirable in this intransigent resistance to the lure of commodity culture, whether in Adorno or in Jameson. But, as Jameson notes of Adorno, the latter's contribution 'is not . . . to be sought in the area of social class . . . for that one goes elsewhere' (Jameson, 1990, p. 9). For Jameson himself, almost as much as for Adorno, the persistence of the dialectic is assured only at the price of an almost complete withdrawal from the empirical realities of class identity and class conflict. For Jameson, as perhaps not for Adorno, the formal certainty of class politics remains. 'Capital and labor (and their opposition) will not go away under the new dispensation . . .' he insists: 'Whether the word Marxism disappears or not . . . in the erasure of the tapes in some new Dark Ages, the thing itself will inevitably appear' (Jameson, 1990, p. 251). If this is Marxism, then it is a Marxism of a very distinctly Adornian kind, deeply implicated in the wider tradition of *Kulturpessimismus*. As such, it belongs as much to Cultural Studies as to Marxism; and we shall have cause to examine it as such in Chapter 4 below.

If Jameson's work is a contribution to Cultural Studies, or at least to 'cultural critique', as much as to Marxism, then both Wright and Westergaard are as much sociologists as Marxists. Neither would have any sympathy for Jameson's aggressively Hegelian style of Western Marxist 'high theory': both tend to see Marxism as a set of empirically defensible social-scientific propositions. Philosophically, this is at its clearest in Wright's adherence to the 'Analytical Marxism' of G.A. Cohen, John

Roemer and others, the distinguishing characteristic of which has been a willingness to subscribe to the logical rigours of Anglophone analytical philosophy (Cohen, 1978; Roemer, 1986). Wright's own sympathies with this self-described 'Non-Bullshit Marxism' date from at least the mid 1980s (Wright, 1985 p. 2) and have been restated with some force only recently. As he explains, the 'school' is committed to *'conventional scientific norms* in the elaboration of theory and the conduct of research' (Wright, 1994, p. 181). For a professional philosopher like Cohen, this might mean little more than a subscription to analytical philosophy *per se*, but for a theorist who defines Marxism as 'the social science of class analysis' (Wright, 1994, p. 210), these conventional norms are almost unavoidably those of the discipline of sociology. Westergaard is much less interested in such questions of epistemology, as indeed are most sociologists. But when he insists that Marxism is a 'continuingly significant source of hypotheses or hunches to be explored by empirical research', it is clear that the empirical research in question will be conventionally sociological in character (Westergaard, 1995, p. 11). Wright has been engaged in a long-run empirical inquiry into patterns of class consciousness in 15 countries, which draws heavily on closely replicated social surveys (Wright, 1989a; Wright, 1994, p. 11). Each of Westergaard's two major studies of class inequality in Britain makes extensive use of conventional sociological data, not least that drawn from official British Government statistics (Westergaard and Resler, 1975; Westergaard, 1995). It is as sociology, then, that such work asks to be judged and we shall judge it thus in the chapter that follows.

There is no doubting the scale of the political disaster that overcame the Marxist Left during the last two decades of the twentieth century. As one of its own erstwhile supporters, the historian Eric Hobsbawm, describes it:

> The collapse of the USSR . . . also undermined the aspirations of non-communist socialism . . . Whether . . . Marxism . . . would continue remained a matter of debate. However, . . . none of the versions of Marxism formulated since the 1890s as doctrines of political action

and aspiration for socialist movements were likely to do so in their original forms. (Hobsbawm, 1995, p. 563)

It is difficult to dissent from this judgement. For Hobsbawm, however, it is the desirability and feasibility of the idea of a non-market economy that was most clearly thrown into doubt by the failure of Soviet Communism.[12] I am much less persuaded by this particular emphasis than by the more general tenor of his conclusions. For, as Ralf Dahrendorf has argued, the velvet revolutions were better characterized by their commitment to openness and democracy than to capitalism (Dahrendorf, 1990, pp. 40–41). Our subject is class, however, rather than democracy, and this brings me to my own provisional conclusions. To observe that Communism was anti-democratic is the merest cliché; but to suggest that this antipathy to democracy might originate in its distinctive class character, as a party of the intelligentsia rather than the proletariat, is much less so. It seems to me no accident that, from Kronstadt to the East Berlin workers' rising, from the Hungarian Revolution to Polish Solidarity, the most powerful forms of internal opposition to Soviet Communism were pre-eminently working-class in character. This 'elective affinity', to borrow Weber's borrowing from Goethe (Weber, 1948a, p. 284), between a certain kind of elitist Marxism and the intelligentsia as a class can be traced back at least as far as Lenin and very plausibly to Kautsky, but not to Marx. Lenin's *What Is To Be Done?* is thus the paradigmatically anti-democratic text in the Marxist tradition. Its status as such derives, not from its formulation of a 'democratic-centralist' theory of the party, as many anti-Leninists have supposed (Heller, 1990, p. 6), but from its peculiarly idealist theory of consciousness, which led almost inescapably to the denigration of empirical working-class belief and thought. No doubt, there was much more than this both to Bolshevism and to post-Leninist Marxism more generally.[13] But from Lenin on, proletarian Marxism had to contend with elitist Marxism, both within parties and movements and in the minds of individual Communist and Socialist militants. The kind of theorized contempt for proletarian consciousness announced in *What Is To Be Done?* remained a more or less permanent feature of the

Marxist legacy thereafter, whether Communist or Western, humanist or structuralist, only finally to be bequeathed from Althusserianism to postmodernism by way of Laclau and Mouffe. Ironically enough, Lenin himself turns out to be the true founder of 'post-Marxism'.

Notes

1 Neither class nor class conflict is strictly universal, at least not for Engels, who inserted a footnote in the 1888 edition of the *Manifesto* to the effect that class struggle belonged only to '*written* history'. Social organization prior to recorded history, he added, had been characterized by 'primitive Communistic society' (Marx and Engels, 1967, p. 79).

2 See, for example, Hilton, 1978; Anderson, 1974.

3 The Communist revolutions in Eastern Europe and Asia neither confirm nor refute Marx's prophecy. These developed, not in the advanced capitalist societies as Marx had expected, but on the system's backward periphery, and their eventual shape bore very little resemblance to his distinctly libertarian vision of a community of equals in which the state, class inequality and even ideological false consciousness would all wither away. From the standpoint of Marx's own Marxism, the Bolshevik Revolution should simply never have happened. This was the view explicitly argued by the anti-Bolshevik Marxist, Karl Kautsky, in 1919: 'It is only the old feudal large landed property which exists no longer. Conditions in Russia were ripe for its abolition but they were not ripe for the abolition of capitalism. Capitalism is now once again celebrating a resurrection, but in forms that are more oppressive and harrowing for the proletariat than of old' (Kautsky, 1983, p. 146). But Kautsky did little more than apply in practice Marx's own theoretical observation that: 'development of productive forces . . . is an absolutely necessary practical premise [for Communism] because without it *want* is merely made general, and with *destitution* the struggle for necessities and all the old filthy business would necessarily be reproduced'. For Marx, as for Kautsky, this led necessarily to the conclusion that 'communism is only possible as the act of the dominant peoples' (Marx and Engels, 1970, p. 56). Even the Bolsheviks themselves, whose Marxism had derived from that of the Second International, initially insisted that the Russian Revolution would be bourgeois, rather than socialist, in character. This is a central line of argument in Lenin's 'Two tactics of social-democracy in the democratic revolution': 'The democratic revolution is bourgeois in nature . . . But we Marxists should know that there is not, nor can there be, any other path to real freedom for the proletariat and the peasantry, than the path of bourgeois freedom and bourgeois progress' (Lenin, 1975a, p. 503).

4 On Second International Marxism, cf. Gay, 1962; Nettl, 1969; Salvadori, 1979.

5 Weber himself had insisted that ideal-typical constructions were peculiarly suited to the analysis of certain kinds of collective consciousness (cf. Weber, 1949, pp. 95–96).

6 These subdivisions are the work of the editor of the English translation rather than Sartre's own.

7 'It does not make any difference whether we are dealing with a trade union or a party; what is important is the relation of the *objectified class* (the trade union or any other institutionality) to the fused class' (Sartre, 1976, pp. 685–686n). Although most of the footnotes to the English translation were provided by the editor, this is Sartre's own (Sartre, 1960, p. 649n).

8 At one point Sartre pointedly compares French and Italian revolutionary 'normality' with the peculiarities of British reformism (Sartre, 1976, p. 797).

9 This intellectual pre-eminence was to prove surprisingly shortlived: Althusser was effectively excluded from intellectual respectability after the death of his wife in 1980. As Grosz recalls, 'he murdered his wife – a well-known feminist. He never came to trial but was hospitalised. His name is consequently rarely mentioned today, and always in hushed tones' (Grosz, 1989, p. 235). But there are also other more sympathetic appraisals (cf. Kaplan and Sprinker, 1993). Althusser's own posthumously published last work is in that most French of genres, the politically motivated confession (Althusser, 1992).

10 There are passing references to the concept of class in *Reading Capital*, but these are by Étienne Balibar (Althusser and Balibar, 1970, pp. 232–233, 267–269).

11 Strictly speaking, Gramsci was still a member of the Italian Socialist Party at this time: the breakaway Communist Party wasn't founded until January 1921. His politics were nonetheless clearly those of a communist, if not yet a Communist.

12 Which is not to suggest a sudden conversion to market economics. To the contrary, Hobsbawm also judges the liberal utopia of the unrestricted market economy 'demonstrably bankrupt'.

13 As Victor Serge, an anarchist turned Bolshevik turned near-Trotskyist, had concluded in 1939: 'It is often said that "the germ of all Stalinism was in Bolshevism at its beginning". Well, I have no objection. Only, Bolshevism also contained many other germs – a mass of other germs' (Serge, 1967, p. xv).

3

Sociological Theories of Class

Like Marxism, sociology has often been preoccupied with social class. For if sociology can be said to have any one 'core' subject matter, then it is the study of structured social inequality. Social inequality is by no means necessarily synonymous with class: the early Italian 'elite' theorists sought to explain it through the dynamics of interaction between 'elites' and 'masses' (Mosca, 1939, pp. 51–53; Pareto, 1976, pp. 247–250); American 'structural-functionalist' sociologists theorized 'social stratification' as the distribution of unequal statuses according to the functional requirements of the social system as a whole (Davis and Moore, 1945; Parsons, 1954); more recently, feminist sociologists have tended to argue that the relations of patriarchal dominance between men and women are at least as important, and in some ways much more fundamental, than those between social classes (cf. Walby, 1986, pp. 5–49).[1] But in Britain at least the sociological profession has generally remained loyal to 'class analysis', so much so that Goldthorpe, one of its leading contemporary exponents, can still cheerfully predict for it a 'promising future' (Goldthorpe and Marshall, 1992). Like most contemporary class analysis, Goldthorpe's work owes a clear and acknowledged debt to two main 'classic sources', Marx and Max Weber (Erikson and Goldthorpe, 1992, p. 37). In the larger world of politics and ideology, revolution and counter-revolution, history-making in short, Weber has been a much less significant figure than Marx. Here, as elsewhere, however, sociologists tend to dissent from the judgements of 'history', for if there is any one figure widely acknowledged as the 'founding father' of their discipline, then it is Weber. One contemporary sociologist even suggests that, since the collapse of Communism, Weber can now be considered 'the primary theorist of modernisation and modernity' (Turner, 1996, p. xvii). For Turner, this clearly entails a rejection of class analysis, even in its more explicitly Weberian formulations (Holton and Turner, 1994, pp. 802–803). This seems a sorry conclusion for an erstwhile devoted Weberian, given Weber's own strenuous attempts to develop a deliberately non-Marxist theory of class.

My main concern here will be with Anglophone sociology, primarily British, to some extent American, in passing Australian. No doubt a more comprehensive survey of recent German or French sociology, for example, would have been instructive. But sociology remains a much less cosmopolitan discourse than Marxism, essentially a set of relatively discrete national disciplines, separated by language and, typically, by preoccupation with the peculiarities of particular 'national' societies. Such discretion has been especially characteristic of the English speakers, moreover, in part because of the predominance of the United States over 'the West', in part that of American over European sociology, during the second half of the twentieth century. In any case, Anglophone sociology has provided an important part of the intellectual context, if only as an immediately cognate discipline, for what became Cultural Studies, itself an overwhelmingly Anglophone intellectual formation. Paradoxically, Cultural Studies has been less indebted than sociology to the 'classical' sociological canon, especially Weber, but more receptive to the work of contemporary European sociologists, for example Pierre Bourdieu. From the admittedly very peculiar vantage point of these admittedly local concerns, it will make more sense to discuss Weber along with Anglophone sociology, Bourdieu with British Cultural Studies. It is to Weber, then, and to the work of subsequent Weberian, post-Weberian and post-Marxist sociologists, that we now turn.

Weber on Class

Though Connell described Weber as 'the quasiparent of stratification theory', he was also quick to recognize that the latter's concept of class was 'based on transactions between people which do not and cannot obey the postulates of the stratification model' (Connell, 1983, pp. 85, 90). In fact, there is much to be said for a view of Weber's sociology as essentially 'generative' in character. Like Marx, Weber was concerned to define the specific nature of capitalism, as part of a comparative historical sociology: the sociology of religion, for which he is justly famous, is organized around the problem of how different religious ethics inhibit or stimulate capitalist forms of economic organization. For Weber, capitalism was above all else a system based on the rational calculation of profit. As he explained in *The Protestant Ethic and the Spirit of Capitalism*, 'a capitalistic economic action' is 'one which rests on the expectation of profit by the utilization of opportunities for exchange, that is, on (formally) peaceful chances of profit' (Weber, 1930, p. 17). Such behaviour is not in itself distinctive to modern capitalism, he acknowledged, but 'in modern times the Occident has developed . . . a very different form of capitalism which has appeared nowhere else: the rational capitalistic organization of (formally) free labour' (Weber, 1930, p. 21). This stress on 'free labour' is similar to Marx's emphasis on wage labour, except that Weber views the capitalist labour contract as distinctively 'rational'. This 'purposive' or 'instrumental' rationality, *Zweckrationalität* in the German original, is based on a system of means–ends calculations, and can be contrasted with 'value-rationality', or *Wertrationalität*, where an absolute end, such as salvation, precludes any possible calculation of costs. For Weber, purposively rational action can be defined

> in terms of rational orientation to a system of discrete individual ends . . . that is, through expectations as to the behaviour of objects

> . . . and of other . . . individuals, making use of these expectations as 'conditions' or 'means' for the successful attainment of the actor's own rationally chosen ends . . . (Weber, 1964, p. 115)

He views this particular type of action as characteristic of modern Western capitalism.

There is no equivalent concept in Weber to the mode of production in Marx, no general process canvassed as fundamentally constitutive of social reality in general. Nor does Weber identify any one individual process as generating capitalism in particular: his analyses are both multi-causal and based on factors conceived as in principle contingent. As he insisted in *The Protestant Ethic*, 'it is . . . not my aim to substitute for a one-sided materialistic an equally one-sided spiritualistic causal interpretation of culture and of history' (Weber, 1930, p. 183). But there is a clearly 'generative' character, nonetheless, to Weber's account of capitalism, once the system has passed beyond its historical point of origin, once capitalist development is already underway. Toward the end of *The Protestant Ethic*, he famously characterized capitalism as an 'iron cage of reason'. 'The Puritan wanted to work in a calling'; he writes:

> we are forced to do so. For when asceticism . . . began to dominate worldly morality, it did its part in building the tremendous cosmos of the modern economic order. This order is now bound to the technical and economic conditions of machine production which today determine the lives of all the individuals who are born into this mechanism . . . with irresistible force . . . In Baxter's[2] view the care for external goods should only lie on the shoulders of the 'saint like a light cloak, which can be thrown aside at any moment'. But fate decreed that the cloak should become an iron cage. (Weber, 1930, p. 181)

This 'irresistible' rationalization is central to Weber's sense of what is most distinctive about modernity and modernization: capitalism is above all a system of rational economic calculation; bureaucracy is the distinctly modern form of rational administration; Protestantism a system of religious belief peculiarly conducive to a radical rationalization of individual ethical conduct; occidental music and its system of notation distinctively and characteristically rationalized (Weber, 1964, p. 279; Weber,

1948b, pp. 215–216; Weber, 1930, pp. 153–154; Weber, 1958, pp. 82–88).

If Weber was the primary theoretical inspiration for contemporary stratification theory, then this is so in part only by way of a series of misreadings of much of his own intent. The famous 'three dimensions', long central to accounts of social inequality in mainstream American sociology, were 'class, status and power', to quote the title of one standard American university textbook (Bendix and Lipset, 1966). These are regularly traced to Weber's own much-cited essay, 'Class, status, party', translated into English from Part III of *Wirtschaft und Gesellschaft*. Interestingly, Weber's own third term is party (*Partei*) rather than power and it is clear that the term is intended, not as some further dimension of social inequality, but as a different type of social group, a political party in much the same sense as in everyday usage (Weber, 1948b, pp. 194–195). Moreover, although Weber had much to say elsewhere on the subject of power (Weber, 1964, pp. 152–153, 324–363), it is also clear that he viewed it as operating within class and status groups, rather than alongside them: ' "classes," "status groups," and "parties" are phenomena of the distribution of power', he writes (Weber, 1948b, p. 181). As one neo-Weberian sociologist observes:

> power need not be thought of as something which exists over and above the system of material and social rewards; rather, it can be thought of as a concept or metaphor . . . used to depict the flow of resources which constitutes this system . . . as such it is not a separate dimension of stratification at all. (Parkin, 1972, p. 46)

If there are dimensions of inequality in Weber's model, then these are only ever twofold: class (*Klasse*) and status (*Stand*).

Weber's definition of class is well worth quoting in full:

> We may speak of a 'class' when (1) a number of people have in common a specific causal component of their life chances, in so far as (2) this component is represented exclusively by economic interests in the possession of goods and opportunities for income, and (3) is represented under the conditions of the commodity or labor markets. (Weber, 1948b, p. 181)

Thus defined, class situation is in effect identical to market position. It follows necessarily that classes are historically specific social groups, the presence of which requires the prior existence of a market economy. Class is thus especially important to capitalism since this is the most thoroughly commodified of all historical social systems. For Marx, by comparison, classes were present in virtually all societies, if only because they were defined in relation to the ubiquity of exploitative production rather than the specificity of market relations. The difference is definitional rather than substantive, but interesting consequences follow therefrom nonetheless. Whereas for Marx there can only ever be a limited number of classes in any given mode of production, since there is necessarily only a limited number of possible relations of production, for Weber there can be as many classes in any given market economy as there are differences in income. In principle, then, Weberian classes should be much smaller than Marxian. Much subsequent neo-Weberian stratification theory has indeed made use of a relatively large number of classes. But in practice, as Giddens rightly observed, Weber himself worked with a much tighter model, in which 'only certain definite combinations, organised around the ownership and non-ownership of property' were 'historically significant' (Giddens, 1971, p. 165). In Part I of *Wirtschaft und Gesellschaft*, Weber had distinguished between: 'property classes', the class situation of which is determined by the relative absence or presence of property-holding, for example as between slave-owners and slaves; 'acquisition classes', determined by the relative absence or presence of opportunities for the exploitation of services on the market, as between entrepreneurs and workers; and 'social classes', amongst which regular social interactions normally occur (Weber, 1964, p. 424). The combined effect of these distinctions is to move toward models of the class structure of capitalist and pre-capitalist societies much closer to Marx than those suggested in Weber's formal definition of class situation. Property classes, it should be apparent, are more obviously characteristic of pre-capitalist than of capitalist social formations.

The most interesting notion here is that of 'social class', for it is this that most closely approximates to Marx's sense, not of what classes are, but of what they do. For Weber:

the 'social class' structure is composed of the plurality of class statuses between which an interchange of individuals on a personal basis or in the course of generations is readily possible and typically observable. (Weber, 1964, p. 424)

The examples Weber gives are, with one exception, predictably close to Marx's own: the 'working class'; the 'lower middle class' (the German *Kleinbürgertum* is very close to the French *petite bourgeoisie*); the 'privileged' classes; and, the exception, the 'intelligentsia' (Weber, 1964, p. 427). Weber was aware of this closeness: he specifically cites the last chapter of *Capital* as an unfinished account of proletarian class unity, offering his own suggestions as to the conditions in which such unity might be likely to occur. Moreover, his analysis leads, in turn, to an account of the more general conditions under which social classes become effective social actors. These are fourfold, he argues: a capacity to concentrate on rival class opponents over issues in which the immediate conflict of interest is vital; a common class status shared by large masses of people; the technical possibility of coming together physically; and a leadership directed towards readily attainable goals (Weber, 1964, pp. 427–428). Much of this is entirely compatible either with Marx or with subsequent Marxism: Weber's first and third conditions echo Marx himself on the difference between workers and peasants; the insistence that leadership comes from 'persons, such as intelligentsia, who don't belong to the class in question' (Weber, 1964, p. 428) is reminiscent of Lenin. The crucial difference remains that, whereas Marx saw capitalism as necessarily generating such class consciousness, Weber recognized this as only one possibility amongst many: in short, it might happen, but need not.

Much subsequent Weberian sociology treated 'class' and 'status' as dimensional indices of inequality. It should now be apparent, however, that one central theme in Weber, as in Marx, is that of the possibility for classes to act as groups: and a group is something very different from an index. For Weber, status was even more obviously associated with the capacity for group action, if only because it is itself primarily an effect of group consciousness. By a 'status situation' he meant

every typical component of the life fate of men that is determined by
a specific, positive or negative, social estimation of *honor*. (Weber,
1948b, p. 187)

Clearly, whilst market situation is a matter of objective fact,
much akin to Marx's 'class in itself', social estimations of honour
are essentially matters of interpersonal subjectivity. And for
Weber this is no random effect of merely personal worth, but
a distinguishing feature of certain kinds of social structure.
Hence, his recognition that status groups, unlike classes, are
normally social actors or, as he has it, 'communities' (Weber,
1948b, p. 186). Status groups, then, are social groups organized
around non-market principles of social hierarchy. This is not to
suggest that they are thereby 'non-economic', for as Weber
himself insists: 'Property as such is not always recognized as
a status qualification, but in the long run it is, and with extra-
ordinary regularity' (Weber, 1948b, p. 187). Moreover, as Weber
readily concedes, any status attribute may be used to monopolize
'specific, usually economic opportunities', so as to achieve the
'closure of social and economic opportunities to *outsiders*'
(Weber, 1968, p. 342). If regularly defined in relation to property,
but not to markets, then what exactly are these status groups?
The short answer is that, for the main part, they are what Marx
had meant by pre-capitalist classes. Mainstream sociology has
tended to think of status as a separate dimension of inequality
functioning alongside class within contemporary society, as, for
example, in the standard contrast between the curate with high
status but low income and the bookmaker with low status but
high income (Runciman, 1972, p. 45). It is clear, nonetheless,
that this is not what Weber intended: the examples in his discussion include the chieftain in a subsistence economy, Indian
castes and the Jewish diaspora, Hellenic and Roman aristocracies, medieval knights, peasants, priests and guilds (Weber,
1948b, pp. 187, 189, 193). His one contemporary example, that of
the American 'gentleman' (Weber, 1948b, pp. 187–188), is also
putatively archaic.

For Weber, status groups are defined in relation to a specific
style of life, a specific notion of honour, and these typically
entail clear patterns of restriction on intercourse with non-

members, for example the taboo on exogamy (Weber, 1948b, pp. 187–188). The extreme instance of an entirely closed status system, he notes, is the caste system (Weber, 1948b, pp. 188–189). Here, he introduces the interesting notion that some societies are in effect stratified according to status criteria, rather than class or market criteria. Indeed, he specifically argues that

> where stratification by status permeates a community as strongly as was the case in all political communities of antiquity and of the Middle Ages, one can never speak of a genuinely free market competition as we understand it today. (Weber, 1948b, p. 193)

Status groups certainly continue to exist in capitalist societies: the obvious examples in Weber's own time were the Anglo-Saxon and Latin hereditary aristocracies.[3] But their status pretensions tend to become progressively marginalized by the central political and economic mechanisms of a rationalized society. As Weber observed, 'the market and its processes "knows no personal distinctions" . . . it knows nothing of "honor" ' (Weber, 1948b, p. 192). Comparing stratification by status and by class, he concluded that:

> When the bases of the acquisition and distribution of goods are relatively stable, stratification by status is favored. Every technological repercussion and economic transformation threatens stratification by status and pushes the class situation into the foreground. (Weber, 1948b, pp. 193–194)

This has been read as suggesting that the further development of capitalism beyond its socially traumatic origins will eventually produce a restrengthening of status distinctions. But Weber's overall characterization of capitalist development as a process of continuing rationalization, and of capitalism itself as a social system based on the market, suggest to the contrary a view of class as the predominant form of stratification for the foreseeable future. Unlike Marx, Weber made few attempts to predict the likely course of subsequent history. However, his gloomily pessimistic speculation that machine production might perhaps determine our lives 'until the last ton of fossilized coal is burnt' (Weber, 1930, p. 181) appears to imply a vision of the immediate future as capitalistic as any in Marx. The fundamental difference between them concerns neither the subjective dimension in stratification nor the existence of non-class societies: Marx knew all about 'false consciousness'; and he knew too that pre-capitalist class systems had been organized around institutions very different from the market. Rather, the basic point at issue is Marx's insistence on the mode of production as an invariable determinant of the structure of social inequality, as compared to Weber's sense of rationalization as a historically unique, albeit very far-reaching, dynamic within modern Western capitalist societies.

That said, certain clear differences do indeed persist between their respective conceptions of the relationship between 'objective' social structure and 'subjective' social consciousness. For Weber, ideas and beliefs play a much more significant role in the overall structure of social determination than for Marx. Weber's general stress on the social effectivity of belief is especially relevant to his theory of legitimation. Despite their own acknowledgement of the power of the 'ruling ideas', Marx and Engels had tended to explain social order as the effect either of the mode of production itself or of state power. Weber, by contrast, stressed what he termed legitimate authority, that is, the 'probability that a command with a given specific content will be obeyed', resting on the acceptance by subordinates of the right of superordinates to give such commands (Weber, 1964, pp. 152, 324–325). For Weber, the search for legitimacy is a near-ubiquitous feature of hierarchical social organization:

> no system of authority voluntarily limits itself to the appeal to material or affectual or ideal motives as a basis for guaranteeing its continuance. In addition every such system attempts to establish and to cultivate the belief in its 'legitimacy'. (Weber, 1964, p. 325)

In short, the 'ruling ideas' rule effectively: insofar as authority is legitimate, it is necessarily uncontested. Moreover, there is for Weber no necessary succession of different types of class rule, and hence of ruling ideas, as there had been for Marx: in principle, at least, a legitimate authority might last indefinitely.

Weber sketches out a typology of three main kinds of legitimation: rational authority, which rests 'on a belief in the "legality" of patterns of normative rules and the right of those elevated to authority under such rules to issue commands'; traditional authority, resting 'on an established belief in the sanctity of immemorial traditions and the legitimacy of the status of those exercising authority under them'; and charismatic authority, which rests on 'devotion to the specific and exceptional sanctity, heroism or exemplary character of an individual person, and of the normative patterns or order revealed or ordained by him' (Weber, 1964, p. 328). Of these, only the first two could sustain relatively stable and enduring social orders. Charismatic authority typically represents a powerful challenge to social routine and is therefore peculiarly suited to facilitate social change, including revolutionary change. But, precisely because it depends on a particular person, it is inherently unstable and will normally either collapse in on itself or become routinized into one of the other two forms (Weber, 1964, pp. 363–364). Rational and legal authority, by contrast, are 'specifically forms of everyday routine control of action' (Weber, 1964, p. 361) and are, therefore, in principle more or less indefinitely extensible. Although both are presented merely as 'ideal types', which cannot 'usually . . . be found in historical cases in "pure" form' (Weber, 1964, p. 329), it should be apparent that traditional authority systems tend to predominate in pre-capitalist (status) societies, legal authority in capitalist (class) societies.

As it stands, this ideal typology appears little more than a set of classificatory analytical tools, devices with which to measure, as it were, three dimensions of authority. But in the analysis of rational legality, in particular, Weber again moves towards what Connell would recognize as generative analysis. This generative component is at its most apparent in the treatment of bureaucracy, the distinctive organizational form through which legal authority is expressed. For Weber, bureaucracy is increasingly characteristic of all complex organizations, not only the state, but also private clinics, hospitals, the Catholic Church, large-scale capitalist corporations, political parties, the modern army, and so on (Weber, 1964, pp. 334–335). The development of this characteristically modern type of administration is, in his view, a direct corollary of the progress of capitalism. He discusses a whole range of factors that contribute to the genesis of bureaucracy, but three especially are inseparable from this more general history: the money economy, the class system and the mass-democratic political system. A 'developed money economy' is necessary to the maintenance, if not the initial establishment, of bureaucratic structures, he argues, so as to pay the salaries of officials: payment in kind, he hypothesizes, tends 'to loosen the bureaucratic mechanism, . . . to weaken hierarchic subordination' (Weber, 1948d, pp. 207–208). Stratification according to class criteria is necessary so that these officials can discharge their duties objectively, without 'regard of persons': 'consistent execution of bureaucratic domination', he writes, 'means the leveling of status "honor" . . . it means the universal domination of the "class situation" ' (Weber, 1948d, p. 215). As for mass democracy, it is not so much that bureaucracy requires democracy as that both democracy and bureaucracy require 'equality before the law', an antipathy to 'privilege' and a principled rejection of doing business 'from case to case'. Bureaucracy may well function perfectly adequately without democracy, but it 'inevitably accompanies modern *mass democracy*' (Weber, 1948d, p. 224) whenever and wherever the latter appears. What we have here, then, are the outlines of a generative analysis both of bureaucracy as a mode of organization and of rational legality as a mode of authority. There is an important element in Weber's comparative historical sociology that is indeed 'dimensional' or classificatory, in Connell's terms, and it is this which provided the analytical framework for much subsequent stratification theory. But there are the beginnings of a 'generative' theory here too: in the account of market society as generating stratification systems based on class rather than status; and alongside this, and closely bound up with it, in that of the progressive bureaucratization of modern systems of organization. This is a much more cautiously stated version of generative theory than anything in Marx. The generative component is there, nonetheless, and it is this that has provided vital inspiration to contemporary neo-Weberian class analysis, from Dahrendorf through to Parkin and beyond (Dahrendorf, 1959; Parkin, 1979).

Neo-Weberian Sociology: Class Identity and Class Consciousness

There is a vast amount of accumulated sociological research on the subject of structured social inequality, especially for the Western world. Over the past 20 years or so this has increasingly tended to include material on race, ethnicity and gender. Historically, however, its major focus had been provided by social class, in either the Marxist or the Weberian sense of the term, or by some alternative concept, such as status or stratification, deemed analytically superior, but also in a sense functionally equivalent, to class. Whatever the theoretical apparatus, most of this research had a threefold empirical focus. Firstly, much work was designed to produce relatively 'objective' measures of the distribution of given resources between families or heads of households over a given population, most commonly income and wealth but sometimes, for example, factors such as educational opportunity or life expectancy. Secondly, there was a whole series of attempts to measure rates of 'social mobility', or movement, between 'working-class' (or 'blue-collar') and 'middle-class' (or 'white-collar') occupations, either 'intragenerationally' (that is, within a working life) or 'intergenerationally' (that is, from father to son to grandson, and so on). Thirdly, much work was carried out on forms of 'class consciousness', to borrow a Marxian term, that is, on the extent to which images of society, and especially perceptions of social inequality itself, varied between different social classes. This final question will be our main concern here because of its much greater relevance to the more general questions of cultural meaning that concern contemporary Cultural Studies.

The study of structured social inequality in mainstream sociology (as distinct from feminist critique thereof) has been an overwhelmingly Weberian affair. Until well into the 1970s, the main lines of argument within the discipline had tended to run between 'stratification theory', which employed an essentially consensual account of social structure, and neo-Weberian 'class analysis', which employed an essentially conflictual account. Both rested on relatively strong propositions concerning the cultural meaning of social inequality: consensus theorists saw stratification as integrative, because it arose from the supposedly common values that bound the different strata together; conflict theorists as producing conflict, because it arose from kinds of coercion that divided the strata against each other, thereby producing mutually antipathetic forms of social consciousness (Heller, 1969, p. 479). Both happily acknowledged some debt to Weber, both with apparent good cause. For stratification theory, this centred on the so-called three dimensions of inequality – class, status and power: in this account, stratification consists in 'a ranking in three separate dimensions – the economic, the social . . . and the political' (Runciman, 1974, p. 56). For conflict theory, by contrast, it centred on the quasi-Nietzschean element in his work, something barely acknowledged by Parsons and the American functionalists. Here, social inequality becomes the effect of a struggle for power and the struggle to legitimize that power through authority.

If for stratification theory social inequality was essentially a matter of 'ranking', then the obvious question arose: who is it that does the ranking? There were basically two alternative answers: either it is the work of the sociologist, in which case it becomes an essentially arbitrary heuristic device; or it is the work of society, in which case it is itself an 'objective social fact'. The first, which was Runciman's, avoids the temptation to imagine society as possessing a Durkheimian 'collective conscience', but only at the price of a retreat from explanation into measurement. Hence, his understanding of the research problem as one of 'plotting', in the sense of mapping (Runciman, 1974, p. 58). The second insists on the knowability of social structure, but can only imagine it as radically consensual. The most famous instance here is Parsons, for whom social stratification was 'the ranking of units in a social system in accordance with the standards of the common value system' (Parsons, 1954, p. 388). If this sounds Durkheimian rather than Weberian, then it is worth recalling how insistent Parsons had been that the two perspectives had converged on 'the conception of a common system of ultimate values as a vital element in concrete social life' (Parsons, 1949, p. 469). We may perhaps dispute Parsons's reading of Weber, but we cannot reasonably doubt its sincerity: indeed, it was Weber, rather than Durkheim, who had provided Parsons's *The Structure of Social Action* with its primary subject matter.

The clearest early example of neo-Weberian conflict theory, albeit untypical in the degree to which it reduced both class and status to power, was Ralf Dahrendorf's *Soziale Klassen und Klassenkonflikt*. For Dahrendorf:

> in every social organization . . . there is a differential distribution of power and authority . . . this . . . invariably becomes the determining factor of systematic social conflicts of a type that is germane to class conflicts . . . The structural origin of such group conflicts must be sought in the arrangement of social roles endowed with expectations of domination or subjection. Wherever there are such roles, group conflicts . . . are to be expected. (Dahrendorf, 1959, p. 165)

Inequality is thus not so much the effect of social consensus as the source of social conflict: by virtue of their relationship to each other, the dominant and the subjected hold 'interests which are contradictory in substance and direction' (Dahrendorf, 1959, p. 174). In these initial formulations, Dahrendorf had imagined his conflict theory as somehow ultimately compatible with Parsonian consensus theory, since a truly general sociology would require explanations for both. In later reformulations, however, he moved towards a more radical rejection of consensus theory: 'the "value system" of a society is universal', he would later write, 'only in the sense that it applies to everyone (it is in fact merely dominant)' (Dahrendorf, 1968, p. 177). In lines that echo Marx as much as Weber, Dahrendorf proceeded to the conclusion that: 'Inequality always implies the gain of one group at the expense of others; thus every system of social stratification generates protest against its principles and bears the seeds of its own suppression' (Dahrendorf, 1968, p. 177).

The crux of the matter at issue between consensus and conflict models hinged on what was ultimately an almost entirely empirical question, that of the absence or presence of a discernible degree of social agreement concerning the unequal distribution of social rewards. Sociology has enjoyed precious little in the way of a reputation for the empirical testing of its major theoretical propositions. Uncharacteristically, however, in this particular instance a great deal of the relevant data were in fact available. The social distribution of attitudes to social inequality had provided Anglo-American sociology with one of its central empirical preoccupations during the post-Second World War period. There is little doubt as to the direction in which these findings point: summarizing much of the enormous Anglophone literature on research into values conducted prior to 1970, Mann concluded that 'value consensus does not exist to any significant degree' (Mann, 1970, p. 432). Even such classically functionalist studies as Almond and Verba's *The Civic Culture* had provided ample evidence for the absence of value consensus in Western societies.[4] Most non-functionalist or quasi-functionalist studies came up with very clear and very direct evidence for widespread value dissensus (Young and Willmott, 1956; Hyman, 1966; Chamberlain, 1983). In retrospect, the only surprise is that any sociologist anywhere could ever have imagined structured social inequality to be the occasion for anything other than systematic social disagreement.

By far the more fertile lines of inquiry were those suggested by the prior assumption of a divided rather than unitary social consciousness. This resulted in a whole series of variously Marxian, post-Marxian and Weberian answers to a set of essentially Marxist questions concerning the relationships between 'being' and 'consciousness'. Typically, this work set out from definitions of class much less complex than those in Marx or Weber, essentially a simple tripartite distinction between, respectively, an 'upper class' of very wealthy capitalists, landlords and their families, a 'middle class' of non-manual workers and their families, and a 'working class' of manual workers and their families. Relatively little attention was directed at the culture of the 'upper class' itself, in part because of its assumed visibility in the dominant institutions, in part because of the relative difficulty of securing access to its truly private affairs. In practice, the central empirical focus typically concerned, firstly, the differences at any one time between 'middle-class' and 'working-class' class consciousness and, secondly, the ways in which each of these had changed internally over time. As to the former, most reports recorded fairly widespread middle-class perceptions of social inequality as hierarchical and based on prestige rather than power. By contrast, traditional forms of working-class consciousness were found to be either dichotomous and based on power or deferential and based on prestige (Lockwood, 1966, pp. 249–255). Other supposedly emergent sub-variants of working-class consciousness were variously characterized as 'embourgeoisified' (Zweig, 1961), 'egoistic' as distinct from 'fraternalistic' (Runciman, 1972), or 'instrumental' as distinct from 'solidaristic'. The latter characterization is that proposed in the still classic British study, Goldthorpe and Lockwood's three-volume *The Affluent Worker* (Goldthorpe et al., 1968a; Goldthorpe et al., 1968b; Goldthorpe et al., 1969). Their general findings – to the effect that even affluent manual workers showed little evidence of becoming 'embourgeoisified' (that is, becoming culturally middle-class), but that they were both more privatized and less solidaristic than those in traditional working-class communities – seem close to incontrovertible, some Marxist point-scoring to the contrary notwithstanding.[5] Other studies focused on the growth of 'secularist', or instrumental as distinct from deferential, forms of working-class Conservatism (McKenzie and Silver, 1968), yet others on the 'new middle class' of salaried, white-collar employees and on its possibilities for 'proletarianization'. We shall have cause to return to this latter question.

Neo-Weberian Class Analysis: Goldthorpe

For the moment, however, let us consider in a little more detail the work of the most prominent British representative of this kind of sociology, John H. Goldthorpe. As we have seen, Goldthorpe had become, along with David Lockwood, perhaps the leading exponent of neo-Weberian empirical class analysis in British sociology. He later designed the so-called 'Hope–Goldthorpe occupational scale' and later still the 'Goldthorpe class schema', the first version of which identified seven main social classes, the latest 11 (Goldthorpe and Hope, 1974; Goldthorpe, 1980, p. 39; Erikson and Goldthorpe, 1992, pp. 38–39). One recent commentator, writing in the official journal of the British Sociological Association, describes the schema as 'the most influential measure of social class in use among European sociologists . . . developed over a long period of research into class structure and social mobility in Britain and comparatively . . . devised, defended and applied with considerable sophistication' (Evans, 1996, p. 209). As we noted in passing in Chapter 2, Goldthorpe's approach is, in Connell's terms, clearly 'dimensional' rather than 'generative'. For Goldthorpe, class analysis can be distinguished, not by any distinctive logic, but by its stress on the empirical significance of social class – as distinct from, say, 'status' or gender – as an independent variable within the wider social matrix. By class Goldthorpe means, in the first instance, an aggregation of occupational categories, the members of which occupy 'typically comparable' market situations (income, economic security, chances for advancement) and work situations (place in the system of authority, degree of autonomy in the performance of work-tasks) (Goldthorpe, 1980, p. 39). The debt to Weber should be obvious. The original seven-class model comprised: Class I, the higher 'service' class (higher-grade professionals, managers of large businesses, large proprietors); Class II, the 'subaltern' service class (lower-grade professionals, managers of small businesses, supervisors of non-manual employees); Class III, the 'white-collar labour force' (routine non-manual employees); Class IV, the 'petty bourgeoisie' (the self-employed); Class V, the 'aristocracy of labour or "blue-collar" élite' (lower-grade technicians, supervisors of manual workers); Class VI, the skilled manual working class; and Class VII, the semi- and unskilled manual working class (Goldthorpe, 1980, pp. 39–42). Later variants distinguished between routine non-manual employees in administration and commerce (IIIa) and personal service workers (IIIb); between small proprietors with employees (IVa), small proprietors without employees (IVb) and farmers, smallholders and fishermen (IVc); and between non-agricultural (VIIa) and agricultural manual workers (VIIb) (Goldthorpe, 1987, pp. 280, 305).

These are clearly 'dimensional' categories, with which to locate the position of individuals in relation to a class 'map'. But the purpose of the analysis is by no means merely classificatory. To the contrary, Goldthorpe is insistent that social classes can have a real existence quite apart from their construction within sociological discourse; that these occupational aggregates can in fact acquire both 'demographic' and 'socio-cultural' identity (Goldthorpe, 1982, pp. 171–172). This is why he defines class, much to the annoyance of many feminist sociologists, not simply as an aggregate of individuals, but as an aggregate of families, the 'heads' of which work in particular occupations (Goldthorpe, 1983, p. 468). For Goldthorpe, the family is the 'major unit of . . . class fate' and, insofar as social classes form relatively stable collectivities, they do so by virtue of 'the continuity with which individuals and families have been associated with particular class positions over time' (Goldthorpe, 1983, pp. 469, 483). The primary focus for much of his work has been the empirical study of comparative social mobility rates, both over time and internationally. He and his various co-workers regard social mobility as of central sociological importance, both in itself as a measure of liberal 'openness' and by virtue of its substantial 'implications for class formation and class action' (Goldthorpe, 1987, p. 28). For Goldthorpe, as for Marx, classes are at once both analytical categories and social collectivities. As collectivities, they consist in aggregates of individuals and families, who are to varying degrees exposed to the competing claims of class identity and social mobility: other things being equal, the higher the social mobility rate, the more open the social structure, and hence the more attenuated the forms of class identity. But Goldthorpe's findings point very clearly towards the persistence of relatively stable and enduring forms of class inequality: the net association between present class position and class of origin was much the same in Britain in the 1970s as in the inter-war years; measurable inequality in life chances was of such a kind as to identify it as the effect of class structure rather than of individual difference; and such inequality was significantly compounded for working-class men by the re-emergence of large-scale unemployment during the

1980s (Goldthorpe, 1987, pp. 327–329). Moreover, comparative analyses of social mobility in the United States, Australia and Japan found little evidence of any exceptional 'openness' in these 'new' countries, as compared to British (and other European) patterns (Erikson and Goldthorpe, 1992, pp. 371–372). Of the 15 'nations' under analysis, the USA, Japan and Australia were ranked respectively 12th, 13th and 14th in the order of 'overall fluidity', whilst Scotland ranked first, that is, it exhibited the highest level of opennesss, and England eighth (Erikson and Goldthorpe, 1992, p. 381).

Goldthorpe concludes that the persistence of class structure as closure makes for a corresponding persistence in patterns of class formation and identity. He argues that it is possible to detect, at the demographic level, at least two clear instances of class formation in modern Britain, respectively the service class (Class I and Class II) and the working class (Class VI and VII), and a possible third, the petty bourgeoisie (Class IV) (Goldthorpe, 1987, p. 338). At the socio-cultural level, too, he concludes that both the service class and the working class display evidence of a strengthening cultural identity, partially offset during the 1980s only by the emergence, from within the working class, of a new underclass of the long-term unemployed and their families (Goldthorpe, 1987, pp. 341, 344–345). Confronted by a series of postmodern arguments to the effect that class has increasingly been superseded by other forms of identity (Pahl, 1989; Holton and Turner, 1989, pp. 160–196), Goldthorpe has insisted, in a paper co-authored with Gordon Marshall, that:

> there is in fact no reason to suppose that over recent decades, classes in Britain – the working class included – have shown any weakening in either their social cohesion or their ideological distinctiveness. This conclusion is . . . consistent with a variety of . . . findings on . . . trends . . . in patterns of class mobility, in levels of class identification, and in class differences in political attitudes and values. (Goldthorpe and Marshall, 1992, pp. 391–392)

On the specific question of the articulation of class identity and political action, Goldthorpe's conclusions run directly contrary to the 'class dealignment' thesis, which had become something of a received wisdom amongst British sociologists during

the long years of Thatcherism. Goldthorpe and Marshall are, of
course, aware of the Labour Party's dismal electoral performance during the 1980s and early 1990s. But they cite a very
substantial body of technically sophisticated empirical research
and analysis, making use of the distinction between relative and
absolute rates of class voting, which shows that there is 'no
secular tendency for the class-vote association to decline': if
Labour failed in the 1980s, then this was for essentially contingent reasons, much more open to 'political' than sociological
explanation (Goldthorpe and Marshall, 1992, p. 391). It is thus
stability, rather than dynamism, that most clearly characterizes
the pattern of class relations in contemporary British society. If
Goldthorpe is right, then the practical political implications also
tend to contradict much of the received wisdom of Tony Blair's
New Labour Party. For, as Goldthorpe himself observes, 'socialist politics . . . must, if they are to have any chance of success,
remain in some sense class politics; that is, must rest on an
awareness of class identities and interests and on the mobilization of class-based support' (Goldthorpe, 1990, p. 402).

Neo-Weberian Class Theory: Parkin, Giddens, Mann

Where Goldthorpe and his colleagues had pursued a primarily
empirical research programme, other recent neo-Weberian work
has often been largely theoretical in character. One of the
interesting developments in British academic sociology during
the 1970s and 1980s was the emergence of a distinctive school
of neo-Weberian class theorists, notably Frank Parkin, Anthony
Giddens and Michael Mann. All three started from the shared
conviction that class was central to the social structures of
advanced capitalist society, but that this centrality was better
theorized in Weberian than Marxian terms. Ironically, as it
turned out, Giddens was initially less enthusiastic in this Weberianism than either Parkin or Mann, going to some lengths to
insist on his own quasi-Marxist credentials: 'Parkin's conception
is much closer to an unreconstructed Weberian position than

my own', he wrote: '. . . My conception – drawn from Marx . . . diverges substantially from Parkin's views' (Giddens, 1981, p. 300). As we shall see, this enthusiasm for Marx would not stand the test of time. But Parkin's work was more obviously Weberian in inspiration. Nonetheless, even he had insisted, in terms that might have done justice to the *New Left Review*, that social inequality was both 'systematic . . . and grounded in the material order' (Parkin, 1972, p. 17). This was a politically 'radical' Weberianism, then, much affected by quasi-Marxist motifs from the then contemporary mood, as refracted both in social theory (Althusserian Marxism) and in social practice (the wave of industrial militancy that characterized the 1970s).

For Parkin, as much as for any Marxist, class provided 'the backbone of the reward structure' (Parkin, 1972, p. 24). Following Weber, he chose to define class in terms of market position and 'occupational order' on the one hand, property on the other. As to occupation, he substituted a conventional six-class model for Weber's four classes, respectively: professional, managerial and administrative; semi-professional and lower administrative; routine white-collar; skilled manual; semi-skilled manual; and unskilled manual (Parkin, 1972, p. 19). The crucial 'break' in this hierarchy was that between manual and non-manual occupational categories (Parkin, 1972, p. 25). As to property, he saw this as generally complementing the occupational order, but with the additional complication of a small 'propertied *élite*' at its apex (Parkin, 1972, p. 24). This led to a 'dichotomous or two-class model': a dominant class, consisting of the elite combined with the non-manual workers, and a subordinate class of manual workers (Parkin, 1972, p. 26). Moreover, he also concluded that contemporary industrial societies are organized around class rather than status:

> as the occupational order comes increasingly to be the primary source of symbolic as well as material advantages, so the areas for potential discrepancy between the different dimensions of equality tend to diminish . . . industrial societies . . . have a more unitary reward system than . . . non-industrial societies. And it is for this . . . reason that a multi-dimensional model of stratification has to be handled with particular caution. (Parkin, 1972, pp. 39–40)

The Affluent Worker studies had concluded that the new 'instrumental collectivism' represented a form of working-class consciousness generated by very specific conditions of employment,
affluence and residence. But the coexistence within the selfsame workplaces and neighbourhoods of competing forms of
consciousness, ranging at the very least from 'solidaristic'
Labourism through to 'deferential' Conservatism, posed the
problem of how exactly to understand the relationship between
competing meaning systems within any one class. Parkin's *Class
Inequality and Political Order* provided perhaps the most
elegant of all neo-Weberian solutions to the problem. He argued
that the working-class normative order could be analysed in
terms of three competing meaning systems: the dominant value
system, which has its origins in the major societal institutions
and stimulates both deferential and aspirational responses in
the working class; the subordinate value system, which has its
source in the local working-class community (wherever this
exists) and promotes essentially accommodative responses to
the social status quo, including both solidaristic and instrumental forms of collectivism; and the radical value system,
which has its institutional source in the mass working-class
political party, whether Labour or Communist, and promotes an
essentially oppositional consciousness, based on class rather
than community (Parkin, 1972, pp. 79–102). There is no suggestion here that such meaning systems are mutually exclusive
in social practice. To the contrary, Parkin likens the overall
class culture to a 'reservoir' fed by three major 'normative
streams': 'Attitudes towards the social order held by any given
members of this class', he writes, 'would be likely to reflect the
influences of this normative mix, rather than the kind of rigorous intellectual consistency which would be produced through
exposure to only one major meaning-system' (Parkin, 1972,
p. 100). Hence, the apparently contradictory nature of much
empirical working-class consciousness. Hence, too, the crucial
role of the Labour Party as a source of political mobilization or
demobilization:

> the mass party is one of the very few social agencies which has the
> potential to condition the outlook of the working class in a radical

direction. If . . . it chooses not to utilize this potential, then we might expect a gradual de-radicalization . . . to set in. (Parkin, 1972, p. 102)

Elsewhere, Parkin approached the problems of class formation and class consciousness by way of a notion of social closure deriving directly from Weber. Classes establish and maintain themselves, he argued, through strategies of social 'closure', which can be based either on the power of 'exclusion', if aimed at the subordination of other groups, or that of 'solidarism', if aimed at the insubordination of already superordinate groups (Parkin, 1974, pp. 4–5). Later, he would reformulate this distinction as that between exclusion and 'usurpation', where the latter term refers to a type of closure 'mounted by a group in response to its outsider status and the collective experiences of exclusion' (Parkin, 1979, p. 74). For Parkin, the dominant class in contemporary capitalist societies, the bourgeoisie, exercises exclusionary powers based either on the property rights of the owners and managers of capital or on the credentialism of the learned professions (Parkin, 1979, p. 58). Both property and qualifications are defined by bourgeois law and ethics as properly attaching to individuals rather than collectivities. Bourgeois class consciousness is thus essentially individualist in character, he argues, and its exclusionary strategies have become progressively more so over time (Parkin, 1979, p. 69). Hence, the primarily meritocratic character of 'bourgeois' notions of justice. Although also intended as applicable to the new social movements, the central focus for Parkin's account of usurpation is provided by the confrontation between capital and labour, that is, by the most quintessentially class-based of all social conflicts. Since in capitalist societies the subordinate working class is both propertyless (that is, it owns no capital, as distinct from mere possessions) and uncredentialled, it follows that its attempts at social closure will be primarily usurpationary rather than exclusionary. Even the most modest forms of such usurpation, he notes, will tend to draw upon 'alternative standards of distributive justice to those solemnized by the rules of exclusion' (Parkin, 1979, p. 74). Working-class industrial leverage can be derived either from skill and market capacity or from what

Parkin terms 'disruptive potential' (Parkin, 1979, p. 80).[6] If the former, then it will remain compatible with an expanded version of the bourgeois conception of distributive justice. In the latter case, however, usurpation is much more directly incompatible with the moral claims of the dominant and exclusionary classes. Interestingly, he toys with the notion that disruption of this kind can itself be read as testimony to the existence in the working class of a 'subterranean theory of distributive justice', where rewards are ideally allocated according to a group's 'functional importance', as measured by the extent of the dislocation that would be caused by the withdrawal of labour (Parkin, 1979, pp. 76–77).

As we have seen, Giddens was unhappy with descriptions of his work as Weberian, yet his early writings on class theory are clearly neo-Weberian in character. The debt to Weber is most apparent in the emphasis on the market: for Giddens, classes are formed, not simply around property, but around a more generalized market capacity, comprising '*all forms of relevant attributes which individuals may bring to the bargaining encounter*' (Giddens, 1981, p. 103). For Giddens, as for Weber, class is an effect of the market, rather than of the mode of production, and classes are therefore peculiarly characteristic of distinctively capitalist stratification systems: 'Capitalism is a "class society" in a more fundamental sense than feudalism or other types of society that have previously existed in history' (Giddens, 1981, p. 298). In a later formulation, Giddens would rework this distinction as that between pre-capitalist 'class-divided societies' and capitalist 'class society' proper. There are social classes in many non-capitalist societies, he concedes, but only under capitalism does class 'serve as a basis for identifying the basic structural principle of organization' (Giddens, 1995, p. 108). In direct contradiction to most American neo-Weberian sociology, then, but in accordance with much in Weber's own logic, Giddens concluded that class actually takes on a greater analytical significance as capitalism develops:

> Class conflict (in the sense of endemic opposition of class interests . . .)
> and active class struggle have a centrality in capitalism which they
> do not have in class-divided societies. (Giddens, 1995, p. 129)

For Giddens, however, neither class conflict nor class struggle carried any necessary connotation of class consciousness, in anything like a Marxist sense of the term. Indeed, his more recent work betrays a growing conviction that 'class is less a basis of communal action than it used to be' (Giddens, 1995, p. xvi). But even if this so, Giddens remains insistent that:

> with the stripping away of many forms of traditional solidarity, including class solidarities, the labour market assumes . . . a greater role in the lives of most individuals than before. Class relations become more 'biographical', but nonetheless remain structured by the imperatives of capitalist production. (Giddens, 1995, p. xvi)

This sense of the differential effectivity of both class position and class solidarity rehearses yet another Weberian distinction, that between class location as market position and social class as a form of group identity. The distinction persists throughout Giddens's work, but with very different inflections in its early and later stages. In his earlier writings he had remained pre-occupied with the ways in which class location generates forms of class identity, especially but not only in the working class; in the later work, class position is still seen as determining life chances, but only rarely as generating class identities *per se*. In *The Class Structure of the Advanced Societies*, for example, he had attempted to theorize the transition from the one to the other, the 'structuration of class relationships' as he termed it, as an effect of the degree of closure of the chances for mobility. 'In general', he writes:

> we may state that the structuration of classes is facilitated *to the degree to which mobility closure exists in relation to any specified form of market capacity.* (Giddens, 1981, p. 107)

In capitalist societies there are normally three important kinds of market capacity – property, educational or technical qualification, and manual labour; and hence three basic social classes – an 'upper', 'middle' and 'working' class. These three sources of 'mediate' class structuration are, in turn, supplemented by three 'proximate' sources: the division of labour within the workplace; authority relations within the workplace; and 'distributive groupings', that is, relationships involving shared patterns of consumption, especially those formed through community or neighbourhood segregation (Giddens, 1981, pp. 107–109). Giddens argued that class structuration normally produces class awareness, that is, 'a common awareness and acceptance of similar attitudes and beliefs, linked to a common style of life' (Giddens, 1981, p. 111) but that it need not – and in the case of the middle class typically does not – produce any conscious recognition of class affiliation. By contrast, class consciousness, in the sense of a recognition of one's own class affiliation and of the existence of other classes, is much more characteristic of working-class people (Giddens, 1981, p. 112).

Giddens had originally intended to pursue these questions of class and class consciousness into the third volume of a projected trilogy that would include *The Nation-State and Violence* as its second volume (Giddens, 1995, p. ix; cf. Giddens, 1985). However, by the time this third volume appeared in 1994, his interests had moved elsewhere. Though still insistent that capitalism 'remains a class society', he had become convinced that the links between class and collective social engagement had 'quite sharply lessened' (Giddens, 1994, pp. 18, 143). In *The Class Structure of the Advanced Societies* he had distinguished three levels of 'class consciousness', termed respectively 'class identity', 'conflict consciousness' and 'revolutionary class consciousness' (Giddens, 1981, pp. 112–113). Conflict consciousness is primarily an effect of the visibility of differentials between classes, he argued, revolutionary consciousness of the kind of 'relativity of experience' which arises at the cutting edge of social change, especially where one mode of production competes directly with another (Giddens, 1981, p. 116). Conflict consciousness is common amongst working-class people, he had concluded, but revolutionary consciousness is not. For the later Giddens, however, neither form of consciousness remained at all typical of the contemporary working class:

> Class for the most part is no longer experienced as class, but as constraints (and opportunities) emanating from a variety of sources. Class becomes individualized and . . . is experienced less and less as a collective fate . . . Lifestyle and taste . . . become as evident markers of social differentiation as position in the productive order. (Giddens, 1994, p. 143)

What explains this shift? On Giddens's own account, the changes had arisen in the social reality, rather than in his own theorizations: 'class-based movements', of the kind Marx expected to lead a global political revolution, had actually turned out to be inextricably connected to the fate of the nation-state and so increasingly irrelevant to 'conditions of intensifying globalization' (Giddens, 1994, pp. 143, 149).

Yet there is also a largely unacknowledged change in Giddens's own theoretical position. Initially, he had insisted that revolutionary class consciousness was essentially a phenomenon of early capitalist development. Where Marx had assumed that conflict consciousness gave rise to revolutionary consciousness, Giddens argued that there was no intrinsic connection between the two and that, to the contrary, revolutionary consciousness was more typically an effect of the initial transition from rural to factory production (Giddens, 1981, pp. 117, 212). The relativism that might prompt revolutionary consciousness is much more likely to occur, he argued, not where Marx had located the social cutting edge, that is, at the point where a mature capitalism confronts an immanent post-capitalism, but rather at the much earlier moment when an emergent capitalism meets resistance from what Giddens termed 'post-feudalism' (Giddens, 1981, p. 207). In Giddens's recent work a similar archaism now attaches to all forms of class consciousness, whether conflictual or revolutionary, and to the labour movements that have borne them: in a pointed comparison with the new social movements, he observes that labour movements possess a peculiar 'strategic importance' only 'early in the development of modern institutions and capitalistic expansion' (Giddens, 1990, p. 159). This particular judgement may well have been overdetermined by its immediate occasion: a series of lectures delivered at Stanford University, that is, in one of the very few late-capitalist societies which possesses no well-established political party of the Left; and by the British Labour Party's own long exclusion from government during the 1980s. But it remains cognate with a more general emphasis, in Giddens's later work, on how lifestyle choices become increasingly important for the making of identities within what he terms 'high modernity' (Giddens, 1991, p. 5).

Both the early assessment of revolutionary consciousness, and the later assessment of labourism, seem strangely deterministic conclusions, however, for a theorist whose reputation has hinged on the attempt to reconcile the rival claims of agency and structure. Moreover, both remain open to theoretical and empirical objection. In the case of revolutionary consciousness, an obvious problem arises: how to explain its persistence into the later stages of capitalist development, as in French or Italian working-class Communism. Giddens, like Parkin, attributed such radicalism in part to the impact of the mass political party: there was a substantial 'feed-in', he conceded, from Communist union leadership to French working-class attitudes (Giddens, 1981, p. 209). But even this was essentially a delayed effect of early industrialization. The 'mode of rupture with post-feudal society creates an institutional complex,' he argued:

> within which a series of profound economic changes are accommodated, *that then becomes a persisting system, highly resistant to major modification.* (Giddens, 1981, p. 214)

But this is far too neat a solution, clearly belied by a number of obvious contra-instances. Early British industrialization had produced quasi-insurrectionary forms of oppositional consciousness, amongst both the Luddites and the 'physical force' Chartists for example, which in no way anticipate the relative 'moderation' of the later Labour Party. Conversely, the strength of the French and Italian Communist Parties during the period from the late 1940s through to the mid-1980s is more plausibly explained as a legacy of their contribution to the anti-Fascist Resistance than as an effect of the moment of transition to capitalism. Their subsequent decline has had similarly contingent sources (the fall of the Soviet Union, the splits in Italian Communism, and so on). We might even recall that the largest of the Western Communist Parties had been neither the French nor the Italian, but the German during the 1920s and early 1930s, which was subsequently almost entirely destroyed by the combination of Nazi repression, military defeat and partition into two states, one claiming to be a 'people's democracy'. If the political effects of early industrialization are as highly resistant to subsequent modification as Giddens suggests, then one would

expect to find more persistent patterns of political and ideological alignment than are historically observable. In the case of
conflict consciousness, the problem is even more obvious: there
is ample empirical evidence for the stubborn persistence of
strongly 'instrumental' forms of conflict consciousness amongst
British working-class voters (Marshall et al., 1988, pp. 225–261;
Goldthorpe and Marshall, 1992, pp. 390–393). The mobilization
and demobilization of different forms of working-class consciousness, and the creation and destruction of different forms of
working-class organization, have often been more historically
contingent processes than Giddens allows. As a discipline,
sociology betrays a characteristic and often entirely under-
standable unease in the face of contingency. Hence its predisposition towards what Goldthorpe calls 'reverse sociologism',
where supposed changes to the underlying social structure are
mistakenly deduced from what are actually short-term shifts in
party-political fortune (Goldthorpe, 1990, p. 426). Contingency
remains a historical fact of immense importance, nonetheless,
and one that no 'social science' can ever properly ignore.

By comparison with Parkin, Giddens's accounts of what are,
after all, forms of political consciousness seem oddly unpolitical
in character. For all the significance he has attached to the
nation-state and to the social organization of military violence,
his sociology seems unable to accommodate the socio-historical
agency of political parties and movements *per se*: for Giddens,
revolutionary consciousness was an effect of early industrialization rather than of Communist intervention; and the supposed
decline in conflict consciousness an effect of globalization
rather than of Labourist (non-) intervention. There is probably
some connection between this 'sociologism' (reverse and otherwise) and the strangely anodyne quality that attaches even to
the most declaredly political of his writings. His 1994 *Beyond
Left and Right*, misleadingly subtitled *The Future of Radical
Politics*, would surely have been more accurately entitled
Between Left and Right. Where the early work on class had
enacted a long, coy flirtation with Marxism, performed at a
suitably respectable distance from the object of its attractions,

so the later work improvised much the same role in relation to postmodernism. In each case, a wide range of currently fashionable nostrums is marshalled and organized into as inoffensive and apolitical a guise as possible, paraded as theoretical wisdom of the first order, and then systematically immunized against the possibility of test by either empirical evidence or political relevance. Roger Scruton once unkindly described Habermas as 'a thinker of world-wide reputation, who has yet to have a thought of his own' (Scruton, 1985, p. 127). It is a good line, but one much better directed at Habermas's supposed English counterpart.

The most explicitly political and also the most intellectually exciting of these neo-Weberian encounters with Marx's theory of class consciousness is almost certainly that in Mann, beginning with the early *Consciousness and Action among the Western Working Class* and proceeding through the magisterial *Sources of Social Power*, the first two volumes of which are already published, a third in progress and a fourth promised. Following Weber rather than 'Weberian' stratification theory, Mann regards power, not as a third dimension of inequality, but as an aspect of all social organization. Societies are best understood as '*multiple overlapping and intersecting sociospatial networks of power*', he argues, and the major sources of all such social power can be located in the four main systems of '*ideological, economic, military, and political* (IEMP) *relationships*' (Mann, 1986, pp. 1, 2). This 'IEMP model' clearly derives from Weber, but with the added complication of a distinction between military and political power. Mann's account of economic power is much less Weberian, however: he argues that its sources can be located either in production, as Marx suggested, or in exchange, as had Weber, and that any group formed around either or both can usefully be termed a class (Mann, 1986, p. 24). Like Marx, Mann treats the emergence of class, civilization and the state as roughly contemporaneous; unlike Marx, he regards them as exceptional and abnormal developments, the effect not so much of the neolithic revolution in general, as of alluvial agriculture and irrigation in particular (Mann, 1986, p. 124). But given their initial appearance, 'class struggle between landlords and peasants' becomes 'a ubiquitous feature of all agrarian societies' (Mann, 1986, p. 527).

Mann distinguishes four phases in the development of class relations and class struggle, which he terms respectively 'latent', 'extensive', 'symmetrical' and 'political' (Mann, 1986, p. 24). Class struggle is 'latent' whenever it is confined to a local level and subordinated to other non-class forms of organization; it becomes 'extensive' whenever more or less uniform patterns of consciousness and organization extend throughout a given territory; 'political' whenever a class attempts to rule through a state; and 'symmetrical' when both superordinate and subordinate classes organize themselves collectively. Extensive, political and symmetrical class struggles, of the kind Marx had assumed to be normal, occurred in the city states of ancient Greece, in Republican Rome and in modern Europe, Mann observes, but they are far from ubiquitous. The history of class, he concludes, is essentially similar to that of the nation:

> class and nation . . . are universal communitites, dependent on the diffusion of the same social practices, identities, and sentiments across extensive social spaces . . . Societies capable of this will develop both classes and nations. (Mann, 1986, p. 530)

Hence, the central theme of Volume II – which focuses on the histories of France, Britain, Austria, Prussia/Germany, the United States and, in some sections, Russia during the period 1760–1914 – that of the 'rise of classes and nation-states'. Mann argues that modern capitalism creates potentially extensive, political, symmetrical and 'dialectical' (by which he means entailing a head-on clash of opposites) classes: 'Rare in earlier societies, such classes have been ubiquitous ever since' (Mann, 1993, p. 27). He identifies six main 'class actors' in modern capitalist societies: the 'old regime' of monarchy and court, established church, aristocracy, gentry and merchant oligarchies; the early 'petite bourgeoisie' of small capitalists and artisans; the capitalist class; the working class; the mid-Victorian 'middle class', comprising petite bourgeoisie, professionals and careerists; and the peasantry (Mann, 1993, pp. 28, 96–99). These were never simply economic, he insists, but were always also moulded by ideological, military and political power relations, especially those entailed in the newly developing nation-states (Mann, 1993, pp. 29–30).

Mann's early *Consciousness and Action among the Western Working Class* had been designed quite expressly to 'test' Marxist notions of class consciousness. There, he had summarized Marx's own account as entailing four distinct components: a simple sense of common 'class identity'; 'class opposition', that is, an awareness of opposed class interests; 'class totality', or the acceptance of class identity and opposition as defining characteristics both of society and of one's own place within it; and finally, the conception of an alternative society as a goal toward which one's class interests finally lead. 'Marxism provides a theory of escalation of consciousness from the first to the fourth', he wrote, leading to something like an 'explosion of consciousness' in conflict situations (Mann, 1973, pp. 13, 18). Comparing data from Britain, the United States, France and Italy, Mann found that a sense of working-class identity and class opposition was widespread in all four countries, but that the sense of class totality was normally absent. Moreover, in Britain and the United States, at least, there was no evidence for any widespread conception of any viable social alternative.[7] This 'IOTA model', as Mann terms it, reappears in *The Sources of Social Power*, but in a more nuanced application. In particular, he stresses the role of the militant as the bearer of class consciousness: 'When decribing classes "acting" ', he writes, 'I am usually describing a few militants who really are so motivated, able to move large numbers by persuading them that their class sentiments are a more significant part of themselves than they had previously believed' (Mann, 1993, p. 28). With this proviso, he concludes that, in each of his six states, working-class 'class loyalties' had in fact emerged, albeit alongside competing 'sectional' and 'segmental' loyalties; that in each case class identities were centred on skilled and semi-skilled metalworkers, miners and transport workers in large towns; and that this 'core' was overwhelmingly masculine (Mann, 1993, pp. 681–682). He also identifies six major working-class (and peasant)

alternatives to capitalism, three pairs, each respectively industrial or political in focus: from the most 'moderate', protection-
ism and mutualism; through the 'reformist', economism and
social democracy; to the most 'revolutionary', syndicalism and
Marxism (Mann, 1993, pp. 513–515). Which became predominant
in any particular national instance was primarily the effect of
already existing 'political power crystallizations', he explains:
'similar emerging labor movements were deflected by different
available state institutions along different tracks' (Mann, 1993,
p. 729).

Mann's conclusion in *Consciousness and Action among the
Western Working Class* had been that such escalations as Marxism predicts rarely if ever occur in the traditional working class:
'The explosion of consciousness is trapped in a vicious circle
(from identity to opponent to totality, and then back to identity),
and so does not make a revolution' (Mann, 1973, p. 69). Socialism is thus a learned philosophy, requiring for its practical
efficacy the interpretation of working-class experience 'by organised groups over a considerable period of time' (Mann, 1973,
p. 71). Without such interpretation, he surmised, 'it is improbable that working-class protest can be directed toward the
creation of a new society' (Mann, 1973, p. 71). His central initial
finding was thus quite specifically anti-Marxist, though not anti-
Leninist, in character: 'The "dialectic" of class consciousness is
circular, not progressive . . . It seems . . . unlikely that the
proletariat carries *in itself* the power to be a class *for itself*'
(Mann, 1973, pp. 72–73). In *The Sources of Social Power*, the
formulation is less decisively Leninist:

> Lenin was partly correct . . . economic experiences on their own
> produced far less than revolutionary socialism, even usually less
> than reformism, and . . . less class than sectional agitation . . . But
> the second half of Lenin's argument . . . is not correct . . . Working
> classes, as well as intelligentsia, *have* generated socialism, though
> only when diverse productive experiences are fused by experience
> of common political exploitations. (Mann, 1993, pp. 629–630)

The second volume of *The Sources of Social Power* concludes
with the outbreak of the First World War in 1914. But it is clear
from more recently published preliminary findings that he

intends to develop this argument, concerning the special significance of both conservative and socialist political leaderships,
for the subsequent history of the twentieth century. He sees
proletarian class consciousness, whether reformist or revolutionary, as sustained by the 'macro-community' of the working-
class areas of industrial towns and cities, a community overwhelmingly masculine in character, which, at its most extensive,
never embraced more than half of European workers (Mann,
1995, pp. 17, 19). In the inter-war period socialism stalled, on
Mann's account because of a successful conservative counter-
mobilization, organized around the three relatively distinct
themes of (mainly Catholic) religion, nationalism and the technocratic claim to greater administrative competence (Mann, 1995,
pp. 27–34). The 'proletarian working class' was thus thrown on
to the defensive and, by 1939, seemed close to losing the ideological battle for the middle classes, for women, and for the half
of the working class that lived and worked outside the macro-
community (Mann, 1995, p. 49). After the Second World War,
although moderate socialism re-emerged right across Western
Europe, the working class appeared increasingly pragmatic and
calculative in its political and industrial behaviour. Moreover, it
was only in the overwhelmingly Protestant states of north-
western Europe (Britain, Denmark, Norway, Sweden) that left
voting had a higher correlation with class-related factors than
with religion or region (Mann, 1995, pp. 52, 46).[8] Mann's provisional general conclusion is thus that:

> In a world still characterized by capitalism . . . I find no sense in
> notions that 'class is dead'. But then classes have never had a full,
> pure and independent life. Class has been, first, a heuristic tool for
> the limited goal of positional measurement and, second, an actually
> limited and impure social actor, in a constant state of development
> and flux. Both roles will probably survive. (Mann, 1995, pp. 53–54)

In different ways and to varying degrees, Parkin, Mann and
Giddens have been attracted by Weber's own proto-Leninist
view of socialist consciousness as the effect of political intervention into the working class by middle-class intellectuals,
organized in mass political parties (although Giddens seems no

longer persuaded of even this possibility). There is some substance to the case, no doubt: people of all classes and groups
are normally more rather than less inclined to follow their own
already acknowledged political leaders. But the implied account
of working-class voters and trade unionists as more or less
passive respondents to party activism is, as Mann came to
recognize, both one-sided and static. It begs the question as to
why these particular people were recognized as political leaders
in the first place. Historically, working-class political parties,
whether Communist, Labour or Social-Democratic, were created
by working-class activists so as to pursue their own political
demands. There is, of course, much inertia in political life and
great changes, such as the creation or destruction of political
parties, only occur in exceptional circumstances. Presumably,
however, what has been done can always be undone, at least in
the long run: if nothing else, the recent precipitate decline of the
French Communist Party suggests as much.

Neo-Marxist Sociology: Westergaard and Wright

In Chapter 2 we noted in passing the existence of a kind of
'sociological' Marxism, which chooses to defend Marx's theory
of class, as against Weber's, on grounds of empirical adequacy
measured according to conventionally sociological criteria.
Whether this is 'really' Marxism I leave for others to decide, but
it is certainly sociology. The obvious instances are provided by
Westergaard in Britain and Wright in the United States. Consider
each in turn. In Westergaard's earlier formulations, co-authored
in 1975 with the late Henrietta Resler, the rhetoric of class
analysis was couched in the most orthodoxly Marxist of
terms: 'class in itself' and 'class for itself'; the political reality of
'proletarian unity'; and the key role of 'property and property
relations' (Westergaard and Resler, 1975, pp. 2–3, 27–28). They
were careful to insist, nonetheless, that the empirical complex-
ities of class structure were 'matters for inquiry and demonstration; not for specification in advance by preconceived
definitions' (Westergaard and Resler, 1975, p. 28). The three-

class model they eventually adopted was thus in essence a generalization from the mass of their own accumulated empirical data, much of it reworked from official sources, on matters such as income distribution, property ownership and social mobility. Each of their three classes is an aggregate of occupations, very much like Goldthorpe's, sometimes sharing a common relation to the means of production, but more characteristically a common set of life chances. Constituted around two main 'lines of cleavage' in the social structure, the three classes comprise respectively: a small layer of 'directors, managers, established professionals and high officials'; an intermediate cluster of 'those who sell their labour at a premium . . . [L]ow-level managers and supervisors, technicians, . . . the "junior" and "auxiliary" professions'; and the 'broad mass of ordinary [wage] earners' (Westergaard and Resler, 1975, pp. 92–96). Westergaard and Resler were much less interested in the cultural corollaries of class than in the patterns of material inequality. Their cursory survey of the available empirical research did lead, however, to the conclusion that 'well-marked divisions of consciousness, organization and everyday culture' run 'in parallel', but 'do not fully coincide', with this threefold class structure (Westergaard and Resler, 1975, p. 380). Their three classes were obviously analogous to Marx's bourgeoisie, petty bourgeoisie and proletariat, but had been subject to substantial empirical modification, especially the intermediate stratum, here characterized as high-salary-earning rather than small-property-holding. Nonetheless, Westergaard and Resler's primary concern remained, not so much these comparatively recent modifications to the class structure, as the sheer persistence of older, longstanding patterns of social inequality. The 'picture as a whole' is characterized above all by its 'simplicity', they concluded: 'Class inequality is tenacious' (Westergaard and Resler, 1975, p. 343).

To all intents and purposes, the argument remains substantially unamended in Westergaard's later work. The general approach is still 'Marxist', but only on the understanding that Marxism is a 'source of hypotheses . . . to be explored by empirical research' (Westergaard, 1995, p. 11). The concept of class is still anchored theoretically in the relations of production, but registered empirically primarily by way of differences in life chances (Westergaard, 1995, pp. 32–33). The class structure is still conceived as essentially tripartite: in one version as ' "hightop" versus "careers" versus "jobs" '; in another as a 'salariat' of 'executives and managers, administrators, professionals, semi-professionals' versus a 'petite bourgeoisie' of 'small business and own-account workers . . . [T]echnicians, industrial supervisors . . . and . . . routine-grade non-manual workers' versus a ' "blue-collar", "white-blouse" ' working class of 'people whose economic lives . . . centre overall on mere jobs and mere wages' (Westergaard, 1995, pp. 161–162). Class inequality is still seen as tenacious. More seriously, Westergaard also views it as subject to a process of systematic 'hardening': 'class has . . . been re-declared dead . . . at a time . . . when its economic configuration has become even sharper' (Westergaard, 1995, pp. 113–114). Politically, this perceived hardening has provoked an increasingly socialistic rhetoric on Westergaard's part, an insistence that Labour should 'break the mould leftwards' (Westergaard, 1995, p. 183). Theoretically, however, it appears to have prompted a growing respect for neo-Weberian class analysis, especially of the kind conducted by Goldthorpe. So he willingly admits that Goldthorpe 'stands out for the lead he has taken in knitting facts and inference . . . closely together' (Westergaard, 1990, p. 282). As Westergaard disarmingly confesses elsewhere: 'I am not concerned . . . with . . . subtleties of conceptual distinction between . . . Marx and . . . Weber' (Westergaard, 1996, p. 142).

Wright, by contrast, has been very much preoccupied by such distinctions: indeed, Westergaard takes him to task for his concern to avoid 'contaminating Marxism with Weberianism' (Westergaard, 1995, p. 32). Like Poulantzas and Carchedi, Wright had set out to refurbish the more traditional Marxist class categories so as to account for recent changes in the class structure of advanced capitalist societies. As with Poulantzas and Carchedi, the general import of the approach remained essentially classificatory and hence, in Connell's terms, 'dimensional'. But where Poulantzas had redefined class as constituted as much in ideology and politics as in economics, while simultaneously insisting on a very tight definition of the working class as the class that produces surplus value, Wright sought both to retain a more conventionally politico-economic definition of class and to sidestep the distinction between productive and unproductive labour. For Wright, class in the sense of a relationship to the means of production could be analysed into three relatively distinct aspects: control, respectively, over the physical means of production, over the labour-power of others, and over investment and resource allocation (Wright, 1979, p. 73). Whereas the last is a relation of 'economic ownership' in the full legal sense of the term, the first and second are 'relations of possession', that is, relations of domination, which may or may not be accompanied by formal rights of ownership. Marx's bourgeoisie possessed all three, Wright concluded, the proletariat none, and the classic self-employed petty bourgeoisie the first and third but not the second (Wright, 1979, pp. 73–74). In addition, however, he pointed to the existence of a further series of intermediate strata, each occupying what he termed '*objectively contradictory locations*' between the three main classes (Wright, 1979, p. 61). This theory of 'contradictory class locations' has been the distinguishing feature of Wright's work and has constituted its central theoretical preoccupation. Its immediate effect was to produce a six-class model less obviously at odds with empirical reality than that in Poulantzas: the bourgeoisie; the self-employed petty bourgeoisie; the proletariat, both manual and routine white-collar, 'productive' and 'unproductive'; and the three contradictory class locations, respectively small employers, managers, and credentialled semi-autonomous employees. According to Wright's calculations, the new petty bourgeoisie on Poulantzas's definition would have comprised 70 per cent of the American workforce in 1969, the working class less than 20 per cent; on his own definition, by contrast, managers and supervisors comprised 30–35 per cent of the workforce, semi-autonomous employees 5–11 per cent and the working class 41–54 per cent (Wright 1979, pp. 55, 84).

There seems little doubt as to the greater efficacy of Wright's schema, as a predictor of social behaviour, by comparison with that of Poulantzas. Hence, Westergaard's acknowledgement of the greater cogency of Wright's departures from Poulantzan class theory (Westergaard, 1977, pp. 168, 185n).[9] But this was only a beginning: as Wright's work fell increasingly under the influence of Roemer's Analytical Marxism, so too his earlier theoreticist formulations became progressively more exposed to empirical testing of a conventionally sociological kind. Inspired by a need to rethink class theory 'in a way suitable for incorporation into middle-level theories and empirical research', he redefined the concept of class as grounded in exploitation rather than domination (Wright, 1985, p. 283). Wright now distinguished three main forms of exploitation, based respectively on ownership of capital assets, control of organizational assets, and possession of skill or credential assets. This led to a 12-class model comprising: three capital-owning classes, the bourgeoisie, small employers and the petty bourgeoisie; three managerial classes, expert managers, semi-credentialled managers and uncredentialled managers; three supervisory classes, expert supervisors, semi-credentialled supervisors and uncredentialled supervisors; and three classes of non-managing employees, expert non-managers, semi-credentialled workers and proletarians (Wright, 1985, p. 195). In all its essential features, this is the model Wright continues to use in his most recent work (Wright, 1997, p. 25). I have grouped the non-owning classes here according to their capacity to exploit organizational assets, but for Wright they can just as easily be represented according to the capacity to exploit skill or credential assets, which would give us three expert classes, three semi-credentialled classes and three uncredentialled classes. Initially, he tested the adequacy of his reconceptualized notion of class by way of a systematic empirical comparison between an American sample of 1,499 working adults and a Swedish sample of 1,145 adults (Wright, 1985, p. 160). These studies were later subsumed into the much larger, 20-year-long 'Comparative Class Analysis Project', involving closely replicated social surveys in 13 other countries – the United Kingdom, Canada, Norway, Australia, Denmark, Japan, New Zealand, West Germany, Russia, South Korea, Spain, Taiwan and Portugal (Wright, 1989a, p. 3; Wright, 1997, p. xxix).

Much of this material has now been incorporated into what is for the moment his last word on the subject, *Class Counts: Comparative Studies in Class Analysis* (1997). In both books, analysis is focused on the relationships between class structure, class as process and class consciousness; in the later work, this is augmented by an extended treatment of the relationship between class and gender. However, it is the nexus between class structure and class consciousness that remains most pertinent to our purposes here.

Wright defines class consciousness as entailing three analytically distinct elements: perceptions, theories of consequences and preferences (Wright, 1985, p. 247; Wright, 1997, pp. 385–386). In the earlier study, he had compared the mean values scored on a 'consciousness scale' for each of his 12 classes, both in the United States and in Sweden; in the later study, comparable data are added for Japan. Wright discovered patterns of variation in all three countries which he judges 'quite consistent' with the notion that class structure, as understood through the exploitation-centred concept, tends to shape the overall pattern of class consciousness: in each case, the working class is the most ideologically 'anticapitalist', the bourgeoisie the most ideologically 'procapitalist', the other classes located somewhere in between, roughly in accord with their respective capacities to benefit from one or more of the three forms of exploitation (Wright, 1997, pp. 417–419). But there were significant differences between the patterns identified in each of the three countries. In the earlier study, Wright had found that the level of working-class consciousness was consistently higher in Sweden than in the United States. So, for example, whereas 81 per cent of the Swedish proletarians in his sample believed that managements should be prohibited by law from hiring non-union labour during a strike, only 55 per cent of American proletarians and 25 per cent of both the Swedish and the American bourgeoisie agreed with this proposition (Wright, 1985, pp. 262–263). He concluded that there was something like 'an international consensus within the capitalist class on class-based attitudes', but an international dissensus amongst the working classes, dependent in part on 'the extent to which political parties and unions adopt strategies which help to crystallize workers' experiences in class terms' (Wright, 1985, p. 264). By comparison with the United States, Swedish classes were more polarized ideologically and the 'working class coalition' built on the basis of that polarization much larger.[10] The later study found Japanese classes to be less ideologically polarized than either the American or the Swedish. Moreover, this greater consensuality exhibited an oddly anti-capitalist character: all 12 Japanese classes, including even the capitalists themselves, produced mean scores that counted as 'proworker' rather than 'procapitalist' on Wright's scale (Wright, 1997, p. 418). He also records a surprising absence in Japan of ideological cleavage with respect to authority, as distinct from expertise (Wright, 1997, p. 429). Just as he had sought to explain class polarization in Sweden as the effect of social-democratic party and union intervention, so too Wright speculates that the relative absence of polarization in Japan might arise from the 'company union' quality of its labour movement (Wright, 1997, p. 440). His later sociology is thus simultaneously sensitive both to the underlying strength of the structural connections between class and consciousness and to the range of empirical variation in the nature of these connections.

As conducted both by Westergaard and by Wright, Marxist sociology has become increasingly empirical in its content and increasingly eclectic in its theoretical formulations. Westergaard's work was always distinctly empirical in tenor and tone: even at its most expressly 'Marxist', contributing a largely 'theoretical' piece to a largely 'theoreticist' collection, he had insisted that 'class is in essence a matter of inequality' and that Marxism should be concerned primarily with 'the concrete differential impact of capitalist economic processes on people's lives and prospects' (Westergaard, 1977, pp. 165, 168). Westergaard and Resler's *Class in a Capitalist Society* was above all an empirical account of social inequality in Britain. Westergaard's own *Who Gets What?* wears its heart very clearly on its jacket sleeve. The point, of course, is that such distributive inequalities are measurable according to straightforwardly sociological procedures, often effectively indistinguishable from those used by writers like Goldthorpe. Wright's work, by contrast, was formed initially in the shadow of Althusserian structuralism and hence exhibited a distinctly theoreticist inflection. But it has progressively acquired a more empirical tenor, so much so in fact that he can now urge his findings on non-Marxist readers:

> If the conceptual justifications for the categories are unredeemably flawed, it might be thought, the empirical results . . . will be worthless. This would be . . . a mistake. The empirical categories . . . can be interpreted in a Weberian or hybrid manner. Indeed, as a practical set of operational categories, the class structure matrix used in this book does not dramatically differ from the class typology used by Goldthorpe. (Wright, 1997, p. 37)

For Wright, as for Westergaard, class analysis may well still be 'Marxist', but it is also, and above all else, sociological. Both are agreed that 'there are important problems of class analysis in which knowledge can usefully be generated with systematic quantitative research' (Wright, 1997, p. 546). No doubt, there are. But this knowledge is not so much distinctively Marxist or socialist as generically sociological; and this may well be its great strength.

This developing convergence of neo-Weberian and neo-Marxist versions of sociological class analysis appears to derive from two main sources: a stubborn commitment to the value and significance of systematically acquired, quantitatively measured, sociological data; and a dawning recognition that many of the more fashionable nostrums in contemporary social theory are almost entirely at odds with the weight of the evidence produced by such data. As to the first, the empirical record is very clear: 'there has been no secular decline in the tendency for collective identities and collective action to develop on a class basis' (Marshall et al., 1988, p. 268). This is a finding that has been confirmed by almost all large-scale, quantitative research into the subject. As to the second, the interesting question is why it should be that so many social theorists are so convinced of propositions so unsupported by relevant empirical data. At one level, we are confronted by the perennial hiatus between theory and evidence in sociology. Wright Mills's deft summary of Parsonian systems theory, as '50 per cent verbiage; 40 per cent

. . . well-known textbook sociology . . . 10 per cent . . . of possible – although rather vague – ideological use' (Mills, 1970, p. 59), is perhaps generalizable to other theoretical perspectives, quite apart from political persuasion. But there is almost certainly something else at work here too. Many of the more enthusiastically theoreticist critics of class analysis have been recruited from amongst the ranks of disillusioned erstwhile New Left Marxists. Noting the correlation, Goldthorpe and Marshall pointedly observe that 'having lost faith in the Marxist class analysis that had once commanded their allegiance . . . [they] now find evident difficulty in envisaging any other kind' (Goldthorpe and Marshall, 1992, p. 381). Now, social theorists are as entitled as anyone else to their enthusiasms and disillusions, and to learn from their mistakes. Nonetheless, the trajectory of New Left (post-)Marxism, which has run from exaggeratedly wild expectations of working-class insurrection – the 'storming-of-the-Winter-Palace' model (Goldthorpe and Marshall, 1992, p. 384) – through to a systematic and determined opposition to any and all forms of 'classism', bears more than a passing resemblance to the earlier history of Bolshevik and Western Marxisms we traced in Chapter 2. If cynicism is merely disillusioned idealism, then perhaps such theoretical recidivism is unsurprising. But, as Marx knew well, whenever history repeats itself, it will tend to do so the first time as tragedy, the second as farce (Marx, 1973a, p. 146).

Notes

1 Walby herself treats patriarchal relations as in part class relations: 'housewives and husbands are classes,' she writes, 'but . . . men and women are not . . . there are two class systems, one based around patriarchy, the other around capitalism' (Walby, 1990, p. 13).

2 Richard Baxter (1615–91), the seventeenth-century English Presbyterian divine.

3 In Germany itself the nearest equivalent, the *Junker* class, was in Weber's view an 'essentially "bourgeois" stratum . . . entirely dependent upon working as agricultural entrepreneurs' (Weber, 1948c, p. 386).

4 This was a study in comparative political sociology, comparing large samples of respondents from the United States, Britain, Italy, Western Germany

and Mexico, so as to test for the absence or presence of a 'civic culture' assumed to be peculiarly appropriate to liberal democracy. The study compared national sample with national sample, in effect assuming that each of the five cultures was in fact relatively unified. Their own findings often suggested the contrary, however. For example, they asked their respondents whether they were able to do anything about a local regulation they considered unjust. The percentage answering 'yes' was much higher in the United States and Britain than in Mexico, Germany and Italy: 95 per cent of American respondents with some college education said 'yes', but only 76 per cent of Italians; 60 per cent of Americans with primary education said 'yes', but only 45 per cent of Italians. Almond and Verba deduced from such data that the civic culture was much less present in Italy than in the United States. In fact, the difference of 35 percentage points between American college-educated and primary-educated respondents far exceeds that of 19 percentage points between American and Italian college-educated respondents. The degree of dissensus within each culture, which barely discussed, was thus significantly greater than that between national cultures, which provided the book with its central theoretical focus (cf. Almond and Verba, 1965, p. 162).

5 Westergaard's insistence that Goldthorpe and Lockwood's 'instrumentalism' was merely Marx's 'cash nexus' rediscovered was entirely valid, but didn't in any way detract from the force of their study's empirical findings (Westergaard, 1970). Blackburn's pointed comparison between the *Affluent Worker* findings and the quasi-insurrectionary character of a subsequent strike at exactly the same factory had much polemical force, no doubt (Blackburn, 1967). But, as Mann astutely observed, these events could very plausibly be read in terms of their intended demonstration effect, that is, as deliberately designed to impress management and unions (Mann, 1973, p. 49).

6 Parkin was writing toward the close of a relatively long period of successful trade union militancy both in Britain and elsewhere: as he notes, the decade 1965–75 witnessed a 13 per cent increase in the real wages of the average British manual worker, but a substantial decline in the real income of various professional groups. Very plausibly, he viewed this as the effect of successful 'closure from below'. But Parkin was quick to add that: 'It is altogether possible that the present tendency could be reversed and labour's gains gradually wiped out' (Parkin, 1979, p. 80). This is more or less exactly what has happened in the subsequent period, in part, of course, as a direct result of the Conservative election victory of the same year in which *Marxism and Class Theory* was published.

7 In France and Italy, by contrast, a belief in the socialist alternative was widespread, but unaccompanied by any practical sense of how to achieve it.

8 Mann speculates that class may be similarly important in Australia and New Zealand, but presents no data to support this (Mann, 1995, p. 51). The history of the Australian Democratic Labor Party, a separate Catholic workers' party, might suggest otherwise.

9 Westergaard is here referring to an earlier version of the argument (Wright, 1976) that would eventually be incorporated, in only slightly amended form, into *Class, Crisis, and the State.*

10 Thus, whereas in Sweden a majority of respondents supported a legal prohibition on 'scabbing' in all classes other than the bourgeoisie and the small employers (and even a full half of them supported it), in the United States majorities existed only amongst the proletarians and the semi-credentialled workers (Wright, 1985, pp. 262–263).

4

Cultural Studies and Class

From its modest British origins in the late 1950s and early 1960s, Cultural Studies has developed into an internationally significant academic growth industry. If not quite the 'genuinely global movement' Simon During imagined (During, 1993, p. 13), it has nonetheless grown into a putatively international discipline, with a serious intellectual presence in Australia and Canada, France, India and the United States, Taiwan and Korea.[1] As we noted in Chapter 1, the origins of British Cultural Studies lay in a decidedly 'classist' critique of the unitary conception of culture deployed by Leavisite English. For Williams and Hoggart, as also for Thompson, it was social class that provided the central marker of what we have since come to know as 'difference'. The revalorization of mass civilization into popular culture, which Cultural Studies effected, was thus itself the effect of an inquiry into and qualified defence of British working-class culture. This shift in focus from the canonical to the popular amounted to something like a 'sociological turn' in what had previously been an almost entirely 'literary' discourse (Milner, 1996, pp. 11–18). Certainly, Williams himself came to regard his own work as a kind of sociology: hence, the decision to include *Culture* (Williams, 1981) in the 'Fontana New Sociology' series. But

Cultural Studies has also become increasingly important as a peculiarly fertile source of 'post-Marxist' alternatives to 'class analysis': the theoretical vocabularies of postmodernism, post-colonialism, post-humanism, and so on, have normally been tested on Cultural Studies well in advance of their subsequent incorporation into sociology. This may explain Goldthorpe's nomination of Stuart Hall's work as a prime example of 'data-free' analysis (Goldthorpe, 1990, p. 431). The peculiar trajectory of this 'strange death of class', as we described it in Chapter 1, will provide the central subject matter for this chapter. We begin with an account of the theorizations of class deployed by early British Cultural Studies; we proceed thence to an account of three especially influential versions of theoretical postmodernism – those developed by Hall, Baudrillard and Jameson; and we conclude with the return of the repressed to Cultural Studies itself, as represented by Bourdieu's 'culturalist' reworkings of class analysis.

Early British Cultural Studies: Williams, Hoggart and Thompson

Despite their often marginal status in contemporary Cultural Studies, there is no doubting the centrality of Hoggart, Williams and Thompson to the early evolution of the new proto-discipline. The shift from canonical 'Literature' to working-class 'culture' registers very clearly in all three. Hoggart's *The Uses of Literacy* combined a sympathetically ethnographic account of North of England working-class culture with a blistering critique of the damage done to it by more recent forms of print media: 'The old forms of class culture are in danger of being replaced', he warned, 'by a poorer kind of classless . . . culture' (Hoggart, 1958, p. 343). Competitive commerce had undermined the older order, he argued, by manipulating its own resources against itself, thus learning 'to express our habitual moral assumptions . . . in such a way that they weaken the moral code they evoke; to say the right things for the wrong reasons' (Hoggart, 1958, p. 244). Thompson's *The Making of the English Working Class* set out to produce 'a biography of the English working class' that would 'rescue the poor stockinger, the Luddite cropper, the "obsolete" hand-loom weaver, the "utopian" artisan . . . from the enormous condescension of posterity' (Thompson, 1963, pp. 11–12). A graduate of Cambridge English, Thompson had already met such condescension in its more extreme forms. Neatly sidestepping the elitism of Leavisite anti-utilitarianism, and turning Leavis's own admiration for Blake to more appropriate use, he pointed to the parallels between working-class and Romantic critiques of utilitarianism. The early labour movement, he wrote, had 'met Utilitarianism in their daily lives, and . . . sought to throw it back, not blindly, but with intelligence and moral passion . . . After William Blake, no mind was at home in both cultures, nor had the genius to interpret the two traditions to each other' (Thompson, 1963, p. 832). It was in Williams's two most influential early works, however, in *Culture and Society* and in *The Long Revolution*, that this shift toward the study of working-class 'right things' was most effectively theorized.

In the earlier book, Williams had sought to redefine the anti-utilitarian tradition in English thought, so as to make it more amenable to radical and socialist interpretation; in the later, to map out the historical emergence of modernity through the interrelated processes of the democratic revolution, the Industrial Revolution and the 'cultural revolution' of increasingly democratized communications. In the first, he had discovered in William Morris a 'pivotal figure', whose significance derived precisely from an attempt to attach the more 'general values' of the tradition to 'an actual and growing social force . . . the organized working class' (Williams, 1963, p. 153). In the second, he would persist in the hope that the long revolution could be carried forward by 'the institutions of the labour movement' (Williams, 1965, pp. 328–329). The conservative reaction to cultural democratization, conventionally troped as the opposition between 'minority culture' and 'mass civilization', thus appeared to Williams as an essentially false solution to a set of very real problems. As such, it eventually becomes complicit with the very philistinism it seeks to critique (Williams, 1963, pp. 299–300). Hence his famous insistence that: 'There are in fact no masses; there are only ways of seeing people as masses' (Williams, 1963, p. 289). If Williams was too Leavisite a critic to opt for either 'proletarian art' or 'popular culture' *per se*, he would still conclude that culture is just as 'essentially' a 'whole way of life' as a 'body of intellectual and imaginative work' (Williams, 1963, p. 311). This argument led directly to the defence of the 'collective democratic institution' as the central 'creative achievement' of working-class culture (Williams, 1963, p. 313).

The reference to creativity should alert us to an important common theme in Williams, Hoggart and Thompson: a 'cultural-ist' understanding of class as constituted pre-eminently in class consciousness. Hoggart's working class were defined above all by their 'sense of being in a group of their own . . . they feel . . . they are "working-class" in the things they admire and dislike, in "belonging" ' (Hoggart, 1958, p. 19). For Thompson, the 'making' of the class had been essentially 'an active process, which owes as much to agency as to conditioning . . . Class is defined by men as they live their own history, and, in the end, this is its only definition' (Thompson, 1963, pp. 9, 11). For Williams, the crucial distinction between the middle and working classes lay in 'alternative ideas of the nature of social relationship' (Williams, 1963, p. 311). All three were suspicious of supposedly 'objective' notions of class, as a 'category' or 'structure', whether deployed by Marxism or by sociology (Hoggart, 1958, p. 17; Thompson, 1963, p. 9; Williams, 1965, pp. 312–313). For all three, the nexus between what Marxists had termed being and consciousness came to occupy a peculiar theoretical centrality. Where most post-Leninist Marxism had tended to treat this as essentially un-problematic, given appropriate political leadership, both Williams and Thompson attempted to theorize its dynamics in deter-minedly non-Leninist fashion. For Thompson, the emphasis fell quite explicitly on the processes by which 'experience' mediates between being and consciousness. 'Class eventuates as men and women *live* their productive relations,' he wrote, 'and as they *experience* their determinate situations . . . with their inherited culture and expectations, and as they handle these experiences in cultural ways' (Thompson, 1978a, p. 150). This stress on the importance of the experiential clearly underwrote much of his extended theoretical polemic against Althusserianism. But, if the main target here was Althusser, then Thompson also freely acknowledged Marx's own failure to explain the 'genetics' of historical process. The missing term from Marxism was 'experience', he insisted: 'Men and women . . . return as subjects, within this term . . . as persons experiencing their determinate productive situations and relationships, as needs and interests and as antagonisms, and then "handling" this experience within their *consciousness* and their *culture*' (Thompson, 1978b, p. 356).

For Williams, the central theoretical focus fell on the complex articulation of cultural tradition and subordinate class identity, an articulation theorized primarily through the twin concepts of 'selective tradition' and 'structure of feeling'. In his earlier work, a strong sense of the 'classed' nature of cultural production and consumption had prompted a reading of Leavis's 'great tradition' as necessarily a 'selective tradition'. In *Culture and Society*, he had described this process of selection as 'related to and even governed by the interests of the class that is dominant' (Williams, 1963, pp. 307–308). In *The Long Revolution*, he would observe how tradition simultaneously creates a 'general human culture', 'the historical record of a particular society' and 'a rejection of considerable areas of what was once a living culture'. These selections 'will be governed', he concluded, 'by many kinds of special interest, including class interests' (Williams, 1965, p. 68). If tradition creates what is in part a truly general 'human' culture, then it does so in ways that are defined according to class-specific criteria. In *The Long Revolution*, Williams also began to theorize the notion of a 'structure of feeling' connecting the 'imaginative work' to the 'way of life' or, as we might now say, the text to its context. Structure of feeling, he wrote, 'is the particular living result of all the elements in the general organization' (Williams, 1965, p. 64). The art of a period is of fundamental importance to an understanding of its structure of feeling, he continued, because there 'the actual living sense, the deep community that makes . . . communication possible, is naturally drawn upon' (Williams, 1965, p. 65). In this initial formulation, Williams seemed more interested in the generational character of structures of feeling than in their more class-specific properties. Hence the distinction between structure of feeling, as 'a very deep and very wide possession', and 'social character', as 'the abstract of a dominant group', in this specific instance the 'industrial and commercial middle class' (Williams, 1965, pp. 65, 78). But he would proceed to argue that a structure of feeling 'is primarily evident in the dominant productive group' and that it also 'corresponds to the dominant social character' of the period (Williams, 1965, p. 80). The important difference between social character and structure of feeling is that the latter articulates the interaction of different social characters, dealing 'not only with the public ideals but with their omissions and consequences, as lived' (Williams, 1965, p. 80).

At first sight, 'structure of feeling' appears merely one of a family of concepts that denote the connection of text to context, roughly equivalent to 'ideology', 'world vision', 'problematic', or 'discursive formation'. Indeed, there are times when Williams employs it thus. But the repeated use of 'living' and 'lived' should alert us to its peculiarly and distinctively experiential aspects. As Pickering rightly observes, the concept's real cutting edge 'lies in its application to liminal forms of experience, as a category of pre-emergence' (Pickering, 1997, p. 45). Paradoxically, this becomes much clearer in Williams's later more explicitly 'theoretical' writings, where he effects his own version of the more general 'turn to Gramsci'. Both Thompson and Hoggart have paid their theoretical respects to Gramsci (Thompson, 1978a, pp. 162–164 ; Hoggart, 1995, p. 185), but for Williams alone of the three the encounter became crucial. The notion of hegemony appeared to deliver exactly the theoretical resolution he had sought: the integration of a near-Leavisite sense of the wholeness and livedness of culture into a quasi-Marxian sense of the interestedness and structuredness of ideology. In Gramsci, Williams discovered a sustained attempt to understand culture as simultaneously both transcending class and irredeemably marked by it. Hegemony, he explained, is 'in the strongest sense a "culture", but a culture which has to be seen as the lived dominance and subordination of particular classes' (Williams, 1977, p. 110). For Williams, as for Gramsci, the counter-hegemonic moment became especially significant: hence, his attempt to distinguish between the 'dominant', the 'residual' and the 'emergent' (Williams, 1980, pp. 39–42; Williams, 1977, pp. 121–127). For Williams, as for Gramsci, a primary source of cultural emergence was the formation of a new social class (the other main source is what he terms 'the excluded social [human] area'); for Williams, as for Gramsci, the exemplary contemporary instance of this process had been the development of the modern working class (Williams, 1977, pp. 124–126). An emergent culture, he argued, requires not only distinct kinds of immediate cultural practice, but also new forms or adaptations of forms. Innovation at the level of form, he continued, is thus best understood as '*pre-emergence*, active and pressing but not yet fully articulated' (Williams, 1977, p. 126). And it is precisely at this level that structures of feeling operate: they are 'social experiences *in solution*', he wrote, 'and it is primarily to emergent formations . . . that the structure of feeling, *as solution*, relates' (Williams, 1977, pp. 133–134). Structures of feeling are thus quite specifically counter-hegemonic; that is, they denote the particular elements within the more general culture that most actively anticipate subsequent mutations in the general culture itself.

As contemporary Cultural Studies has acquired an increasingly postmodern coloration, so it has tended to consign history and class, experience and culture, humanism, Marxism and even literature, into the discard tray labelled 'modernity'. The resultant theoretical marginalization clearly marks Hoggart, Williams and Thompson's later work. In the wonderfully vindictive 'Foreword' to *The Poverty of Theory*, Thompson insisted that the previous 10 years had been 'a time for reason to sulk in its tent' (Thompson, 1978b, p. ii). In his last unfinished work, Williams asked exasperatedly of cultural theory whether it was 'hard enough' to look for its 'own double edges', so as to recognize 'works and . . . theories' that are based only on 'negations and forms of enclosure' (Williams, 1989a, p. 175). More recently, Hoggart has bemoaned the way Cultural Studies juggles 'with new theoretic language . . . that is both a kind of game and an indication that they have joined a club, an in-group, a mystery, a modish clique' (Hoggart, 1995, p. 176). For all their apparent marginalization, all three remained committed to the centrality of class analysis of one kind or another: Thompson's last book 'places' Blake definitively and authoritatively 'in the strongest centre of tradesman and skilled artisan *independency* in the kingdom' (Thompson, 1993, p. 111); Hoggart dismisses the claim that 'we are all classless nowadays' as 'blind to evidence all around of the enduring power of the English sense of class-divisions' (Hoggart, 1995, pp. 198–199); and, even as he acknowledged the importance of the new social movements, Williams remained adamant that these 'new issues', followed through, 'lead . . . into the central systems of the industrial-capitalist mode of production and . . . its system of classes' (Williams, 1983, pp. 172–173). It has become something of a commonplace to complain of a 'disconcerting lack of objective coordinates' in 'culturalist' writing of this kind, to borrow Anderson's description of Thompson (Anderson, 1980, p. 33). But if this were really so, then one would have expected to find in their work some impress of the supposed decentring of class from the experience of postmodernity. This is not the case, however. Certainly, Williams registered the danger of a political demobilization of organized labour, which might extend even into a possible 'final incorporation . . . into a capitalist bargaining mechanism' (Williams, 1983, p. 173). And Hoggart, at least, has toyed with the notion of a 'move from class to status' (Hoggart, 1995, p. 202), although it is clear that he intends by this almost exactly the opposite of what a Weberian sociologist would mean.[2] But all three seem persuaded of the continuing importance of the experience of class. As Hoggart has it, 'a new form of class' this may be, but the 'gates have closed against openness' nonetheless (Hoggart, 1995, p. 202). Theirs is a different kind of experience, then, from that which underpins postmodernism.

Postmodernism: Stuart Hall

As we noted in Chapter 1, Stratton and Ang's 'mythic history' nominates Stuart Hall as the third father of Cultural Studies,

after Hoggart and Williams. There is an obvious appropriateness
to the nomination: Hall was Hoggart's chosen successor as
Director of the Birmingham Centre; and, on his own account, he
and Williams had found themselves 'shaping up to the same
issues . . . from the same directions' (Hall, 1989a, p. 54). But for
all these apparent continuities, Hall's central achievement was
to preside over the theoretical postmodernization of British
Cultural Studies. For Colin Sparks, this means above all a break
from Marxism, but also and in my view more interestingly a
break from the more general 'concern with the ways in which
material life and culture were . . . interwoven' (Sparks, 1996,
p. 98). For Marxists and non-Marxists alike, this concern had
been intimately bound up with the problem of class. Hall had
shared these preoccupations and, like Williams, he had sought
to theorize them, initially by way of left-Leavisite culturalism,
later neo-Gramscian Marxism. Hence the linkage between the
concepts of hegemony and culture, clearly reminiscent of
Williams, in the co-authored overview of subcultural theory that
opens *Resistance through Rituals* (Clarke et al., 1976, pp. 10–
13). There were few doubts here as to the centrality of class in
cultural analysis: 'In modern societies,' wrote Hall and his collaborators, 'the most fundamental groups are the social classes,
and the major cultural configurations . . . "class cultures" '
(Clarke et al., 1976, p. 13).

But Hall was much more sympathetic than either Williams
or Thompson to Althusserian and other structuralisms. His
early much-cited 'Encoding/decoding' essay had displayed a
clear interest and fluency in semiotic theory (Hall, 1980c). As
Anglo-Althusserianism gathered momentum, his formulations
increasingly situated Gramsci in relation to Althusser rather
than to Thompson or Williams (Hall, 1978; Hall et al., 1978).
Eventually, he would characterize the Anglo-culturalists' work
as improperly eliding the distinction between active consciousness and determinate conditions; and as mistakenly turning
experience into the 'authenticating position' in cultural analysis
(Hall, 1980a, p. 63). The 'disabling theoretical effects' of Williams's culturalism, Hall wrote, included 'an inevitable theoretical pull' towards reading structures as 'expressively correlated

with one another' (Hall, 1989a, p. 62). In short, the culturalists were guilty of the peculiarly humanist vice defined by Althusser as the sin of expressive causality. Structuralism, by contrast, had recognized the presence of constraining relations of structure and successfully replaced the category of experience with that of ideology (Hall, 1980a, pp. 67, 69). At times, Hall clearly caricatured both Williams and Thompson. Neither had been anything like so empiricist or so unaware of structural determinacy as he suggested: as he had cause to remark elsewhere, Williams's work was in many respects intensely theoretical; and Thompson's account of the dialogue between theory and evidence is very much more nuanced than its title suggests (Hall, 1980b, p. 19; Thompson, 1978b, pp. 197–242). The point, however, is that Hall's reading of Gramsci had developed along very different lines from that in Thompson and Williams. If hegemony is a culture, as Williams and Thompson supposed, then it is materially produced by the practices of conscious agents, and can be countered by counter-hegemonic practice. But if hegemony is a structure of ideology, as Hall and the Althusserians supposed, then it will determine the subjectivity of its subjects in ways that radically diminish the prospects for such practice, except in the characteristically attenuated form of a plurality of post-structuralist resistant readings. Hegemony as culture is thus a matter of material production, reproduction and consumption; hegemony as structure, a matter for textual decoding.

There was always a certain inherent improbability in the choice of the martyred Italian Communist leader as a source of theoretical inspiration for this mainly Anglophone academic proto-discipline. It is difficult to avoid the suspicion that something of the enthusiasm for Gramsci derived from the notorious opacity of the *Quaderni*, occasioned in the first instance by the necessity to evade the Fascist censorship. As Hall candidly observed: 'What was undoubtedly a limitation from a textual point of view – namely, the fragmentary nature of his writings – was . . . a positive advantage' (Hall, 1991, p. 8) for subsequent Gramscian theory. As he later recalled of the Birmingham Centre during the 1970s: 'we were trying to find an institutional practice that might produce an organic intellectual . . . We were organic intellectuals without any organic point of reference . . . with a nostalgia or will or hope . . . that at some point we would be prepared in intellectual work for that kind of relationship, if such a conjuncture ever appeared' (Hall, 1992, p. 281). There is a certain disingenuousness to this formulation, since whatever else Hall's Centre aspired to, it was certainly not to an institutionally organic relationship with either the existing working class or the existing labour movement. In a strange caricature of the vanguardist pretensions of would-be Leninists, these would-be Gramscians were ready to 'organize and lead' only the ideal proletariat that never was, in Hall's phrase 'the emerging historical movement' that couldn't be found (Hall, 1992, p. 281). And even if Hall himself might have been prepared to 'simulate such a relationship in its absence' (Hall, 1992, p. 281), the more general tendency was to give up on the working class altogether. If the Centre's graduates were to become organic intellectuals, then it would only ever be as organic to the new social movements: Marxist-feminists applied the Althusserian theory of ideology to gender relations (Marxist-feminist Literature Collective, 1978; Harrison, 1978; Barrett, 1988, pp. 84–113), whilst Hall argued for Gramsci's relevance to the study of race and ethnicity (Hall, 1986). For such purposes, only a radically rewritten Gramscianism could suffice, such as neither Gramsci himself nor even Williams would have been able to recognize. Where Williams's interpretation of Gramsci's work remained resolutely culturalist, Hall progressively assimilated it to the developing structuralist and post-structuralist paradigm. Hence, his eventual view of Gramsci as anticipating 'many of the actual advances in theorizing' brought about by 'structuralism, discourse and linguistic theory or psychoanalysis' (Hall, 1988, p. 56).

These theoretical differences between culturalism and (post-) structuralism gradually devolved on to a particular substantive issue, that of 'Thatcherism'. During the 1980s and early 1990s, Hall and many of his colleagues remained fascinated by the problem of how to analyse the particularities and peculiarities of Thatcherite Toryism. The issues at stake were claimed for Cultural Studies, rather than, say, political science, because they appeared to pertain to the social construction of consent: 'What is particularly significant for our purposes', wrote Hall, 'is Thatcherism's capacity to become popular, especially among those sectors of society whose interests it cannot possibly be said to represent in any conventional sense of the term' (Hall, 1988, p. 41). His analyses commenced from the assumption that Thatcherism was substantially different from earlier forms of Conservatism, and that this difference centred on the particular ways in which hegemony was established and maintained. What was at issue, Hall argued, was the 'move toward "authoritarian populism" – an exceptional form of the capitalist state which . . . has been able to construct around itself an active popular consent' (Hall, 1983, pp. 22–23). His approach was strongly influenced by Laclau and Mouffe, whose work he would describe as 'seminal' and 'extraordinarily rich' (Grossberg, 1996, p. 145). Hence, the central contention that popular consent had been secured through the effective 'articulation' of Thatcherism with key elements from traditional working-class culture. According to Hall, Thatcherism operated directly 'on popular elements in the traditional philosophies and practical ideologies of the *dominated* classes' (Hall, 1983, p. 30). This was possible, he explained, because such elements 'have no intrinsic, necessary or fixed class meaning' and can therefore be recomposed in new ways, so as 'to construct the people into a populist political subject: *with*, not against, the power bloc' (Hall, 1983, p. 30). In subsequent reformulations, the account was modified and augmented by a theory of postmodernism redefined, in peculiarly British terms, as 'New Times'. Hall now sought to 'disarticulate' the politics of the Anglo-American New Right from economic and cultural postmodernity: Thatcherism, he insisted, 'represents . . . an attempt . . . to harness and bend to its political project circumstances . . . which do not necessarily have a "New Right" political agenda inscribed in them' (Hall, 1989b, pp. 116–117).

No doubt, Hall was right to insist that the British Left could neither revive nor survive if 'wholly cut off from the landscapes of popular pleasures, however contradictory and "commodified" ' (Hall, 1989b, pp. 128–129). But some critical distance, some continuing sense of the 'classed' nature of (even postmodern late) capitalism, was surely necessary were the Left to go on being left. There are good empirical reasons, moreover, to treat Hall's approach with some caution. Alternative explanations were available, after all: Williams himself had suggested that the scale of Conservative electoral victory was more plausibly explained by the 'first-past-the-post' electoral system, than by a successfully Thatcherite ideological mobilization (Williams, 1989b, p. 163); he had shown that pro-Labour loyalties persisted amongst union members, the unemployed, and manual workers (Williams, 1983, pp. 156–157); and that the fall in the Labour vote was as much a consequence of the splits in the party as of any direct transfer to the Conservatives (Williams, 1983, p. 155). We might note that Williams was dealing here with precisely the kind of 'objective coordinates' or 'structural determinants' that culturalism was supposed to ignore. Indeed, it is Williams's explanation, rather than Hall's, that seems the more readily compatible with mainstream empirical sociology. As Goldthorpe observed of Hall:

> Not only is no evidence provided of the supposed 'hegemony' at work, but the argument for it involves ignoring the . . . quite substantial findings to indicate that Thatcherism *cannot* be linked with any very significant belief and value changes within British society, and that many Conservative policies are well out of line with prevailing opinion. (Goldthorpe, 1990, p. 431)

The political risks in any such 'block diagnosis of Thatcherism' were apparent to Williams: that it 'taught despair and political disarmament in a social situation which was always more diverse, more volatile and more temporary' (Williams, 1989a, p. 175). But now that the despair – and perhaps something at least of the political disarmament – has passed, the more straightforwardly academic problem remains: to determine the theoretical and empirical adequacy of Hall's analysis. Whatever we make either of postmodernism in general or of 'New Times' in particular, the accumulating empirical data on the continuing resilience of the connections between class identity and politics increasingly cast his intervention as a theoretical overreaction to short-term contingencies. Theoretically, we need to ask why it was that Williams was able to read Thatcherism more accurately than Hall. At one level, the answer might rest with the legitimacy accorded the proper claims of experience. When Williams identified the striking miners as the 'point of growth for a reviving socialism' (Williams, 1989b, p. 127), for example, he clearly invoked the lived experience of the class and place of his birth and upbringing. But experience alone had never been *the* authenticating test, either in his own work or in Thompson's. The older culturalists had in fact persisted in a longstanding commitment, inherited from Leavisism ironically enough, not so much to experience *per se*, as to the analysis of the connections between being, consciousness and experience. By contrast, Hall and the younger post-Althusserians progressively abandoned all three, initially in favour of the notion of ideology as structure, later still the even more 'immaterial' notion of discursive formation. In truth, structuralism never had paid very much attention to the structural determinants of culture, except insofar as they occurred within ideology or within language. And to the extent that these were made available for analysis, they were understood as present, neither in experience nor in the empirical data produced by history and sociology, but in the deep structures of textuality. Even the Leavises had known that historical reality could never simply be deduced from a close reading of the literary text. But as Sparks observes, contemporary Cultural Studies has increasingly regressed 'beyond Hoggart and Williams, beyond the Leavises and the British marxists, to an essentially textualist account of culture'. If this has been Hall's achievement, then it is surely, as Sparks concludes, a quite 'fundamentally regressive step' (Sparks, 1996, p. 98).

Postmodernism: Baudrillard and Lyotard

All things are relative, however, and by comparison with French postmodernism Hall remains the very model of a scrupulously empirical probity. Indeed, almost every British vice seems magnified tenfold when projected on to the screen of the French intelligentsia's fascination with things American. The term 'postmodern' is an American coinage, subsequently inserted into French 'theory' only by way of Lyotard's *La Condition postmoderne,* which was itself originally commissioned for a Canadian audience.[3] The term's American connotations have persisted, most obviously in the sense of the American present as an anticipation of Europe's near future. The Americans, wrote Baudrillard, 'were a marginal transcendence of that Old World', but 'are today its new, eccentric centre . . . It will do us no good to worry our poor heads over this. In Los Angeles, Europe has disappeared' (Baudrillard, 1988a, p. 81). Along with Europe, so too goes class and class struggle. In countries 'with liberal or advanced liberal management', observed Lyotard, these 'struggles and their instruments have been transformed into regulators of the system' (Lyotard, 1984, p. 13). For Lyotard, class seems little more than a narrative effect of Marxism, itself a grand narrative stripped of all credibility in contemporary culture, not only in its Stalinist versions, but even as Frankfurt School critical theory (Lyotard, 1984, pp. 36–37). If he has remained critical of capital and capitalism, then it is from the standpoint of a 'socialism' that betrays very little enthusiasm for organized labour: witness his dismal history of the 'labour movement' as in effect identical to that of Marxist politics (Lyotard, 1989a, p. 322). For Baudrillard too the working class has been subsumed under the 'code of normality': 'the proletarian is a "normal" being,' he wrote, 'and . . . he seizes onto every dominant discrimination: he is racist, sexist and repressive . . . he has sided with the bourgeoisie' (Baudrillard, 1993, p. 29). As for Marxism, it 'no longer furnishes . . . a real alternative to capitalism' (Baudrillard, 1975, p. 29).

Both Lyotard and Baudrillard were at one time members of a small non-Communist Marxist group, Socialisme ou barbarie,[4] and for all the vehemence of their later objections to Marxism, their work betrays something of this earlier Marxist inspiration. Both insist on a logic of periodization, by which the 'post-modern' (for Lyotard) or the 'hyperreal' (for Baudrillard) succeeds to and proceeds from a past imagined much as Marxists had tended to describe capitalism. Both seek to explain post-modern culture as in some sense the effect of a change in what Marxists had meant by 'the mode of production'. For Lyotard, 'the status of knowledge is altered as societies enter . . . the postindustrial age' (Lyotard, 1984, p. 3). For Baudrillard, the shift from the second to the third 'order of simulacra', that is, from industrial production to 'simulation', is an effect of capitalist development: 'it is *capital itself*', he writes, 'which abolishes the determination of the social according to the means of production' (Baudrillard, 1993, p. 8). Once achieved, however, this 'end of production' radically reverses the productivist logic described by Marx and Marxism. For Lyotard, postmodernity exhibits the 'atomization' of the social 'into flexible networks of language games' (Lyotard, 1984, p. 17). The decline of meta-narrative – for Lyotard, the distinguishing characteristic *par excellence* of the postmodern condition – has entailed a shift in emphasis 'from the ends of action to its means' (Lyotard, 1984, p. 37). The resultant predominance of 'performativity' determines not only the 'normal' functioning of postmodernity, but also the utopian possibilities immanent within it. Hence the aspiration to language games 'of perfect information at any given moment' (Lyotard, 1984, p. 67). For Baudrillard, the shift to a third order of simulation has meant the entry into an 'order no longer of the real, but of the hyperreal' (Baudrillard, 1993, p. 3). Against Marx, but with McLuhan (and also, in his reading, with Benjamin), Baudrillard concludes that 'the real message . . . *lay in reproduction itself*. Production itself has no meaning: its social finality is lost in the series. Simulacra prevail over history' (Baudrillard, 1993, p. 56).

If Lyotard's is essentially a technocratic liberal-individualist utopia with little or no place for class, then Baudrillard's vision, part utopian, part dystopian, eventually substitutes 'the masses' for both the individual and the social class. Despite his own hesitancy as to the validity of the category (Baudrillard, 1990, pp. 20–21), it is in Baudrillard's 'postmodernism', rather than Lyotard's, that we encounter the clearest argument against 'class', against 'the social', even against 'sociology'. As early as *Le Miroire de la production*, the 1973 text which had announced his break with Marxism, Baudrillard had sought to counter Marx's theory of class with the greater 'revolutionary potentiality' of a 'cultural revolution' aiming at nothing less than 'the totality of life and social relations' (Baudrillard, 1975, pp. 152, 151). Here Baudrillard dismissed all notions of class and class consciousness, including Marx's, as essentially 'bourgeois': 'there has always been and there will always be only one class,' he writes, 'the bourgeoisie . . . To make a class of the proletariat is . . . to enclose it in an order of definition . . . in which the model remains that of the bourgeoisie' (Baudrillard, 1975, pp. 157–158). Clearly, there is a sense in which this must be true. Any socially subordinate group, which chooses to organize around and against the fact of its own subordination, necessarily defines itself, at least in part, in the terms of that subordination: this is as true of gay activists or immigrants as of organized labour. But that in no way belies the brute empirical significance of class as a sociological phenomenon. Moreover, its obverse may also be true: that any such subordinate identity is transcendable, in Eagleton's phrase, only by way of passage 'all the way through it and out the other side'. 'To wish class . . . away . . ., to seek to live sheer irreducible difference *now* . . .,' Eagleton observes, 'is to play straight into the hands of the oppressor' (Eagleton, 1990, p. 23). Whatever the leftist utopianism underpinning the initial antipathy to Marxist notions of class, Baudrillard's developing political fatalism gave rise to a growing sense of the social passivity of mass-mediated society. The 'clearest result of the whole media environment', he would conclude in an essay first published in English in 1985, is 'stupor . . . a radical uncertainty as to our own desire, our own choice, our own opinion, our own will' (Baudrillard, 1988b, p. 209). To suffer from stupor of this kind is to be a part of the 'masses', to be 'made up of . . . useless hyperinformation which claims to enlighten . . . when all it does is clutter up the space of the representable' (Baudrillard, 1988b, p. 211). It goes without saying that we are all, Baudrillard included, a part of the masses (Baudrillard, 1988b, p. 212).

According to Baudrillard, we inhabit a hyperreal world of mass media simulation, in which 'the code' no longer refers to an external reality, but only to itself, so that the 'signifier becomes its own referent' and the 'sign no longer designates anything at all' (Baudrillard, 1975, pp. 127–128). This 'implosion of meaning' implies both the 'end of the social' and the decline of the political, since what is true of signs in general is true of political signs in particular. For Baudrillard, both the rational liberal individual subject and the class-conscious proletarian collective subject thereby cease to function: 'there is no longer any social signified to give force to a political signifier' (Baudrillard, 1983, p. 19). The one still functional referent is thus 'the silent majority' or 'the masses'. But since their existence is merely statistical rather than social, they can function only as an imaginary referent for the simulations of the media (Baudrillard, 1983, pp. 19–20). It follows that, in the most fundamental of senses, the media and the masses imply each other: 'Mass(age) is the message' (Baudrillard, 1983, p. 44). In itself, the pastiche of McLuhan is little more than a truism. More interestingly, this mutual implication of masses and media is, for Baudrillard, a matter neither of manipulation nor of democratization, a cause neither for hope nor for regret (Baudrillard, 1988b, p. 207). To the contrary, the inertia of the masses is precisely their strength: '*the masses are a stronger medium than all the media*' (Baudrillard, 1983, p. 44). Hence his eventual conclusion that, since 'the system' itself aims to maximize speech, meaning and participation, the 'actual strategy of the masses', their strategic resistance, is that of 'the refusal of meaning and the refusal of speech' (Baudrillard, 1988b, p. 219). The masses, as distinct from both the individual and the class, thereby become the repository of Baudrillard's hopes and expectations for 'a finally delusive, illusive, and allusive strategy', the 'correlative' of an 'ironic, joyful, and seductive unconscious' (Baudrillard, 1988b, p. 217).

This is something less than the 'celebratory mode' Hall deplored in Baudrillard (Grossberg, 1996, p. 131), something more than the Weberian sobriety admired by Smart (Smart, 1992, p. 137). More persuasively than either, Bauman takes the measure of Baudrillard's work in its overly televisual character: 'Baudelaire's stroller has turned into Baudrillard's watcher', he observes, but 'there is life after and beyond television' and for many 'reality remains what it always used to be: tough, solid, resistant and harsh' (Bauman, 1992, p. 155). This is nicely put both in itself and as a pointer to what has emerged as one of the characteristic weaknesses of contemporary Cultural Studies, its excessive textualism. Baudrillard himself had initially hoped to develop a 'sociological perspective' that would account for the 'cultural class logic' of bourgeois society (Baudrillard, 1981, pp. 33–62). The subsequent shift, away from quasi-sociological forms of analysis and towards an impressionistic reading of media texts, was very clearly a matter of quite explicit choice. Glancing towards the 'more subtle' categories of ' "sociological" understanding', such as 'class' and 'cultural status', he readily concedes that 'mass' is not so much 'a concept' as 'a soft, sticky, lumpenanalytical notion'. But that is precisely its great merit, he continues: 'it is by prowling around these soft and acritical notions . . . that one can go further than intelligent critical sociology' (Baudrillard, 1983, p. 4). The point is made more explicitly in a later interview: 'sociology . . . became a kind of stereotype, an analysis for which you have to produce facts . . . what's the use of producing facts? . . . This sort of conformity to facts, this compliance with truth is . . . never going to contest anything' (Baudrillard, 1990, p. 31). Here, then, right at the heart of theoretical postmodernism, we find something suspiciously close to a self-conscious defence of 'data-freedom', to borrow Goldthorpe's description of Hall. Of course, neither Hall nor any of the British post-Marxists is prone to such deliberate academic solecism. But there is no reason in principle to suppose that the anti-empirical logic of an overwhelmingly textualist discourse will operate any less effectively in English than in French.

Hall's own critical commentary on Baudrillard warrants repetition at this point. 'French intellectuals', he caustically observed in a 1986 interview:

> always had a tendency to use 'the masses' in the abstract to fuel or underpin their own intellectual positions. Now that the intellectuals have renounced critical thought, they feel no inhibition in renouncing it on behalf of the masses . . . It is critical intellectuals, locked into their own kind of cultural elitism, who have often succumbed to the temptation to give an account of . . . the masses . . . in terms of false consciousness . . . So the recognition of the masses . . . as significant historical elements is a useful corrective . . . But the politics which follows . . . seems . . . historically incorrect . . . The silent majorities *do* think . . . in spite of the fact that the popular masses have never been able to become . . . the subject-authors of the cultural practices in the twentieth century, their continuing

presence . . . has constantly interrupted, limited and disrupted everything else . . . The masses are like an irritant, a point that you have to pass through . . . postmodernism has yet to go through that point . . . I think Baudrillard needs to join the masses for a while, to be silent for two-thirds of a century, just to see what it feels like. (Grossberg, 1996, pp. 140–141)

There is an awful poignancy to the way Hall's retrospect for Baudrillard also served as his own prospectus. With Hall the argument is more nuanced and more carefully qualified than in Baudrillard. But the 'New Times' explanation for Thatcherism remains, finally, a renunciation of critical thought, on behalf of the 'masses', by a critical intelligentsia similarly predisposed to use the 'masses' as underpinning for its own theoretical positions. How else to explain the enthusiasm for a theory so persistently belied by the available evidence? One is tempted to ask, with Eliot: 'After such knowledge, what forgiveness?'

Postmodernism: Jameson

If there is one American cultural theorist whose name is most closely associated with postmodernism, then it is surely Fredric Jameson, Distinguished Professor of Comparative Literature at Duke University. His various essays on the subject have become standard references (Jameson, 1984; Jameson, 1985; Jameson, 1988b); and his full-length study *Postmodernism, or The Cultural Logic of Late Capitalism* is for many the *locus classicus* of the postmodern debate (Jameson, 1991). So, when Alan Sokal came to select a target for his now famously anti-postmodern academic hoax (Sokal, 1996), which anticipated the more seriously theoretical counter-offensive later co-authored with Bricmont (Sokal and Bricmont, 1998), it was perhaps unsurprising that the chosen journal should have been one Jameson co-edited, *Social Text*. Yet there is an obvious irony in this. For, if Jameson has indeed remained fascinated by the postmodern, there is no doubting the critical edge to that fascination, as registered at the very least in the distance between the appalled theorist and the 'extraordinarily demoralizing and depressing . . . new global space' he seeks to theorize (Jameson, 1991, p. 49). Nor is there much doubting the critical vantage point from which this theorizing has been mounted, that of a 'vocation to explain and to popularize the Marxist intellectual tradition' (Jameson, 1988a, p. xxvi). We noted in Chapter 2 that one available Marxist response to the postmodernist insistence on the disconnectedness of social position and cultural identity would be to treat this as a historical (rather than an ontological or epistemological) proposition, that is, as pertaining to the period culture of a specifically postmodern stage in human history. This is exactly the view canvassed by Jameson. Hence the paradox that the work of this apparently postmodern thinker should have acquired an increasingly Adornian cast, as a kind of *Kultur-pessimismus* for the 1990s. The paradox is more apparent than real, however, for if Jameson has been ready to concede the local theoretical value of postmodernism and post-structuralism, it was only ever on the condition that ' "traditional" Marxism . . . must necessarily become true again when the dreary realities of exploitation . . . and the resistance to it in the form of class struggle . . . slowly reassert themselves' (Jameson, 1988c, p. 208). In the absence of an effective socialist movement, of the kind to which 'traditional' Marxism aspired, there is an almost inescapable logic in Jameson's resort to Adorno and Horkheimer 'to restore the sense of something grim and impending within the polluted sunshine of the shopping mall' (Jameson, 1990, p. 248).

For Jameson, a quite central cultural significance continues to attach to social class and to class struggle, in their absence as well as their presence. This is apparent from the relatively systematic outline of his literary-critical method provided in *The Political Unconscious*. Here he had argued that the object of inquiry for cultural analysis could be located at any of three analytically distinct levels, those of 'text', 'ideologeme' and 'ideology of form'. Each of these has its socio-historical corollary in an equivalent 'semantic horizon', respectively: 'political history', in the sense of a chronicle-like sequence of events; 'society'; and global 'history', in the sense of a sequence and succession of modes of production (Jameson, 1981, pp. 75–76). By ideologeme, Jameson means the kind of collective discourse in relation to which texts function as 'little more than . . .

individual *parole* or utterance'. Since 'society' can be characterized primarily in terms of class struggle, then it follows that the ideologeme should be defined as 'the smallest intelligible unit of the essentially antagonistic collective discourses of social classes' (Jameson, 1981, p. 76). Class thus becomes one of the key analytical tools in Jameson's critical method: witness, for example, his ideologemic analysis of the medieval romance as providing an imaginary resolution to the emergent contradiction between positional ethics and noble class solidarity in twelfth-century Europe (Jameson, 1981, pp. 110–119); or that of *ressentiment* in Gissing and Nietzsche (Jameson, 1981, pp. 185–205). Class analysis of this kind provides the occasion for a 'double hermeneutic', simultaneously embracing both the negative hermeneutic of ideology-critique and the positive hermeneutic of a 'non-instrumental conception of culture' (Jameson, 1981, p. 286). For Jameson, class consciousness is simultaneously a matter both of ideology and of utopia: '*all* class consciousness', he insists, '. . . including the most exclusive forms of ruling-class consciousness . . . is in its very nature Utopian' (Jameson, 1981, p. 289).

On this account, class consciousness arises out of the struggle between classes, essentially as a form of social solidarity: its origins are thus in the exploited classes, although it will reappear amongst the exploiting classes by way of a response that is at once imitative and reactive (Jameson, 1971, pp. 376–390). For Jameson, class consciousness is above all a relational phenomenon: 'each class defines itself in terms of the other', he writes, 'and constitutes a virtual anti-class with respect to the other' (Jameson, 1992a, p. 47). As such, it is also overwhelmingly experiential: 'for genuine class consciousness to be possible', he observes, 'we have to begin to sense the abstract truth of class through the tangible medium of daily life' (Jameson, 1992a, p. 38). Whilst this abstract truth has been a near-universal feature of human society to date, Jameson readily acknowledges that the tangible experience is much less so. So, in a theoretical move that replicates the central preoccupations of the Western Marxist tradition, the relative absence of subordinate class consciousness from contemporary capitalist societies comes to

acquire a peculiar theoretical salience. During the mid-1970s
Jameson had anticipated a 'renewed possibility of class consciousness' in America (Jameson, 1992a, p. 51). By the early
1980s, however, he would describe the 1920s as 'the last period
in which class consciousness is out in the open' (Jameson,
1992b, p. 95). Indeed, his account of the postmodern condition
is couched increasingly in terms of an absence of class consciousness. Jameson has long maintained that class consciousness presupposes the 'narrative figurability' of class inequalities,
their representability 'in tangible form' (Jameson, 1992a, pp. 37–
38). But the capacity for such representation becomes progressively attenuated, he would conclude, as monopoly capitalism
evolves into global capitalism, modernism into postmodernism.
The point is made quite explicitly, in the course of a comparison
between representations of women in Gide's *Counterfeiters* and
in the Taiwanese director Edward Yang's 1986 film *Terrorizer*:

> In our own postmodern world there is no longer a bourgeois or
> class-specific culture . . . but rather a system-specific phenomenon:
> the various forms which reification and commodification and the
> corporate standardizations of media society imprint on human sub-
> jectivity and existential experience. (Jameson, 1992c, p. 131)

As is well known, Jameson posits a historical periodization
according to which there are three main stages in the history
of capitalism, each accompanied by a characteristic 'cultural
dominant'. So aesthetic realism becomes the cultural dominant
of nineteenth-century 'market capitalism', modernism of early
twentieth-century 'monopoly capitalism', postmodernism of
contemporary multinational 'late capitalism' (Jameson, 1991,
pp. 35–36). If late capitalism is 'the purest form of capital yet to
have emerged, a prodigious expansion of capital into hitherto
uncommodified areas' (Jameson, 1991, p. 36), then art itself
is one of these hitherto largely uncommodified areas, postmodernism the form of its commodification. 'What has happened',
Jameson writes, 'is that aesthetic production . . . has become
integrated into commodity production generally' (Jameson,
1991, p. 4). Postmodernism is thus inherently a commodity
culture, distinguishable from earlier modernisms as much by its
'resonant affirmation . . . of the market' as by any distinctive

style (Jameson, 1991, p. 305). As such, the postmodern emerges as a 'field of stylistic and discursive heterogeneity without a norm' (Jameson, 1991, p. 17). One important aspect of this process is what Jameson terms the 'waning of . . . historicity', whereby the past as 'referent' is gradually 'bracketed', so as eventually to leave 'nothing but texts' (Jameson, 1991, pp. 21, 18). Insofar as postmodernism can be said to have a characteristic aesthetic effect, then this is deliberate intertextuality itself, 'our awareness of the preexistence of other versions' (Jameson, 1991, p. 20). In a culture so commodified, so subject to the logic of the simulacrum, what becomes of class consciousness? At one level, the answer is obvious: if its emergence requires that the realities of class structure become representable, then the widening rift between sign and referent will tend to produce formidable structural inhibitors to its development: 'For a society that wants to forget about class . . . reification . . . is very functional indeed' (Jameson, 1991, p. 315).

But there is more to Jameson's argument than this. In the first place, he insists that the transition from monopoly to late capitalism really has, as a matter of fact, entailed a radical transformation in the nature of contemporary class structures (Jameson, 1991, p. 319). Secondly, he registers more powerfully than most previous Marxists, more so even than Lenin, the sheer difficulty and historical rarity of fully realized class consciousness (Jameson, 1991, pp. 345–346). Finally, he toys with the notion that the specific class content of postmodern culture might be derived from a particular new class fraction 'variously . . . labeled as a new petit bourgeoisie, a professional-managerial class, or more succinctly "the yuppies" ' (Jameson, 1991, p. 407). In combination, these propositions tend to suggest that the 'truth' of postmodernism might consist in its peculiar fidelity to the lie which is late capitalism. The preconditions for the emergence of class consciousness are thus effectively postponed, not indefinitely, but for the duration of a 'transitional' period, in which the 'new global economy has not yet allowed its classes to form in any stable way, let alone to acquire genuine class consciousness' (Jameson, 1991, p. 348). In these circumstances, radical politics becomes group politics, the preserve of new social movements, whose characteristic narratives lack 'the allegorical capacity to map or model the system' (Jameson, 1991, p. 349). Noting how difference and identity have come to substitute for each other in the political rhetoric of these movements – as simultaneously the 'politics of difference' and 'identity politics' – Jameson concludes that difference has been made possible only by the prior consolidation of something very close to universal identity. Postmodern politics thus entails a 'ceaseless alternation' between identity and difference, which itself attests to a kind of cultural 'blockage' that obstructs further development through interaction (Jameson, 1994, pp. 65–66, 70). This blockage bespeaks a collective incapacity to imagine change, he concludes, wherein time can be imagined only as 'an eternal present and, much further away, an inevitable catastrophe' (Jameson, 1994, p. 70).

At this point, Adorno's significance for Jameson becomes more readily apparent. Since the emergence of class consciousness has for the moment been structurally pre-empted, the capacity to map or model 'the system' either disappears altogether or must temporarily lie elsewhere. That elsewhere is located somewhere between critical theory itself and a hypothetically postmodern political art. For this is Jameson's solution to the temporary absence of class consciousness from postmodern late capitalism: to posit the need for an 'aesthetic of cognitive mapping', through which to learn how to represent 'the truth of postmodernism – that is . . . the world space of multinational capital' and so 'again begin to grasp our positioning as individual and collective subjects' (Jameson, 1991, p. 54). Cognitive mapping, he explains, is in reality a 'code word' for class consciousness 'of a new and hitherto undreamed of kind', which has not yet come into being. Hence the sense of his own work as the anticipation in theory of what may eventually become class consciousness, that is, as an experiment 'to see whether by systematizing something that is resolutely unsystematic, and historicizing something that is resolutely ahistorical, one couldn't outflank it and force a historical way at least of thinking about that' (Jameson, 1991, p. 418). Despite the obviously American idiom, the rhetorical strategy thus invoked is clearly reminiscent of the Frankfurt School. Adorno and Horkheimer had initially imagined their critical theory as cognate with a proletarian opposition to fascism: witness the latter's own programmatic insistence that 'critical theory . . . is an essential element in the historical effort to create a world which satisfies the needs and powers of men' (Horkheimer, 1972, pp. 245–246). From at least the *Dialectic of Enlightenment* such emancipatory potential increasingly inheres in the immanent logic of critical theory itself, as the attempt to discover 'in the facts . . . the tendency that points beyond them' (Adorno, 1976, p. 257). As Jameson himself notes, this eventually led Adorno to a kind of 'temperamental and cantankerous quietism' that would prove a disabling liability at moments of popular politicization (Jameson, 1990, p. 249). For Jameson, the 1960s were 'the most politicized era in modern American social history' (Jameson, 1994, p. 68). But the times they have a-changed in ways apparently unanticipated by either the young Bob Dylan or the young Fredric Jameson. And so Adorno 'in the postmodern' becomes 'a joyous counter-poison and a corrosive solvent to apply to the surface of "what is" ' (Jameson, 1990, p. 249).

As we noted in Chapter 2, Marxism of this kind functions by way of a great refusal, both of the increasingly totalized late-capitalist system and of the postmodernist ideologies that legitimize it. No doubt, there is a certain grandeur to this intransigent resistance to the lures of commodity culture, whether in Adorno or in Jameson. This is critique of a kind to which properly critical criticism would do well to aspire: criticism 'which refuses to accept what is offered simply at face value,' as Chris Baldick has it, 'which will not rest satisfied with things as they are' (Baldick, 1983, p. 234). But criticism *per se* provides no special warranty as to the adequacy of any attendant theory of class. For Jameson, as not for Adorno, the formal certainty of Marxian class politics remains, but it proceeds virtually unaccompanied by any developed sense of the empirical realities of class identity and class conflct. So when Jameson describes cognitive mapping as a code for class consciousness, he can only mean class consciousness in the specifically post-Marxist

(Leninist or Kautskyist) sense of a socialistic or proto-socialistic consciousness coming 'from without' the empirical consciousnesses of working-class people. Like Lenin and Kautsky, Jameson looks forward to a future time when the working class will attain to such consciousness. In the meantime, however, class consciousness exists only as cognitive mapping, that is, only *in theory*. His observation that, although 'a new international proletariat . . . will re-emerge', we ourselves are 'still in the trough . . . and no one can say how long we will stay there' (Jameson, 1991, p. 417), carries with it the implication that contemporary empirical working-class belief can effectively be discounted. But, as we have seen, empirical sociological research already provides clear testimony to the widespread presence of class consciousness in America and elsewhere. Such beliefs have clear behavioural correlates, moreover: after 30 years of decline, trade union membership has begun to increase in the United States; in 1996 strike rates picked up for the first time in years (Walker, 1997, p. 6; Moody, 1997, p. 53). None of this is strictly precluded by Jameson's model, but nor is it likely to be predicted therefrom. My point is not to argue that nothing changed in the shift from monopoly to late capitalism, which would be absurd; nor even to deny that Jameson can often be very acute, and much more so than either Hall or Baudrillard, on the cultural specificities of late-capitalist society. It is, rather, that the mass-mediated cultures of these societies systematically conceal the realities of their class structure, class consciousness itself definitely not excepted, in ways that are peculiarly unamenable to any merely textual deconstruction of the kind deployed by Jameson in particular and by Cultural Studies more generally.

Culturalism and Class Analysis: Bourdieu

When Baudrillard dismissed sociology as 'a kind of stereotype', his target wasn't so much Goldthorpe or Wright as Pierre Bourdieu, Professor of Sociology at the Collège de France and the doyen of contemporary French sociologists. Baudrillard's distaste for Bourdieu is almost transparent: 'nothing has changed in fifteen years . . .', he comments at one point; 'all it does is constantly verify itself – a tautology which can be found in the very form of Bourdieu's discourse . . . the same conjuring tricks return, without having budged an inch . . . that's sociology: a kind of permanent recurrence' (Baudrillard, 1990, p. 31). Nor is the distaste difficult to explain, for there is an important sense in which Bourdieu's work can be read, in Fowler's phrase, as a 'sociological rebuttal of . . . postmodernist thought' (Fowler, 1997, p. 70). At the core of this rebuttal lies precisely the kind of proposition to which Baudrillard takes most exception: 'But then, what about class? Whatever became of class logic?' (Baudrillard, 1990, p. 31). We might add that there are significant differences between their respective intellectual styles: where Baudrillard made the transition from teacher to writer to celebrity, to borrow Debray's terms (Debray, 1981),[5] Bourdieu has chosen to follow a more strictly academic career. Bourdieu is, however, by no means the caricature sociological empiricist of theoreticist imaginings. The Anglophone reception of his work has been overwhelmingly located in Cultural Studies rather than in sociology (Garnham and Williams, 1986; Frow, 1987; Frow, 1995, pp. 27–47):[6] hence his inclusion in the present rather than the previous chapter. And he is in many respects a quintessentially 'French' theorist, an erstwhile structuralist, whose work sometimes seems to run parallel to Foucault, an erstwhile anthropologist and former student of Lévi-Strauss. But Bourdieu has long since distanced himself from the 'objectivism' of structural anthropology, whilst remaining stubbornly resistant to Derridean deconstruction (Bourdieu, 1977a, pp. 1–30; Bourdieu, 1984, p. 495). Moreover, his work engages very directly with the German tradition in social theory, both Marxist and Weberian. One recent commentator has observed that it 'is best understood as the attempt to push class analysis beyond Marx and Weber' by giving the concept of class 'a genuine *culturalist twist*' (Eder, 1993, p. 63). The term 'culturalism' carries more baggage from recent English debates than Eder perhaps realizes (cf. Hall, 1980a; Johnson, 1979; Milner, 1994, pp. 20–47), but his meaning is clear: for Bourdieu, class analysis has become primarily the attempt to identify and account for class-specific cultural practices.

Even Baudrillard admits to finding Bourdieu's work 'very strong at one time . . . long ago' (Baudrillard, 1990, p. 31). What kind of class analysis is it, then, that excites such antipathy and admiration? It is, in the first place, as Eder suggested, a specifically culturalist kind: for Bourdieu, the 'symbolic power' of culture is not some secondary effect of an economy located elsewhere, but is itself fully material. So, when he rejects the 'crude reductionism' of much Marxism, he does so by emphasizing that ideologies 'owe their structure and their most specific functions to the social conditions of their production and circulation – that is to say, to the functions which they fulfil . . . for the specialists competing for the monopoly of the established competence in question' (Bourdieu, 1977b, p. 116). This sense of culture as itself material, and of its practitioners as themselves materialists, finds many an echo in contemporary cultural theory, with Foucault, for example, or with Williams. But for Bourdieu an important source of inspiration is clearly Weber, whom he describes as having opened the way to a 'radical materialism' that will seek out 'the economic determinants' even 'in areas where the ideology of "disinterestedness" prevails', for example art and religion (Bourdieu, 1993a, p. 12). Secondly, this is a kind of class analysis that seeks to overcome what Bourdieu perceives to be the 'false opposition' between 'objectivism' and 'subjectivism': in his account, social actors 'are both classified and classifiers, but they classify according to (or depending upon) their position within classifications' (Bourdieu, 1987, p. 2). This means that class is neither simply an 'analytical construct' nor simply a 'folk category'. Rather, it exists only to the extent that 'historical agents' are able to transform the latter into the former 'by the magic of social belief' (Bourdieu, 1987, p. 9). The existence or non-existence of classes is thus itself a major stake in the political struggle: 'through this endless work of representation', he concludes, '. . . social agents try to impose their vision of the world . . . and to define their social identity' (Bourdieu, 1987, pp. 10–11).

Bourdieu's key sociological concept is that of 'the habitus', a constraining, but not determining, value context, in relation to which individuals act meaningfully and strategically (Bourdieu, 1977a, pp. 72–95). According to Bourdieu, the concept has a history that can be traced back, through Mauss and Durkheim, to Scholastic translations of Aristotle (Bourdieu, 1993a, p. 86). The habitus, he explains, is 'an acquired system of generative schemes objectively adjusted to the particular conditions in which it is constituted' (Bourdieu, 1977a, p. 95). It is simultaneously structured and structuring, materially produced and very often generation-specific (Bourdieu, 1977a, pp. 72, 78). Elsewhere, he draws the analogy between social life and games, likening the habitus to the 'feel' for a game and its stakes, which encompasses 'both the inclination and the capacity to play the game, to take an *interest* in the game, to be taken up, taken in by the game' (Bourdieu, 1993a, p. 18). The habitus, he writes:

> is a product of conditionings which tends to reproduce the objective logic of those conditionings while transforming it . . . a kind of transforming machine that leads us to 'reproduce' the social conditions of our own production, but in a relatively unpredictable way . . . (Bourdieu, 1993a, p. 87)

Like Marx and Weber, Bourdieu considers contemporary capitalist societies to be class societies. But for Bourdieu, their dominant and dominated classes are distinguishable from each other, not simply as a matter of economics, but also and primarily as a matter of habitus: 'social class, understood as a system of objective determinations,' he insists, 'must be brought into relation . . . with the class habitus, the system of dispositions (partially) common to all products of the same structures' (Bourdieu, 1977a, p. 85). If his understanding of class is substantially 'encultured', then the obverse is also true: his understanding of culture is similarly 'enclassed'. 'Position in the classification struggle', he concludes, 'depends on position in the class structure' (Bourdieu, 1984, p. 484).

Even though Bourdieu is insistent on the central importance of social class, he remains relatively uninterested in detailed class maps of the kind developed by Goldthorpe and Wright. If class remains primarily a matter of cultural classification, the value of such 'objectivist' class schemata will appear strictly limited. Hence, his amused contempt for a study designed to 'count . . . how many *petits bourgeois* there are in France . . . to the nearest digit, without even rounding the figures up!' (Bourdieu, 1990a, p. 50). This is not to suggest that he is insensitive to the claims of quantitative analysis. Quite the contrary, Bourdieu's most widely cited study, *Distinction: A Social Critique of the Judgement of Taste*, is an immensely ambitious exercise in theoretically informed empirical social research, using detailed sociological surveys of the cultural preferences of over 1,200 people from three different urban areas (Bourdieu, 1984, p. 503). Moreover, its analytical logics are quite fundamentally empirical in character, designed 'not to propound a theory of social classes', as he would later explain, 'but rather . . . to uncover principles of differentiation capable of accounting . . . for the largest possible number of observed differences' (Bourdieu, 1990b, p. 117). For Bourdieu, the major social classes are distinguishable according to their 'overall volume of capital' that is, their 'set of actually usable resources and powers – economic capital, cultural capital and . . . social capital'. Within each of these classes, different class fractions can be identified according to the 'different distributions of their total capital among the different kinds of capital' (Bourdieu, 1984, p. 114). The classes thus constructed are 'classes on paper' or 'theoretical classes', he reminds us, rather than 'groups which would exist as such in reality'.[7] In practice, however, they turn out to be aggregates of occupations: in the extended version, 24 'class fractions' combined into four classes; in the more condensed, 16 fractions combined into three classes (Bourdieu, 1984, pp. 504, 16–17).

Analysing his sample data by way of the latter version, Bourdieu identified three main 'zones of taste': 'legitimate' taste, which is most widespread in the educated sections of the dominant class, where the predominant musical preferences included *Well-Tempered Clavier*, *Art of Fugue* and *Concerto for the Left Hand*; 'middle-brow' taste, which is more widespread amongst the middle classes (*les classes moyennes*), where musical preferences included *Rhapsody in Blue* and *Hungarian*

Rhapsody; and 'popular' taste, most widespread in the working classes (*les classes populaires*), where preferences included the *Blue Danube, La Traviata* and Petula Clark (Bourdieu, 1984, pp. 16–17). Bourdieu describes legitimate taste primarily in terms of its 'aesthetic disposition' to assert the 'absolute primacy of form over function' (Bourdieu, 1984, pp. 28, 30). Artistic and social 'distinction' are thus inextricably interrelated, he concludes: 'The pure gaze implies a break with the ordinary attitude towards the world which, as such, is a social break' (Bourdieu, 1984, p. 31). The 'popular aesthetic', by contrast, is based on an affirmation of continuity between 'art and life' and on a 'deep-rooted demand for participation' (Bourdieu, 1984, p. 32). The characteristic detachment of this 'pure gaze', Bourdieu argues, is part of a more general disposition towards the 'gratuitous' and the 'disinterested', in which the 'affirmation of power over a dominated necessity' implies a claim to 'legitimate superiority over those who . . . remain dominated by ordinary interests and urgencies' (Bourdieu, 1984, pp. 55–56). In Bourdieu's account, especially as represented diagrammatically, the statistical correlation between zone of taste and class affiliation appears very strong (Bourdieu, 1984, p. 17). But, as John Frow has convincingly demonstrated, the strength of the correlation is dependent on a 'sleight of hand', by which educational hierarchy is tacitly substituted for economic (Frow, 1995, pp. 40–42). For Frow, this substitution of cultural for economic 'capital' forms part of a more general and 'systematically misleading conflation of the intelligentsia and its culture with the bourgeoisie and its culture' (Frow, 1995, p. 40).

Exactly how misleading the conflation is remains to be seen, but there is no doubting its existence. The issue at stake here is essentially straightforward: that of whether or not the intelligentsia should be distinguished from the bourgeoisie as a separate 'social class'. Bourdieu's general sociology posits that 'all practices, including those purporting to be disinterested or gratuitous' can be treated as 'economic practices directed towards the maximizing of material or symbolic profit' (Bourdieu, 1977a, p. 183). Hence his inclination to treat the intelligentsia as self-interested traders in cultural capital. For Bourdieu, but not for Frow, it follows from this that professional intellectuals are best considered as a subordinate fraction of the same social class as the bourgeoisie itself. Defining the dominant class as that possessed of a high overall volume of capital, whatever its source – whether economic, 'social' or cultural – Bourdieu locates the intellectuals in the dominant class by virtue of their access to the latter. A comparison of the degree of 'closure', or social immobility, displayed by each of the different fractions in the dominant class then leads him to identify three higher-ranking fractions – industrial employers, commercial employers and the professions – and three lower-ranking – engineers, public-sector executives and teachers in higher and secondary education (Bourdieu, 1984, p. 120). The dominant class thus includes a dominant fraction, the bourgeoisie proper, which disproportionately controls 'economic capital', and a dominated fraction, the intelligentsia, which disproportionately controls 'cultural capital'. These will have a common interest in maintaining their privileges *vis-à-vis* the dominated classes. Moreover, insofar as the symbolic system is necessary to the social order, the bourgeoisie cannot simply dispense with cultural capital. The two fractions will be drawn into conflict, nonetheless, over the relative value of, and the rates of exchange between, economic and cultural capitals (Bourdieu, 1984, pp. 315–316). For Bourdieu, the dominant class is thus the 'site par excellence of symbolic struggles' (Bourdieu, 1984, p. 254). *Prima facie*, his argument possesses much greater plausibility than Frow will allow. As yet, however, it would be premature to accord Bourdieu the theoretical last word: we shall return to this matter of the class position of the intellectuals in Chapter 5.

For the moment, suffice it to note how insistently Bourdieu detects the presence of class distinction even in the most apparently disinterested of cultural practices. In the struggle between bourgeoisie and intelligentsia, he observes, the dominated fraction will typically invoke against the dominant precisely those values of disinterestedness, in opposition to necessity, that the dominant class as a whole deploys against the dominated classes. This explains the bourgeoisie's capacity to utilize even the most self-consciously oppositional art as a means to demonstrate its own cultural distinction (Bourdieu, 1984, p. 254). More fundamentally, however, it also attests to the underlying structural affinity between bourgeois and intellectual class positions. Whether economic or cultural in character, all capital bestows upon its possessors 'the capacity to satisfy the demands of biological nature or the authority . . . to ignore them' (Bourdieu, 1984, p. 255). This is why the bourgeoisie cannot dispense with its intelligentsia:

> the dominant fractions . . . need to draw on what they are offered by the dominated fractions, in order to justify their class domination, to themselves as well. The cult of art and the artist . . . is one of the necessary components of the bourgeois 'art of living'. (Bourdieu, 1993b, p. 44)

Even when analysing the more 'purely artistic' forms of literary activity, the 'anti-economic economy' of the field of 'restricted' as opposed to 'large-scale' cultural production, Bourdieu notes how '*symbolic, long-term profits* . . . are ultimately reconvertible into economic profits' (Bourdieu, 1993b, p. 54) and how avant-garde cultural practice remains dependent on the 'possession of substantial economic and social capital' (Bourdieu, 1993b, p. 67). In the case of the academic intelligentsia the structural connections to the dominant fraction are even stronger. The academic profession is itself a competitive struggle for legitimacy and cultural distinction, he argues, which functions to reproduce the wider structures of social class inequality: whether applied to the world, to students, or to academics themselves, academic taxonomies are 'a machine for transforming social classifications into academic classifications' (Bourdieu, 1988, p. 207). More recently, he has set out to explain the central significance to the French bourgeoisie of its elite graduate schools, the so-called *grandes écoles*, stressing how their credentialism operates as a kind of 'state magic' for a supposedly rationalized society (Bourdieu, 1996, p. 376). Tracing the growing incidence of academic credentials amongst the chief executives of the top 100 French companies during the period 1952–72, he concludes that this apparent substitution of academic for property titles actually performs a crucial legitimizing function: company heads 'no longer appear . . . the heirs to a fortune they did not create,' he writes, 'but rather the most exemplary of self-made men, appointed by their . . . "merits" to wield power . . . in the name of 'competence' and "intelligence" ' (Bourdieu, 1996, p. 334).

In Chapter 3 we traced the growing divergence between an increasingly postmodern and 'anti-classist' social theory and the empirical findings of sociological class analysis. In this chapter, we have found roughly analogous processes at work in Cultural Studies: on the one hand, textualist and/or theoreticist work, which tends to read late-capitalist culture as essentially postmodern and lacking in class consciousness; on the other, more experiential and/or conventionally 'sociological' work, which continues to locate class at the centre of the cultural stage. There are important differences between sociology and Cultural Studies nonetheless. Insofar as the term 'textualist' has any relevance to sociology, it can only be as an aspect of social theorizing. But for Cultural Studies textual analysis is a mode of empirical inquiry in its own right. So when Jameson deduces an absence of class consciousness from his analyses of postmodern cultural texts, he registers an important empirical finding, rather than a merely theoretical construct of the kind deployed by Giddens or Holton and Turner. Much the same might be said for the 'experiential'. Insofar as personal experience enters into sociology, it does so at worst as distorting bias, at best as a kind of inspirational 'value-relevance' (Weber, 1949, pp. 21–22). For Cultural Studies, by contrast, remembered experience is again a source of empirical evidence in its own right. So when Hoggart recalls the class character of working-class Hunslet, he too registers a set of important empirical findings. However, Hegel's judgement on public opinion, as Adorno's on opinion polls, can and should be generalized to embrace both experience and textuality: 'it deserves equally to be respected and despised . . . Respected because even ideologies . . . are an element of social reality . . . But despised: that is, their claim to truth criticized' (Adorno, 1976, p. 256).

In Chapter 3 we noted how many of the more enthusiastically theoreticist critics of class analysis were either erstwhile New Left Marxists or at least strongly influenced by such Marxism. This has been as true of Cultural Studies as of social theory: compare Hall, Baudrillard and Lyotard with Bauman and Giddens, Heller and Fehér, Hindess and Holton. Arguing against such celebrations of the 'decline of class' amongst sociologists and social theorists, Goldthorpe has defined his own research enterprise thus:

> It is not research undertaken in the interests of Marxism, nor yet of anti-Marxism . . . What those who engage in such research have chiefly in common is a commitment not to some political world-view but rather to a particular conception of social science . . . Central to this is the insistence that . . . the attempt . . . be made to conduct it according to the best available methodological standards – *and* that such standards *can* be specified . . . the debate on class and politics is perhaps as much about whether or not such a conception of social science is to prevail as it is about socio-political realities. (Goldthorpe, 1996, p. 207)

Goldthorpe is almost certainly right to place the stress here, on social science rather than on socio-political reality. But his enthusiasm for quantitative research techniques must be handled with some care by a discipline as necessarily qualitative in character as Cultural Studies. Textual analysis, of the kind that rightly concerns much Cultural Studies, simply cannot be conducted according to this model. Nor can ethnography, which has nonetheless proven immensely fertile for research both in Cultural Studies and in anthropology. More modestly, we might wish to stipulate merely that those generalizing propositions, which arise from and inform such qualitative research, should be subject to some test of minimal compatibility with the relevant quantitative data. The real achievement of Bourdieu, as of Williams, consists precisely in the attempt to bring into active interrelationship the qualitative and the quantitative, the theoretical and the empirical, the textual, contextual and experiential. And if my own formulation appears pedantic, then consider the alternative: that Cultural Studies should take as its basic datum the television screen, social theory the shared assumptions and prejudices of senior common room gossip. For it is difficult to see what else other than television-viewing underpins Baudrillard's postmodern fantasia;[8] what other than shared middle-class prejudice Giddens's almost entirely unexplained, let alone theorized, shift from quasi-Marxist class analysis to quasi-postmodern identity theory.

Notes

1 Cf. on Australia, Frow and Morris, 1993; on Canada, Blundell, Shepherd and Taylor, 1993; on France, Forbes and Kelly, 1995; on India, Guha and Spivak, 1988, and Lal, 1996; on the United States, Grossberg, Nelson and Treichler, 1992; on Korea and Taiwan, Stratton and Ang, 1996, pp. 386–388.

2 Hoggart describes a move from 'class' by 'birth and education' (that is, Weber's *Stand*) to 'status based on ability or effectiveness' (Weber's *Klasse*) (Hoggart, 1995, p. 202).

3 Lyotard's 'report' was prepared for the Conseil des Universités of the government of Quebec. As he explained in the 'Introduction': 'the word *postmodern* . . . is in current use on the American continent among sociologists and critics' (Lyotard, 1984, p. xxiii).

4 The personal costs consequent on such a marginal position *vis-à-vis* postwar French political life should not be underestimated. But Lyotard's self-description as one of 'only sixty' in 'the whole world' who 'succeeded in making a fairly radical critique of communist bureaucracy' (Lyotard, 1989b, pp. 129–130) suggests a certain lack of sympathy with the wider non-Communist Left.

5 This is to misappropriate the title of the English translation of Debray's *Le Pouvoir intellectuel en France* (Debray, 1979). Debray actually defined and periodized three distinct 'cycles' in the history of the modern French intelligentsia, each dominated by a characteristic institutional apparatus, respectively the university from 1880 to 1930, publishing from 1920 to 1960, and the media since 1968. On this account, both Baudrillard and Bourdieu inhabit the media cycle. But Debray's evident admiration for the latter suggests a location considerably more distant from the media apparatus (Debray, 1981, pp. 20, 34, 79n).

6 The obvious exception to this observation is the specialist subdiscipline constituted by the 'sociology of education'.

7 They might well become 'real groups', Bourdieu concedes, but only through the political activity of '*group-making*' (Bourdieu 1990b, pp. 117–118). Here as elsewhere, he cites approvingly Thompson's *The Making of the English Working Class* (Bourdieu, 1990b, p. 118; cf. Bourdieu, 1987, p. 8).

8 I admit to being occasionally underwhelmed by the Marxism of Alex Callinicos, but his description of Baudrillard's work as 'largely worthless' strikes me as absolutely right (Callinicos, 1991, p. 99).

5

Class, Postmodernism and the Intelligentsia

We began with a conundrum: how is it that Cultural Studies, originally a discourse about class, the masses and culture, has been transformed into a very different, postmodern, discourse about gender, race, ethnicity, sexuality, in short, about almost all differences *other than* those of class? The most straightforward explanation, we conceded from the outset, would be that social class had as a matter of fact ceased to be of central empirical significance to our culture. I admit to a personal disinclination to subscribe to this view, no doubt in part because I tend to narrate my own biography as a story of upward social class mobility. I hope, nonetheless, that this bias hasn't unduly prejudiced our proceedings. We identified three relatively distinct intellectual formations around which debate on class had tended to centre, respectively Marxism, sociology and Cultural Studies, and we set out to explore the concept's theoretical meaning and significance for each of these. What, then, are our findings to date?

They can be summarized much as follows. By contemporary standards, our conclusions on Marxism were largely uncontentious. At least since Lenin, we concluded, and probably since Kautsky, Marxist theorists have been preoccupied, not so much with articulating and representing empirical working-class consciousness, as with explaining its failure to live up to the political expectations of socialist intellectuals. As a result, proletarian Marxism found itself obliged to contend with elitist Marxism, both within parties and movements and in the minds of individual militants. A theorized contempt for working-class consciousness, first announced in *What Is To Be Done?* and often imagined to be specific to Bolshevism, seems rather to have become a more or less permanent feature of the Marxist legacy, if not of Marx's own. We have traced its presence across a whole range of Marxisms, Communist and Western, humanist and structuralist, finally noting the irony by which Lenin's bequest was passed from Althusserianism to postmodernism by way of Laclau and Mouffe (this is perhaps the contentious sting in the tail). Our findings on sociology appear more interesting. In the first place, we discovered a widespread consensus amongst empirical sociologists to the effect that the class character of culture is as undeniable as ever. Whether measured according to Goldthorpe's neo-Weberian 11-class schema or Wright's neo-Marxian 12-class model, the available sociological evidence clearly shows class position to be a primary determinant of cultural behaviour, attitudes and lifestyle. However, we also noted the absence of any similar consensus amongst social theorists: to the contrary, the more theoreticist the sociology, the less likely it is to accord significance to social class. Many of these social theorists were themselves former Marxists, we noted, which in turn suggested the possibility that social theory has tended to repeat something of the history of Western Marxism, albeit as farce rather than tragedy.

Our conclusions on Cultural Studies ran along roughly similar lines. First-generation Cultural Studies had derived its sense of class from the lived experience of a class society, we observed: hence its characteristic focus on ethnography, whether explicit, as in Hoggart, or implied, as in Williams. But thereafter Cultural Studies learnt to think class through 'theory', initially French Marxism, but later the kinds of post-Marxism to be found in Baudrillard, Lyotard and Hall. Moreover, insofar as Cultural

Studies had also become an overwhelmingly 'textualist' discourse it tended increasingly to deduce social realities from cultural texts. In the whole of contemporary Cultural Studies it would be difficult to find a more subtle and astute textual analyst, nor one more aware of the social realities beyond textuality, than Jameson. And yet even he deduces the absence of class consciousness in contemporary America, not from any sustained account of an appropriate empirical referent – strike rates, for example, or trade union membership statistics[1] – but from movies, books and buildings. The illegitimacy of this procedure, as also its enormous appeal to those trained in text-based disciplines like literary studies and philosophy, are both equally evident from this failure in Jameson. That Bourdieu, the one significant contemporary cultural theorist to insist on the continuing centrality of social class, should also be almost alone in his commitment to extra-textual empirical studies, of a more or less conventionally sociological variety, seems unlikely to be mere coincidence.

We have described both the various theoretical moves by which Cultural Studies learnt to forget class and something at least of the sociological argument that tends to belies them. There is a history outside theory, however, a history that 'hurts', in Jameson's phrase (Jameson, 1981, p. 102), a history that might hurt even theory itself. So the vulgarly 'worldly'[2] question arises as to whether this collective denial of class might not itself be an effect of what Marxists used to call 'class forces'. In Chapter 1, we noted the close connection between postmodernist cultural theory and new social movement identity politics and we speculated as to the possible effect on the theory of the 'middle-class' character of the movements. Later, in Chapter 4, we noted Jameson's view that postmodernist cultures possess a specifically 'yuppie' class content. A worldly account of the strange death of class could doubtless proceed along many different lines: it might well inquire, for example, into the effects of globalization and consumerism, in both academic and everyday practice, on our collective perceptions of such an apparently 'national' and 'productivist' phenomenon as class. But one obvious line of inquiry, suggested by the tradition of class analysis itself, is the possibility that the theoretical retreat from class might in some way express the class interests of its advocates amongst the professional intelligentsia. We are not quite finished with the concept of class, then, nor yet with empirical sociology, since this immediately poses the question as to whether or not the intellectual professions do in fact possess any such common class character.

The Intelligentsia as a Social Class

There can be little doubt that the growth and development of a substantial stratum of white-collar, 'middle-class' employees has constituted one of the central dynamics in the occupational structure of advanced capitalist societies during the twentieth century. In the first half of the century, this growth was concentrated mainly amongst clerical workers employed in administration, in the second amongst professionally credentialled non-administrative employees. Both groups are readily distinguishable from the 'petite bourgeoisie', in the classically Marxist sense of a class of small self-employed capitalists, by virtue of the fact that they are employees, paid salaries or wages. Until about the middle of the century, it would have been reasonable to risk the generalization that almost all salary-earners, whether managers, administrators or routine clerical workers, tended to occupy positions of clear superordinacy in relation to manual labour. The novel element in the post-Second World War period was the growth of a new kind of non-administrative, credentialled, white-collar labour, a 'new middle class', as Giddens and others described it (Giddens, 1981, pp. 177–197), sharing no such relation to manual labour. This stratum of employed professionals tends to work in quite different institutional locations, and in quite different sets of authority relations, from those occupied by manual workers. It should be apparent that cultural producers, the stratum of intellectuals which produces the texts and artefacts that provide Cultural Studies with much of its subject matter, are disproportionately located in exactly this class position. In Williams's terms, the dominant relations of cultural production have moved progressively from 'market professional' to 'corporate professional' forms, so that cultural producers are now more likely to work as salaried employees of one of the 'culture industries', whether in television or radio, publishing or the press, advertising or higher education (Williams, 1981, pp. 47–54). If there is an 'intelligentsia' in contemporary society, in the sense of a social class or at least a definable collectivity of 'intellectuals', then it is disproportionately a class of this kind.

In contemporary common usage, the word 'intelligentsia' denotes a collectivity of 'intellectuals', where both terms clearly function as nouns. But, as Williams points out, from the four-teenth until the nineteenth century, 'intellectual' was more commonly used as an adjective, roughly synonymous with 'intelligent'. Only in the early nineteenth century did the word acquire the meaning of a particular kind of person, someone who 'thinks', then that of a particular kind of occupational role, someone who works with 'ideas' (Williams, 1976, p. 140). These new usages captured an important part of a developing social reality: the emergence of a new layer of increasingly special-ized and professionalized cultural workers. For class analysis, whether Marxist or Weberian, the obvious question arose as to whether or not these 'cultural' professions, taken together in aggregate, constituted a distinct social class. Historically, Marx-ists had argued against this view, on the grounds that intellec-tuals share no common relation to the means of production. Hence, their representation as members of or spokespeople for other social classes, rather than as part of a separate intellectual class. Even Gramsci had tended to think of intellectuals in this fashion: that after all is precisely what makes an organic intel-lectual organic. More recently, however, sociologists have tended toward a view of experts and intellectuals, if not as a separate social class, then at least as occupying a relatively distinct location within some larger class. For Bourdieu, they are the dominated fraction of the dominant class; for most neo-Marxists they are either a 'new working class' or a 'new petite bourgeoisie'; for neo-Weberian sociology either a 'service class' or a 'new middle class'. Taking Bourdieu as the central instance

of a new kind of culturalist class theory, and Wright and Goldthorpe as respectively by far the most influential neo-Marxian
and neo-Weberian class analysts working in sociology, I propose
to consider each of their accounts of the structure and composi-
tion of this putative new class or fraction.

As we have seen, Bourdieu regards the bourgeoisie and the
intelligentsia as different fractions of the same class. However,
he is careful to acknowledge the comparatively recent development of a new kind of intelligentsia, a new dominated fraction, if
one will: '*Bourgeois employees* . . . a group whose development
goes hand in hand with the spread of corporate bureaucratization' (Bourdieu, 1996, p. 336). Moreover, he specifically argues
that this new salaried intelligentsia has been much more effectively integrated into, but also subordinated to, the bourgeoisie
than were previous intellectual formations. The dominant class
can thus be characterized by a form of 'organic solidarity', he
concludes, where the networks of institutions and agents that
compose, respectively, the academic, bureaucratic, economic
and political fields, together 'protect the interests of the domi-
nants while officially rejecting . . . forms of hereditary transfer'
(Bourdieu, 1996, p. 386). This is a single dominant class, then,
united in solidarity by the very fact of its internal divisions. The
notion of organic solidarity derives from Durkheim and denotes
a complex form of mutual interdependence that 'presumes . . .
difference' (Durkheim, 1964, p. 131). But even if internal differences do indeed make for social solidarity, as Durkheim had
argued, they remain differences nonetheless. And when Bourdieu
turns to their substance, his dominated fraction becomes reminiscent of one of Wright's contradictory class locations. 'This is
what distinguishes . . . engineers, researchers, teachers, etc. . . .
from members of the professions,' he writes:

> bourgeois employees, and more generally, those known as *cadres*,
> are doomed by the ambiguity of their position to a profound ambiguity
> in their stances. The advantage they enjoy as holders of cultural
> capital . . . moves them closer to the dominant pole of the field of
> power, . . . while the subordinate position of this kind of capital
> distances them from those who . . . have control over the use of their
> capital. (Bourdieu, 1996, p. 336)

The patterns of interdependence between bourgeoisie and intelligentsia betray a similarly contradictory character: on the one
hand, the bourgeoisie has become more reliant on academic
credentialism as a source of legitimation; on the other, and as its
necessary corollary, as its obverse in fact, the bourgeoisie
makes increasingly successful attempts to extend its control
over the field of cultural production. For Bourdieu, then, the
intelligentsia has become at once both more essential and more
directly subordinated. Both qualities find expression in the shift
from independent self-employment to dependent employment.
So Bourdieu reads the changing structure of intellectual estab-
lishments and the growing complexity of technology as together
propelling the contemporary equivalents of erstwhile independent cultural producers into a salaried dependency that progressively deprives intellectual work of its 'charismatic aura'
(Bourdieu, 1996, pp. 336, 337).

As we noted in Chapter 4, Frow has been very critical of
Bourdieu's conflation of the bourgeoisie and the intelligentsia.
For Frow, professional intellectuals are a separate 'new middle
class', a 'knowledge class' dealing in education-generated information, albeit only *weakly formed as a class*', because formed
around claims to knowledge rather than property (Frow, 1995,
pp. 121, 125). Frow dissents from Bourdieu's account at a
peculiarly significant juncture in the latter's more general theory
of culture, given the intelligentsia's central role within the
processes of cultural production and reproduction. In Frow's
own account, both the intellectuals themselves and their characteristically intellectual virtues enjoy a much greater autonomy
from the bourgeoisie (and from other classes) than Bourdieu
will allow. Indeed, Frow's analytical focus falls on 'the knowledge class's own interests' and on the need to represent their
'cultural politics . . . openly and without embarrassment . . . as
their politics, not someone else's' (Frow, 1995, pp. 165, 169). As
Frow notes, even Bourdieu is by no means entirely immune to
such arguments (Frow, 1995, pp. 166–167; cf. Bourdieu, 1989).
To some extent, the disagreement is merely one of terminology:
where Frow sees a different class, Bourdieu detects a different
fraction of the same class, but both acknowledge the fact of

difference. The disagreement becomes one of substance, however, over the question of whether the bourgeoisie and the intelligentsia share any necessarily common interests. For Bourdieu, the two fractions are bound together by their common and mutually antagonistic rights to capital of one kind or another, and by their common and mutually supportive claims to distinction. Frow takes issue on both counts: economic and cultural capital are neither truly equivalent, he insists, nor reciprocally convertible; intellectual culture is not only a matter of distinction, he argues, but can be both genuinely critical and economically productive as knowledge (Frow, 1995, pp. 40, 38, 91–96). Bourdieu therefore conflates what are in fact quite different positions in the relation of production, Frow concludes, so that an abstract concept of 'privilege' comes to substitute 'for any more rigorous conception of class' (Frow, 1995, p. 43).

It is difficult to dissent from the gist of Frow's critique. Clearly, Bourdieu's account of the class structure of late-capitalist society is far too internally undifferentiated to accommodate adequately the data yielded by his own research. Indeed, his two-class (dominated and dominant) and three-class (popular, middle and dominant) models are analytically less complex even than those used by Marx and Weber. The attempt to produce a culturalist theory of class remains in itself entirely commendable; the social functions of culture are indeed in part as Bourdieu reads them; but the models he deploys are inadequate to the task he asks them to perform. For a more sophisticated account of the class structure itself, we need to turn to the kind of sociological class analysis developed by Wright and Goldthorpe, both of whom work with models of class that are both relatively extensive and inclusive. We can now add that both attempt to theorize the specific class location of the credentialled intelligentsia, albeit in very different ways that accord the question a very different theoretical salience. The empirical problem of the new middle class of semi-autonomous employees, the 'embarrassment' of the middle class (Wright, 1989b, p. 3) as he once termed it, has been central to Wright's work. For Goldthorpe, by contrast, the intelligentsia seems much less significant, merely one class amongst many necesary to fill in the gaps in the overall class map. But the treatment accorded them remains interesting, nonetheless, deriving as it does from the notion of the *Dienstklasse*, or 'service class', developed by the Austrian Marxist (and sometime President of the Republic), Karl Renner, and subsequently redeployed by Ralf Dahrendorf (Renner, 1953; Renner, 1978; Dahrendorf, 1964).

Wright's theory of 'contradictory class locations' was originally formulated precisely to explain the supposedly anomalous status of 'intermediate strata' other than the classic petty bourgeoisie. In its initial version, the three major contradictory locations were inhabited by small employers, managers and supervisors, and 'semi-autonomous employees' (Wright, 1979, p. 63). These latter are located between the petty bourgeoisie and the proletariat, he argued, because like the proletariat and unlike the petty bourgeoisie, they exercise no real control over the physical means of production or investment and resource allocation; but like the petty bourgeoisie and unlike the proletariat, they exercise control over their own immediate labour-process and not over the labour-power of others (Wright, 1979, pp. 80–82, 84). For Wright, the secret of their contradictory class location resided in these relatively autonomous work practices. This is a strange notion for a self-proclaimed Marxist, if only because workplace autonomy has been a recurrent feature of skilled working-class occupations and very often a close corollary of successful socialist and trade union organization.[3] Later versions of the theory, reformulated in terms of exploitation rather than domination, retained the same empirical focus, but represented the occupants of middle-class contradictory class locations as '*simultaneously* exploiters and exploited' (Wright, 1985, p. 285). Determined to avoid any 'economistic' reading of the salaried intelligentsia as part of the working class, Wright defined the new middle class as beneficiaries of either 'skill exploitation' or 'organization exploitation' (Wright, 1985, pp. 56–57, 64–98). Again, the solution seems strangely inappropriate for a Marxist, the entire procedure resting on the notion of 'rent' (Wright, 1985, p. 70), as 'bourgeois' an ideological construct as ever there was, expressly designed to delegitimize landowning as against capitalist profit-taking, and of little apparent use for much else.

Whatever the merits of Wright's more general theory, his specific handling of the problem of the new middle class seems open to serious question. Indeed, he has himself expressed strong reservations as to the full extent to which experts constitute a separate class in relation to non-experts (Wright, 1985, p. 95). More recently, he has also argued that the analysis needs to be supplemented by an account of how class locations are mediated through extra-occupational social relations, such as those of family, and also embedded temporally in different career trajectories (Wright, 1989c, pp. 325–331). These revisions produce only a marginal amendment to the earlier treatment of managers and supervisors, but a fairly substantial modification to that of professionals and experts. In short, Wright now suggests that the middle-class character of the latter arises, not from any property of the expert job itself, but from the way professional careers develop over time. This has three distinct aspects: a growing capacity to convert increasingly high incomes through savings into capitalist property; a career trajectory that tends towards management; and the increasing availability of opportunities for petty bourgeois self-employment (Wright, 1989c, pp. 332–334). These arguments have been repeated and rehearsed elsewhere (Wright, 1994, pp. 251–252). Yet, for all the apparent rigour, Wright's own doubts as to their adequacy are betrayed by his appeal to the 'standard intuition' that professional employment is non-proletarian. Such intuition is based on the 'lived experience' of inequality, he explains, in which working-class people are 'bossed around' and subjected to 'basic powerlessness' (Wright, 1989c, p. 337). By comparison, professionals and experts are 'less alienated . . . and in this sense . . . "middle class" ' (Wright, 1989c, p. 337). Once again, the appeal to experience seems strangely at odds with the general tenor of Wright's own approach and, in any case, it tends to exaggerate the subjective experience of 'alienation', at least as it is lived in sections of the skilled manual working class.

The latest version of Wright's Comparative Class Analysis Project is organized around the exploitation-centred concept of class, modified to account for temporal and mediated class locations. Marxist though the approach still remains, he now admits the theoretical possibility that 'an eclectic hybrid between Marxist and Weberian class analysis' could see 'exploitation as defining the central cleavages within a class structure and differential market capacities as defining salient *strata within classes*'. One important practical effect of any such synthesis, he speculates, would be to represent the middle class as 'privileged strata within the working class' (Wright, 1997, p. 36). Returning to this question in his concluding remarks, Wright concedes that the general conceptual framework 'does not achieve the level of comprehensive coherence, either theoretically or empirically, which I had hoped for' (Wright, 1997, p. 528). Quite specifically, he identifies two especially anomalous findings in his data: the fact that authority boundaries appeared persistently more permeable than skill boundaries, despite authority being more fundamental to the capital–labour relation; and the muting of ideological differences along lines of authority rather than skill in the specifically Japanese case. He notes that both could be accounted for by treating authority and skill, not as aspects of class, but as 'the bases for gradational strata within the class of employees' (Wright, 1997, p. 528). Although Wright declines to pursue this line of inquiry, it remains available to us as one possible way into the sociology of the intelligentsia. In my view, more plausible solutions to Wright's problem with the class of employed professionals (that is, with his – and my – own class position) seem likely to arise from a Marxian-Weberian synthesis of exactly this kind.

If Wright is the most highly regarded of contemporary neo-Marxist class theorists, then Goldthorpe occupies much the same position amongst neo-Weberians. His theorization of the 'service class' derives from Dahrendorf, who had suggested that, from the standpoint of authority and power relations, the middle class is best seen as comprising 'free-floating intellectuals', on the one hand, and a 'service class' of 'those who assist the ruling groups . . . a bridge between rulers and ruled', on the other (Dahrendorf, 1964, pp. 225, 248–249). This service class is employed primarily in bureaucratic hierarchies, he continued, and is thus a stratum preoccupied with its own individual prospects for competitive promotion, rather than with any sense of collective class identity (Dahrendorf, 1964, pp. 251–252). He added that the older free-floating intelligentsia had gradually been reorganized into a service class and that there is a sense in which the social system as a whole can be seen as evolving toward a 'service class society' (Dahrendorf, 1964, pp. 260–263). Whatever the merits of Dahrendorf's general understanding of class as an authority relation, this account of the middle classes seems far too undifferentiated. Moreover, the stress on bureaucratic hierarchy is clearly exaggerated, given that so many of the new professionals work in relatively unhierarchical structures. In retrospect, his expectations of the emergence of a 'post-capitalist' society dominated by 'bureaucratic conservatism' are also belied by the recommodification of social life, we might almost say 'recapitalization', that has occurred in the last two decades of the century. Stripped of its more grandiose applications, however, *Dienstklasse* might still serve as the description for a particular type of middle class, one amongst others. This is the sense of the concept developed by Goldthorpe.

Like Dahrendorf, Goldthorpe borrowed Renner's term to denote the entire 'class of professional, administrative and managerial employees', thus stipulating a 'basic commonality' of employed-professional and managerial work situations (Goldthorpe, 1982, pp. 162, 170). He argued that managers and experts both require considerable autonomy for the effective exercise of their work roles and that the resultant 'service relationship' is necessarily invested with 'an important measure of *trust*', in return for which these employees are rewarded with a range of privileged employment conditions, notably job security and promotion prospects (Goldthorpe, 1982, pp. 167–169). This is, in effect, a rejection of any analytical distinction between managers and experts, such as that proposed by Wright, even in the original six-class model. When Goldthorpe distinguishes different middle classes, the boundary runs between 'higher' professionals and managers on the one hand, and 'subaltern' professionals and managers on the other (Goldthorpe, 1980, pp. 39–40). He is insistent, moreover, that the service class provides a relatively clear

instance of demographic class formation: despite fairly heterogeneous social origins, it displays 'a high degree of . . . inter-
generational stability and work-life continuity' (Goldthorpe,
1987, p. 333). More hesitantly, he also points to the evidence of a
developing sense of socio-cultural class identity (Goldthorpe,
1982, pp. 178–179). This will not be the 'new radicalism' eagerly
anticipated by 1960s Marxism, he suggests, nor that feared by
conservative 'new class' theorists. To the contrary, even middle-
class 'trade unionism' seems likely to become 'an attempt to
prevent proletarianisation and . . . maintain class differentials'
(Goldthorpe, 1982, p. 181) As the service class develops into 'an
increasingly important basis of collective action', Goldthorpe
predicts, 'it will be seen to constitute a primarily conservative
force within modern society, so far at least as the prevailing
structure of class inequality is concerned' (Goldthorpe, 1987,
p. 341). The latter qualification seems especially pertinent: if
Goldthorpe is right, then there are good reasons to suppose that
middle-class radicalism is in principle likely to be directed at
almost anything and everything other than class inequality
itself.

The obvious neo-Weberian alternative to Goldthorpe's work is
the notion of a 'new middle class', as used by Giddens. Although
himself no longer much interested in class analysis, Giddens's
differences with Goldthorpe retain a certain contemporary relevance. For Giddens, following Mills, the new middle class
comprised 'workers whose tasks are not primarily "manual", but
who are not so clearly involved in any . . . identifiable hierarchy,
and who, while they may often be connected with the professions, are not of them' (Giddens, 1981, p. 187; cf. Mills, 1951).
The reference to the professions is instructive: like the older
professions (archetypically, medicine and the law) the market
capacity of the new middle class is almost entirely dependent on
claims to technical or intellectual expertise; but unlike the older
professions, the new middle classes are typically employees
rather than self-employed small businesspeople. Giddens argued
that the middle classes were best understood as internally
differentiated along two major axes: market capacity and the
division of labour. In relation to the former, the new middle

class, like self-employed professionals, possesses 'the capacity to offer marketable technical knowledge, recognised and specialised symbolic skills', as distinct from the merely 'general symbolic competence' characteristic of clerical workers (Giddens, 1981, p. 186). In relation to the latter, the new middle classes, like skilled manual workers, are outside the hierarchy of management (Giddens, 1981, p. 188). Indeed, they may even be subordinated to management, thereby occupying a position in some respects akin to that of traditional manual workers – although this is a possibility Giddens fails to explore. For Goldthorpe, Giddens's stress on the distinction between management and expertise is unimportant, registering merely *'situs* divisions . . . *within* the service class' (Goldthorpe, 1982, p. 170). No doubt, there is good reason to question Giddens's emphasis on scientific and technical knowledge, as distinct from cultural capital more generally, as the key to an account of the new middle class. But the differences between managers and experts in their respective relations to manual labour, which are central both to Giddens and to Wright, surely cannot be dismissed so lightly. More seriously, Goldthorpe himself fails to provide any real evidence of convergence between management and experts at that level of social interaction to which a self-proclaimed 'Weberian' might be expected to pay particularly close attention. As Scott points out, Goldthorpe makes no explicit use of mobility data in the construction of his social classes, preferring to rely on 'professional judgement' to identify their boundaries (Scott, 1994, p. 937). Now it may well be that there are good technical reasons for this strategy, just as Scott suggests, at least at the level of the overall class structure. In the specific instance of managers and experts, however, it appears peculiarly suspect, if only because of the lack of any external evidence for such interchange.

To recapitulate, we have surveyed three different accounts of the class position of the intelligentsia, as deployed respectively by Bourdieu, Wright and Goldthorpe. We have seen how Bourdieu's culturalist reading of the intellectuals, as the dominated fraction of a dominant class, assumes a commonality of

interests between bourgeoisie and intelligentsia which it singularly fails to demonstrate; and how this arises from a prior
insistence on an oversimplified model of class structure. We
have seen how Wright's theory of the new petite bourgeoisie of
salaried employees, as occupying a contradictory class location
between classic petite bourgeoisie and proletariat, successfully
isolates the distinction between management and expertise;
but then flounders through a whole series of unsatisfactory
revisions, occasioned by a presumed need to reconcile fidelity
to Marx, which would ordinarily suggest that non-managerial
employees are proletarians, with an intuitive sense that this
cannot and must not be so. Finally, we have seen how Goldthorpe's notion of the service class brackets together managers
and experts, in a way that belies the general theoretical
sophistication of his overall class schema and, like Bourdieu, in
effect assumes what actually has to be demonstrated, that is,
the commonality of class identity and interests between intelligentsia and management. Strangely enough, Wright insists on a
distinction between intellectuals and workers that would be
better sustained in a Weberian analytical framework than in a
Marxist, Goldthorpe on an identity between managers and
experts clearly belied by Weber's own understandings of 'social
class' as a kind of status group. Conversely, however, there is
much to be said for Bourdieu's notion that cultural capital
provides the basis for whatever social power intellectuals may
possess; much for Weber's stress on the importance of social
interaction between those with immediately cognate market
capacities; much too for Marx's sense of the crucial significance
of relations of economic production (which are also necessarily
authority relations, as Wright rightly recognized).

We noted in Chapter 3 how Weber's and Marx's accounts of
the class structure ran interestingly parallel, except in the
specific instance of the credentialled intelligentsia. The problem
should be apparent: how to reconcile these competing accounts,
especially as they apply to the apparently anomalous position of
the class of cultural producers? The solution must surely com-
mence from a recognition that Marx and Weber each identified
real processes at work in class formation, not all of which

operate on all social classes. It thus becomes possible to distinguish classes like the bourgeoisie and the proletariat, which
share both a common relation to the means of production and a
regular interchange of individuals between market positions;
and classes like the intelligentsia, which share no common
relation to the means of production, but nonetheless experience a regular interchange of individuals between a cluster of
cognate market situations. The intelligentsia is indeed a weakly
formed class, as Frow has it, but this is so primarily because it
shares no common relation to any means of production, not
even to knowledge itself as capital. Clearly, all intellectuals
possess a common interest in the general market value of
cultural capital, most obviously in their collective commitment
to the status of academic titles, degrees and diplomas.[4] But
these degrees and the knowledge and distinction they signify are
mobilized in different ways, for different purposes, by different
fractions of the intellectual class. Some intellectuals, for example
most doctors and lawyers, are self-employed petit bourgeois,
who will use their credentials to legitimize the services offered
for sale by their independent small businesses; others are wage-
or salary-earning proletarians, for example most teachers or
academics, who will use theirs in the collective bargaining
process, as a basis for claims to superior conditions of employment and higher wages; others, school principals or university
deans and senior professors for example, are managers, that is,
occupants of a contradictory class location between capital and
labour, who will use their credentials to justify claims to authority over intellectual labour, and hence to managerial salaries
(which typically include some element of profit in excess of
wages); some intellectuals are even able to transform their
cultural capital into economic capital to the extent that they
become capitalists, credentialled employers of credentialled
employees (in contemporary folklore Bill Gates is often rendered thus, although the reality appears more prosaic). Elsewhere, I have described the intelligentsia as a class for itself, but
not in itself (Milner, 1996, p. 185). The formulation is clumsy, no
doubt, but sensitizes us to the fact that intellectuals possess a
real sense of collective identity, founded on common material

interests, which are nonetheless not those of a shared relation to the means of production.

What exactly are these material interests? What enables this regular interchange of individuals between adjacent market situations? In short, what are the dynamics of class formation? As we have seen, these have been theorized by Bourdieu as a function of the rate of exchange between economic and cultural capitals within a single dominant class (Bourdieu, 1977a, pp. 183–197). Frow too stresses the central importance of definable class interests in the 'institutions of cultural capital' (Frow, 1995, p. 130). But whereas, for Bourdieu, cultural capital had been almost entirely a matter of distinction and of the 'symbolic domination exerted by or in the name of culture' (Bourdieu, 1984, p. 511), for Frow it becomes primarily a matter of knowledge 'as a central productive force' (Frow, 1995, p. 91). This seems to me slightly suspect, if only because the surplus-generating qualities of academic deconstruction are by no means apparent, even to the initiate; still less, the knowledge content of supposedly 'scientific' management. It is clear that certain knowledges are indeed economically productive, in much the fashion Frow suggests, but that others are not. Later, however, he concedes that what is really at issue is 'the *claim* to knowledge rather than its actual possession' (Frow, 1995, p. 117). This suggests a more interesting line of inquiry, which Frow registers but declines to pursue: that of the significance of credentialism. As we observed in Chapter 4, Bourdieu has argued that this 'state magic' is becoming increasingly important to the mechanisms by which the entire bourgeoisie, not only the intelligentsia, legitimizes itself. Indeed, he very nearly suggests that credentialism has superseded the more 'effortless' forms of distinction which once legitimized bourgeois dominance. Doubtless, there is some substance to this argument, especially as applied to the French bourgeoisie, perhaps also the American, but it seems much less applicable elsewhere. By contrast, the intellectual class, as distinct from the bourgeoisie proper, is almost invariably credentialled, so that credentialism *per se* can more plausibly be read as a specific attribute of modern (and postmodern) intelligentsias than of bourgeois distinction in general.

This is the line of argument pursued by Parkin, who has defined the class interests of the intelligentsia as the outcome of a shared monopoly over the means of certification (Parkin, 1979, pp. 47–48). Simultaneously the most interesting and infuriatingly obfuscatory of neo-Weberian attempts to explain the new middle class, Parkin's theory of credentialism as a form of social closure derives directly from Weber's account of the intelligentsia. But where Weber had identified different 'social classes', Parkin sees only a single 'dominant or exclusionary class' formed by the fusion of property and expertise (Parkin, 1979, p. 58). Even more so than in Bourdieu, this conflation of material and cultural capital is radically unhelpful: Parkin almost entirely fails to register the political and cultural significance of social conflict *between* capitalists and expert professionals. That said, his account of the exclusionary logics of credentialism is often very telling. Preoccupied with distribution rather than production, he glosses over the differences between self-employed and employed professionals, but is nonetheless very acute on the ways in which their exclusionary capacities derive from state-supported legal monopolies over the provision of services (Parkin, 1979, p. 57). Where Giddens had seen technical knowledge as providing the basis for enhanced middle-class market capacity, Parkin rightly insists that it is the credential rather than the skill, in semiological terms the sign rather than the referent, that secures effective social closure. Pointedly contrasting professional credentialism with the skills used in sport and entertainment, he observes that:

> Formal qualifications and certificates . . . appear to be a handy device for ensuring that those who possess 'cultural capital' are given the best opportunity to transmit the benefits of professional status to their own children. Credentials are . . . supplied on the basis of tests designed to measure . . . class-related qualities and attributes rather than . . . practical skills and aptitudes that may not so easily be passed on through the family line. (Parkin, 1979, p. 55)

In the specific case of the 'semi-professions', defined by Parkin as possessing formal qualifications but not a state-sanctioned monopoly, closure strategies typically seek to combine exclusionary credentialism with usurpationary trade unionism (Parkin, 1979, p. 102). 'It is characteristic of these intermediate groups', he writes, 'that they strive to maximize their advantages by adjusting the balance between *both* types of closure activity' (Parkin, 1979, p. 107). No doubt this is indeed the case. And, no doubt, Parkin is right to insist that both strategies are equally 'attempts to improve *material* conditions' (Parkin, 1979, p. 107). But this recognition of 'intermediate groups' located between bourgeoisie and proletariat sits uneasily beside his more general preference for a two-class model. More seriously, the resort to trade unionism is surely better explained as the effect of a semi-professional group's status as employees than of their lack of any strict monopoly over the provision of services. After all, modern states do insist that only fully qualified teachers be allowed to teach, that only fully qualified social workers be allowed to do whatever it is that social workers do. The point, however, is that teachers and social workers are also normally salaried employees, unlike either doctors or lawyers. In short, teachers can strike precisely because they have employers, that is, because they are in some non-trivial sense proletarians, whilst lawyers cannot do so because they typically have clients, that is, because they are, in an equally non-trivial sense, petit bourgeois.

I would guess that the social power of the intelligentsia is much more obviously grounded in credentialism than in either cultural distinction or economic productivity. But however we theorize cultural capital – whether as distinction, knowledge or accreditation – it is clear that the universities have been of fundamental importance to the establishment and maintenance of a relatively autonomous intelligentsia: its common class interests and internal bonds of affiliation derive from possession of and continuing access to academically legitimized 'culture'. This is true even of intellectual professions possessed of no formal educational prerequisites.[5] The emergence of a distinct intellectual class, we may then hypothesize, remains crucially dependent on the prior expansion of higher education. It follows that in Marx's own time the intelligentsia almost certainly did not constitute a separate social class, not even as defined by Weber. And it was only in the twentieth century that the central processes of class formation finally occurred, and then mainly in the advanced capitalist societies. As the class has formed and developed, it has progressively acquired common class interests, not only in the legitimacy of credentialism itself, but also in the struggle to delegitimize alternative claims to authority running directly contrary to its own. Typically these have proven to be, not those of property, as many conservatives had once feared, but rather those of (white) race, (dominant) ethnicity, (male) gender and (hetero) sexuality. Whilst inequality in the distribution of property appears compatible with credentialism, which itself denotes a kind of intellectual property, the logic of intellectual class interest appears to require that equivalent certificates be accorded equal treatment, whether they are obtained by black people or Jews, women or homosexuals. As Frow observes, the intelligentsia has 'real, though ambivalent, class interests in the implementation of modernity' (Frow, 1995, p. 165). In practice, moreover, those interests have commonly been associated with what Frow terms the intelligentsia's capacity to speak (uneasily) 'for' others (Frow, 1995, p. 164). It is this very specifically conditioned 'progressive potential of the knowledge class', as Frow describes it, which both informs and inhibits the kinds of radicalism normally available to the intelligentsia.

The New Social Movements and the Intelligentsia

Since the 1960s, this radicalism has typically found organizational form in what are now routinely described as the 'new social movements'. Unlike the labour movement, the 'old' social movement as it came to be represented, these have been quite explicitly organized around social categories other than those of class. Moreover, they have often imagined themselves to provide a radical alternative to proletarian materialism: whereas the old social movement had deliberately pursued the collective self-interests of the working class, the new movements more commonly claimed to pursue quasi-altruistic solutions to more generally 'human' problems. Taken on their own terms, then, they represent something close to the antithesis of a class-based movement. These self-perceptions have found a ready echo amongst radical social theorists. As we noted in Chapter 2, Marcuse himself produced one of the earliest attempts to theorize the turn away from class. Subsequently, however, these and similar notions have become much more generally available. Inglehart described the shift from the materialism of the old politics and the old social movements to the 'post-materialism' of the new as marking nothing less than a 'silent revolution' in values (Inglehart, 1977). Touraine concluded that the labour movement had declined from social movement into mere 'political force' (Touraine, 1981, p. 13). In post-industrial society, he argued, the central conflict is no longer that between capital and labour, but rather 'between the structures of economic and political decision-making and those who are reduced to dependent participation' (Touraine, 1971, p. 9). Offe has insisted that the mere fact of wage labour is now no longer 'a point of departure for cultural, organizational and political associations and collective identities' (Offe, 1985, p. 136). Much of this was directed at Marxism, of course, as much as at the labour movement, in an argument that would reach its apogee in Laclau and Mouffe's 'post-Marxism'. The new social movements, their activists and their theorists, have thus become progressively committed to more diversified and apparently personalized responses to politics, which resonate with the more generally postmodern propensity to represent power as ubiquitous, or 'capillary' in Foucault's phrase (Foucault, 1980, p. 39).

This self-proclaimed classlessness should not, however, be taken at face value. Empirical studies of the new social movements typically emphasize both the extent to which their activists possess intellectual capital and the importance to their growth of increased levels of 'cognitive mobilization', that is, the capacity to understand in abstract and theoretical ways, which is itself largely an effect of higher education (Inglehart, 1990, pp. 336–342, 375–388). Parkin's pioneering study of the British

Campaign for Nuclear Disarmament demonstrated it to be an overwhelmingly 'middle-class' movement (Parkin, 1968). According to Offe, the base of the new social movements comprises 'the new middle class, especially those who work in the human service professions and/or the public sector; elements of the old middle class; and . . . people outside the labor market or only peripherally involved, such as the unemployed, students, housewives, and the retired' (Offe, 1987, p. 72). This preponderance of the intellectually trained within their ranks is almost certainly what has enabled and perhaps even required the new social movements to construct their collective identities in increasingly overt opposition to class-based identity. For, as we observed in Chapter 1, they are typically organized and led, not by a random sample of all women, or all homosexuals, but precisely by a layer of intellectuals whose unrepresentative class position follows a very clear pattern. That unrepresentativeness is most easily legitimized, we may hypothesize, when its significance, which is the significance of class, is systematically denied. The class character of the movements is at its most readily apparent in their developing preference for individualist and consumerist as opposed to structural solutions. So the marketplace has increasingly provided for the needs of their vanguards: high salaries in academia or the civil and public services for the better-educated women; dramatically expanding opportunities for affluent gays to pursue subcultural leisure pursuits; and for ethnic cultural entrepreneurs to cater to the palates of White Anglo-Saxon Protestants.

For all their apparent successes, the new social movements have not challenged the fundamentally class-divided nature of late-capitalist society. It is difficult to avoid the suspicion that this has been so because, insofar as they derive their primary identities from an intelligentsia which is itself a socially privileged class, they remain reluctant to threaten class-based inequalities. Inasmuch as social change is sought, it is change that fine-tunes the existing, class-based order in ways conducive to the interests of the educated professionals who tend to dominate these movements. The new social movements thus articulate most effectively the interests of the least disadvantaged amongst those they purportedly represent, so that the values and priorities of the intelligentsia tend to determine their political agenda. It is in this respect, rather than in their supposedly 'prefigurative' qualities, that they are at their most distinctively postmodern. For, as we noted in Chapter 4, postmodern late capitalism can be understood as a 'purer' form of capital, effecting 'a prodigious expansion' into previously uncommodified areas (Jameson, 1991, p. 36). If we understand postmodernism thus, then the peculiar place occupied within it by the new social movements becomes clearer. They have drawn attention to and challenged social inequalities that had become unnecessary and even dysfunctional to the capitalist social order: super-exploitative but inefficient race-based relations of production; gender relations that systematically under-utilized female labour; taboos on homosexuality that severely restricted the prospects for its commodification; patterns of generational hierarchy that acted as a persistent depressant on the commercial viability of youth subcultures. In short, the marked decline in non-market forms of social hierarchy over the past 30 years has opened up the opportunities for exactly this 'prodigious expansion' of capital into hitherto uncommodified areas. The new social movements greatly facilitated the process: as Melucci has argued, they now play a vital role in modernizing the cultural outlook and procedures of dominant institutions and in selecting new elites (Melucci, 1989, pp. 11–12). Many of those for whom the personal was political have begun to dress for success.

In itself none of this need provide the occasion for much guilt amongst either intellectuals in general or new social movement activists in particular: we are better rid of patriarchy, racism and homophobia, even if on capital's terms. As Jameson rightly insists, the new social movements are neither simply the heroic agents of an entirely new history nor merely a functional response to the trend of social-systemic evolution, but, rather, simultaneously both: hence, 'the possibility of active political commitment along with disabused systemic realism and contemplation . . . not some sterile choice between those two things' (Jameson, 1991, p. 330). But the limits to identity politics should be apparent nonetheless. Jameson spells these out with some precision. In the first place, he observes, postmodern group identities need to be understood as the substitute, not so much for class as for individuality: they bespeak an unprecedented 'organization and collectivization of individuals after the long period of individualism' (Jameson, 1991, p. 321). Unlike social classes, which are typically 'more material, more impure and scandalously mixed', the postmodern group 'is above all anthropomorphic' and so offers 'the gratifications of psychic identity' (Jameson, 1991, pp. 346–347). Hence the apparent paradox that it develops contemporaneously with the 'death of the subject': in truth, Jameson notes, the one is merely an 'alternate version' of the other (Jameson, 1991, p. 348). Secondly, he stresses the way in which identity politics tends ultimately toward 'depolitization and withdrawal' (Jameson, 1991, p. 331). Historically, politics has worked through the allegorical co-ordination of the global and the local, in ways that allow the latter to become vested with wider significances. Once these levels drift apart, however, as in postmodern group politics, the result is a peculiar combination of the 'disembodied and easily bureaucratized abstract struggle for and around the state' with a 'properly interminable series of neighbourhood issues'. Neither singularly nor in combination do these amount to a politics, not even as traditional liberalism imagined it. So the much-criticized 'nostalgia for class politics', Jameson wryly observes, is better understood as a nostalgia 'for politics *tout court*' (Jameson, 1991, pp. 330–331). The irony should be apparent that, in the name of identity and politics, late-capitalist culture becomes simultaneously and progressively both de-individualized and depoliticized. Jameson himself clearly believes that these particular postmodern conditions cannot persist for very long: in a telling analogy, he adds that to speak thus of 'nostalgia' is 'about as adequate as to characterize the body's hunger, before dinner, as a "nostalgia for food"' (Jameson, 1991, p. 331). Whether the main menu will be quite so Marxist as Jameson supposes remains to be seen. What we do know, however, at least from Wright's empirical sociological research, is that, even at the height of this postmodern moment, class consciousness remained a more permanent and enduring feature of American society than even Jameson ever imagined. That too is surely an irony.

Disciplining Cultural Studies

We concluded Chapter 4 with the modest proposal that the kind of generalizing propositions, which arise from and inform the qualitative research done in Cultural Studies, should be subject to some test of minimal compatibility with relevant data generated by such immediately cognate disciplines as sociology (and history, for that matter). This is not intended to suggest that these latter disciplines occupy any peculiarly privileged position as guarantors of some kind of objective 'truth'. Quite the contrary: just as much as literary studies or Cultural Studies, history and sociology are socio-discursive constructs, institutional arrangements for the production of particular 'knowledges', defined according to the generic conventions of the discipline in question. My point, however, is that these institutions and conventions are in fact currently operative in the Western university system and in Western culture more generally; and that Cultural Studies will therefore find itself obliged sooner or later to negotiate some sort of accommodation between itself and these contiguous socio-discursive formations. It is difficult to see how such accommodation can be pursued except according to some notion of minimal mutual compatibility. This raises important questions about the status of Cultural Studies as an academic discipline, or proto-discipline, and about the extent to which disciplinization is either necessary or possible. The suggestion that Cultural Studies should become a formal academic discipline would have seemed absurd to its mythic 'founding fathers'. At its inception, Cultural Studies appears to have been imagined either as a political intervention into the academy and its existing disciplines or alternatively as the paradigmatic instance of interdisciplinary studies. Both conceptions still remain in play. For Hall, who cheerfully admits to having entered it 'from the New Left', the idea of an intellectual practice as a politics is what most clearly defines Cultural

Studies as a project (Hall, 1992, pp. 279, 284). The 'seriousness' of the project is inscribed in its 'political' aspect, he insists: 'there is something *at stake* in cultural studies, in a way that . . . is not exactly true of many other . . . intellectual . . . practices' (Hall, 1992, p. 278). For Hoggart, by contrast, Cultural Studies is essentially a 'field of study' as distinct from a discipline: 'the student should have an initial discipline outside Cultural Studies,' he writes, 'an academic and intellectual training, and a severe one' (Hoggart, 1995, p. 173).

Both conceptions, the political and the interdisciplinary, have been powerfully present in the subject's history. Like Hall, Williams and Thompson also entered Cultural Studies from the New Left; both feminist Cultural Studies and black Cultural Studies were primarily political interventions into a discourse already marked by the pre-existent politics of this British New Left; American Cultural Studies has been preoccupied with queer theory and the cultural politics of AIDS; Australian and Canadian Cultural Studies with problems of nationality, indigeneity and postcolonialism with obviously political implications. It was Hoggart nonetheless, personally neither in nor of the New Left, who established the Birmingham Centre, thereby inaugurating the subject's academic institutionalization. As conceived at Birmingham, Cultural Studies was much as Hoggart still wishes it to be: a postgraduate research field, recruiting from amongst those already trained in 'the social sciences, history, psychology, anthropology, literary study' (Hoggart, 1995, p. 173). More faithfully than the New Left, Hoggart had reworked Leavis's own earlier conception of a university English School that would require its students 'to come to fairly close terms . . . with other fields of special study, other trained approaches and other disciplines' (Leavis, 1948, p. 57). The characteristic weaknesses of both conceptions have become increasingly apparent over time, however. The New Leftist understanding of higher and secondary education, as available to whatever political project groups of intellectuals might choose to prosecute, is simply politically naive. As Tony Bennett rightly cautions: 'the institutions and spaces of public education are . . . contexts which necessarily confer their own logic and social direction on the work that is conducted within them' (Bennett, 1998, p. 49). As for interdisciplinarity, whatever the advantages to be had from continuing thus, in practice Cultural Studies has already long since ceased to be an exclusively postgraduate field. Its students are now much more likely to be undergraduates and thus tend not to have the initial training outside the field Hoggart believed necessary. In short, the choice has already become that between becoming a discipline of a different kind and remaining that 'bringing together of glittering, unordered and unassessed heaps' Hoggart most fears (Hoggart, 1995, p. 173). In Hoggart's own terms, the former is already the lesser evil.

The strongest arguments for disciplinization have tended to come from those interested in the idea of 'cultural policy studies', Bennett himself, for example, or Ian Hunter. Whatever we make of policy studies, there are at least four key points where I suspect their arguments might be right: that the changing norms and practices of secondary school English teaching were more important than the New Left as a primary 'conditioning context' of British Cultural Studies; that Cultural Studies will need to lay claim to some definite set of 'knowledge claims and methodological procedures', convertible into practically utilizable 'clearly defined skills and trainings'; that its subject matter is better defined as 'the relations of culture and power' than as popular culture *per se*; and that public education has developed as an amalgam of two earlier educational projects, the 'bureaucratic' and the 'pastoral', concerned respectively with 'social training' and 'individual salvation', or 'self-realizing personhood' as the latter eventually became secularized (Bennett, 1998, pp. 49, 52–53; Hunter, 1994, pp. 61, 92). Some of the inferences drawn therefrom nonetheless seem to me unwarranted, two in particular: that these skills and trainings need necessarily be policy-oriented; and that the bureaucratic ethos must take precedence over the pastoral. To the contrary, and as Hunter knows well, it is a matter of historical record that English Literature was able to function both without any such policy orientation and as a predominantly pastoral discipline, specializing in self-expressivity, within the more general pedagogic amalgam of the bureaucratic and the pastoral (Hunter, 1994, pp. 80–81, cf. Hunter, 1988, pp. 108–153). I see no good reason why this option shouldn't still remain available to Cultural Studies.

Neither Bennett nor Hunter is at all willing to embrace it: Bennett because he remains determined that Cultural Studies should not become 'the heir of literary studies in its English formation', a prospect he finds positively 'depressing' (Bennett, 1998, p. 52); Hunter because he deems the resultant 'refurbishment of literature departments' likely to result in a parallel renovation of the kind of 'fundamentally aesthetic critique' that Cultural Studies inherited from Romanticism, by way of Leavis and Williams (Hunter, 1993, p. 172; cf. Hunter, 1992). These are reasons, of course, but not necessarily good ones. As I have argued elsewhere, there are two alternative versions of Cultural Studies in play in debates such as these: a 'modest' version, where the discipline is defined in terms of a new subject matter, that is, as the study of popular culture; and an 'immodest' version, defined in terms of a new methodology, which connects the study of the popular to the study of the 'literary' (Milner, 1996, pp. 18–26). We should note that both are equally compatible with Bennett's sense of the discipline as being about the imbrication of knowledge and power. But in applying a self-denying ordinance toward 'Literature', the modest version tacitly agrees to cede back to English (or Comparative) Literature the traditional business of high-canonical literary studies. As a result, it has no alternative but to aspire to become something else, in practice, it seems, something very close to a kind of policy-oriented sociology. For Bennett and Hall, this provides a perfectly adequate theorization of their own personal career paths and biographical choices: both were trained in English Literature, both moved into Cultural Studies, both eventually became professors of sociology, successive occupants in fact of the same chair at the Open University (Bennett took over from Hall in 1998). But this isn't where Cultural Studies in general actually tends to proceed. Much more characteristically, it is evolving into exactly the successor to literary studies Bennett and Hunter feared it might: hence the panic attack it occasions in high-literary circles (cf. Bloom, 1994, p. 519).

This alternative trajectory seems to me fairly predictable, if only because the disciplinary competencies produced by Cultural Studies are of marginal relevance to 'policy workers', who are in any case only a very small proportion of the workforce. Such competencies are much more likely to be relevant to secondary school teaching, where the linkage of novel, film and television is becoming increasingly commonplace. No doubt, Bennett is right to insist, with Bourdieu, that being an intellectual is a job 'like any other', governed by 'mundane protocols' (Bennett, 1998, p. 31). But he misrecognizes the nature of the job in question. The primary business of Cultural Studies is more likely to be teaching and the training of teachers, in higher and secondary education, in a version of literary studies reformed so as to make it more directly relevant to the concerns and interests of the students of the early twenty-first century. No doubt, Hall is right to insist that the discipline 'can't just be any old thing which chooses to march under a particular banner' (Hall, 1992, p. 278). But if the choice is that between becoming an improved version of English (or Comparative) Literature, updated by theory and expanded to embrace the audio-visual media and popular fiction, on the one hand, and becoming a kind of amateur applied sociology on the other, then there seems no good reason to prefer the latter. Since sociology itself already trains properly professional sociologists, the career prospects for the gifted interloper from Cultural Studies are likely to prove strictly limited. That said, it must also follow, precisely *because* Cultural Studies is neither sociology nor history, that it needs to learn to respect the specialist disciplinary competencies of these immediately cognate disciplines. In its various treatments of social class this is what it has singularly failed to do.

Moreover, the strange death of class in contemporary Cultural Studies seems symptomatic of a more general pathology increasingly characteristic of the discipline. In Chapter 4 we noted Williams's hostility to explanations of Thatcherism that had, in his view, 'taught despair and political disarmament'. The remark is from a 1986 essay later included in *The Politics of Modernism*, apparently as Williams himself had planned (Williams,

1986; Williams, 1989a, p. xi). The essay displays its author in uncharacteristically polemical mode: 'Is there never to be an end', he asked, 'to petit-bourgeois theorists making long-term adjustments to short-term situations?' (Williams, 1989a, p. 175). Apparently not, I am tempted to reply, at least for so long as Cultural Studies persists in deducing the existence of a class-lessly pluralist, postmodern society from the media productions of a handful of late-capitalist global megacorporations. Bennett has taken me to task for an earlier inference that he and Hall might both belong in the ranks of the petit bourgeois theorists Williams sought to criticize here (Milner, 1993, p.88). Since I have no desire at all to split hairs over matters of textual exegesis, let me concede immediately that I might be mistaken in my interpretation of Williams. All texts are polysemic and Williams's own are sometimes notoriously opaque. But, what-ever the latter's intentions, both Hall's reading of Thatcherism and Bennett's commitment to cultural policy studies can plausibly be understood as long-term adjustments to short-term situations, respectively those of Labour defeat in successive British general elections during the 1980s, and Labor victory in successive Australian elections at much the same time.[6] It has become clear, from the kind of work conducted by Goldthorpe, Marshall and their colleagues, that Thatcherite Toryism impinged very much less on British popular consciousness than Hall hypothe-sized. I suspect it will become equally apparent that much less will be achieved, by way of micropolitical cultural renovation under a reforming Labour administration, than Bennett believes possible.

To be fair, Bennett is not himself much concerned with textual exegesis for its own sake. Certainly, he is under no illusion as to the distance between himself and Williams. 'In the political and cultural situations which now exist in the societies where cultural studies has made some headway', he writes,

> the long-term vision that Williams proposes . . . loses its coherence and purchase. For this particular petit-bourgeois theorist . . . the issue is not one of making long-term adjustments to short-term situations, but of making long-term adjustments because the long-

term situation itself now has to be thought in new ways. (Bennett, 1998, p. 37)

In itself, Bennett's disclaimer is unsurprising: no matter how ready to confess to petit bourgeois status, no one ever admits to making long-term adjustments to short-term situations. So the matter at issue hinges on how we read the long term, rather than on how we read Williams. This in turn devolves into two analytically distinct questions: that of the relative cultural significance attaching to social class and the labour movement (in practice, the trade union movement) on the one hand, 'difference' and the new social movements on the other; and that of the role of the state in cultural management. Each of these provides Bennett with reason to think the new situation in his own particular new ways: firstly that 'the recognition and promotion of cultural diversity' is now 'a more pressing priority' than the kind of aspiration toward a common culture that inspired Williams and Hoggart; and secondly, that culture has been 'so deeply governmentalised' that it now makes no sense to think of it 'as a ground situated outside the domain of government . . . through which that domain might be resisted' (Bennett, 1998, pp. 37, 30). In short, the business of Cultural Studies will be to negotiate and facilitate the relations between the new social movements and the state bureaucracies; or, as Jameson might have put it, to oscillate between an 'interminable series of neighbourhood issues' and a 'disembodied and easily bureaucratized' struggle around the state.

Bennett seems to me mistaken on both counts. As to the former, it has been a central argument of this book that social class is of considerably greater long-term cultural significance than the kinds of difference addressed by the new social movements. There seems little point in rehearsing the argument yet again at this late stage. As to the latter, I doubt that either culture in general or higher education in particular is anything like as 'governmentalized' as Bennett and Hunter suggest. Their notion of 'governmentality' clearly refers to a much more explicitly 'statist' process than that identified in Foucault (Bennett, 1998, p. 144; cf. Foucault, 1991), which is unsurprising given their interest in government-funded policy studies. But if governmentality is the work of the state in particular, rather than of power in general, then the most striking feature of postmodern late capitalism is surely its opposite: the commodification and consequent 'de-governmentalization' of cultural texts, practices and institutions. Bennett writes as if the great American private universities, into which Cultural Studies has increasingly relocated itself, were an aberrant institutional form (Bennett, 1998, p. 35). Cultural globalization must surely mean, however, that the 'benchmarks' for 'international best practice' in higher education, to borrow the jargon, are more likely to be those established by these American universities than by the local interests of British or Australian state functionaries. All this tends toward the speculative, I know, so that the question must needs remain open: Bennett has tried his hand at cultural policy under an Australian Labor administration and, no doubt, will try it again under a British. It must be apparent that I expect very little in the way of results. But we shall see: as Thompson once observed, of an earlier moment in the structuralist odyssey, 'I may now, with a better conscience, return to my proper work and to my garden. I will watch how things grow' (Thompson, 1978b, p. 384).

Notes

1 The successful Teamsters strike against United Parcel Services (UPS) in August 1997 is exactly the sort of material one might wish to include in a more contemporary account of class consciousness in America. Of course, this postdates Jameson's work on postmodernism by some years. The worry, however, is that this *kind* of material rarely if ever attracts the attention of textual analysts, even declaredly 'Marxist' ones.

2 I borrow the term from Said: 'texts are worldly, to some degree they are events, and, even when they appear to deny it, they are nevertheless a part of the social world, human life, and of course the historical moments in which they are located and interpreted' (Said, 1984, p. 4).

3 So working-class militancy is often in part a struggle against deskilling. The argument has been made theoretically by Harry Braverman, himself both a socialist and a former craftsman (Braverman, 1974). But it provides a recurring theme in much working-class socialist autobiography. Consider, for example, Harry McShane, Glasgow engineering shop steward, socialist militant, anti-war activist and member of the Clyde Workers' Committee, on working at the

Bridgeton Ironworks in 1916: 'the company wanted to keep me because there was one job that only I could do . . . The engines ran perfectly, but the screws in the valves wouldn't hold . . . When I was put on I took the valve to pieces, ground down the bronze plate between them in about five minutes, trimmed the stems, and put them back . . . I was the only person who could ever do it. I did it at night and never told them how' (McShane and Smith, 1978, p. 88).

4 So radical literary critics and insurgent sociologists are as committed to 'academic standards' as conservative economists, lawyers, doctors and dentists. No matter how sisterly the feminism, how brotherly the black activism, how egalitarian the socialism, credentialled radicals almost invariably insist on the use of their titles, 'Professor', 'Doctor', and so on. This is a tradition that dates back at least to the good Dr Marx.

5 Consider writers, for example. Altick's 1962 study of 1,100 British authors over the period 1800–1935 found the great majority to be university-educated: 52.5 per cent in the period 1800–1835, 72.3 per cent for 1900–1935. Coser, Kadushin and Powell's survey of 219 American writers found them over-whelmingly well-educated: 40 per cent of even the general 'trade' authors were actually university professors. A 1983 survey of 183 Australian writers found that 56 per cent were university-educated, 21 per cent to a level resulting in postgraduate academic qualifications (Altick, 1978, p. 53; Coser et al., 1985, pp. 232–233; Australia Council, 1983, p. 15).

6 Bennett taught at Griffith University in Australia for most of the 1980s. Sardar and Van Loon's Mad Max seems to me mistaken to insist that it is 'only in the set of questions that it asks in relation to the national identity that Australian cultural studies differs from British cultural studies' (Sardar and Van Loon, 1997, p. 65). For, as Bennett acknowledges, his work in policy studies remains indebted to 'Australian traditions of government' that 'have historically tended to be more strongly directive and utilitarian – more Benthamite, even – than those associated with British forms of liberal government' (Bennett, 1998, p. 7). Insofar as it proves possible to import cultural policy studies into Britain, this will be so because the Australian Labor Party's combination of 'economic liberalism mixed with conspicuous "yuppie" consumption and cultural liberalism' provides the nearest thing to a practical model for Blair's New Labour (Frankel, 1997, p. 18).

References

Adorno, T. (1976). 'Sociology and empirical research'. (Translated by G. Bartram).
In P. Connerton (ed.), *Critical Sociology*. Harmondsworth: Penguin.

Adorno, T. and Horkheimer, M. (1979). *Dialectic of Enlightenment*. (Translated
by J. Cumming). London: Verso.

Almond, G.A. and Verba, S. (1965). *The Civic Culture: Political Attitudes and
Democracy in Five Nations*. Boston: Little, Brown.

Althusser, L. (1969). *For Marx*. (Translated by B. Brewster). London: Allen
Lane.

Althusser, L. (1971). 'Ideology and ideological state apparatuses (Notes towards
an investigation)'. In *Lenin and Philosophy and Other Essays*. (Translated by
B. Brewster). New York: Monthly Review Press.

Althusser, L. (1972). *Politics and History: Montesquieu, Rousseau, Hegel and
Marx*. (Translated by B. Brewster). London: New Left Books.

Althusser, L. (1992). *L'avenir dure longtemps: suivi de les faits*. Paris: Stock/
IMEC.

Althusser, L. and Balibar, É. (1970). *Reading Capital*. (Translated by B. Brewster).
London: New Left Books.

Altick, R. (1978). 'The sociology of authorship'. In P. Davison, R. Myersohn and
E. Shils (eds), *Literary Taste, Culture and Mass Communication*, Vol. 10:
Authorship. Cambridge: Chadwyck-Healey.

Anderson, P. (1974). *Passages from Antiquity to Feudalism*. London: New Left
Books.

Anderson, P. (1976). *Considerations on Western Marxism*. London: New Left
Books.

Anderson, P. (1977). 'The antinomies of Antonio Gramsci'. *New Left Review*, 100,
5–78.

Anderson, P. (1980). *Arguments within English Marxism*. London: New Left
Books.

Anderson, P. (1992). 'Components of the national culture'. In *English Questions*. London: Verso.

Australia Council (1983). 'Appendix I: statistical tables'. In *The Artist in Australia Today: Report of the Committee for the Individual Artists Inquiry*. Sydney: Australia Council.

Baldick, C. (1983). *The Social Mission of English Criticism 1848–1932*. Oxford: Oxford University Press.

Barrett, M. (1988). *Women's Oppression Today: The Marxist/Feminist Encounter*. London: Verso.

Baudrillard, J. (1975). *The Mirror of Production*. (Translated by M. Poster). St Louis: Telos Press.

Baudrillard, J. (1981). *For a Critique of the Political Economy of the Sign*. (Translated by C. Levin). St Louis: Telos Press.

Baudrillard, J. (1983). *In the Shadow of the Silent Majorities, or, The End of the Social and Other Essays*. (Translated by P. Foss, J. Johnston and P. Patton). New York: Semiotexte.

Baudrillard, J. (1988a). *America*. (Translated by C. Turner). London: Verso.

Baudrillard, J. (1988b). 'The masses: the implosion of the social in the media'. (Translated by M. Maclean). In *Selected Writings*. (Edited by M. Poster). Cambridge: Polity Press.

Baudrillard, J. (1990). 'Revenge of the crystal: an interview by Guy Bellavance'. In *Revenge of the Crystal: Selected Writings on the Modern Object and its Destiny, 1968–1983*. (Edited and translated by P. Foss and J. Pefanis). Sydney: Pluto Press.

Baudrillard, J. (1993). *Symbolic Exchange and Death*. (Translated by I.H. Grant). London: Sage.

Bauman, Z. (1992). *Intimations of Postmodernity*. London: Routledge.

Bendix, R. and Lipset, S.M. (eds) (1966). *Class, Status and Power: Social Stratification in Comparative Perspective*. New York: Free Press.

Bennett, T. (1986). 'Popular culture and "the turn to Gramsci" '. In T. Bennett, C. Mercer and J. Woollacott (eds), *Popular Culture and Social Relations*. Milton Keynes: Open University Press.

Bennett, T. (1992). 'Putting policy into cultural studies'. In L. Grossberg, C. Nelson and P. Treichler (eds), *Cultural Studies*. New York: Routledge.

Bennett, T. (1998). *Culture: A Reformer's Science*. London: Sage.

Blackburn, R. (1967). 'The unequal society'. In R. Blackburn and A. Cockburn (eds), *The Incompatibles: Trade Union Militancy and the Consensus*. Harmondsworth: Penguin.

Bloom, H. (1994). *The Western Canon: The Books and School of the Ages*. New York: Harcourt Brace.

Blundell, V., Shepherd, J. and Taylor, I. (eds) (1993). *Relocating Cultural Studies: Developments in Theory and Research*. London: Routledge.

Bourdieu, P. (1977a). *Outline of a Theory of Practice*. (Translated by R. Nice). Cambridge: Cambridge University Press.

Bourdieu, P. (1977b). 'Symbolic power'. (Translated by C. Wringe). In D. Gleeson (ed.), *Identity and Structure: Issues in the Sociology of Education*. Driffield: Nafferton Books.

Bourdieu, P. (1984). *Distinction: A Social Critique of the Judgement of Taste*. (Translated by R. Nice). London: Routledge and Kegan Paul.

Bourdieu, P. (1987). 'What makes a social class? On the theoretical and practical existence of groups'. (Translated by L.J.D. Wacquant and D. Young). *Berkeley Journal of Sociology*, 32, 1–17.

Bourdieu, P. (1988). *Homo Academicus*. (Translated by P. Collier). Cambridge: Polity Press.

Bourdieu, P. (1989). 'The corporatism of the universal: the role of intellectuals in the modern world'. (Translated by C. Betensky). *Telos*, 81, 99–110.

Bourdieu, P. (1990a). 'Landmarks'. (Translated by M. Adamson). In *In Other Words: Essays towards a Reflexive Sociology*. Cambridge: Polity Press.

Bourdieu, P. (1990b). 'A reply to some objections'. (Translated by L.J.D. Wacquant). In *In Other Words: Essays towards a Reflexive Sociology*. Cambridge: Polity Press.

Bourdieu, P. (1993a). *Sociology in Question*. (Translated by R. Nice). London: Sage.

Bourdieu, P. (1993b). 'The field of cultural production, or: the economic world reversed'. (Translated by R. Nice). In *The Field of Cultural Production: Essays on Art and Literature*. (Edited by R. Johnson). Cambridge: Polity Press.

Bourdieu, P. (1996). *The State Nobility: Elite Schools in the Field of Power*. (Translated by L.C. Clough). Cambridge: Polity Press.

Braverman, H. (1974). *Labor and Monopoly Capital: The Degradation of Work in the Twentieth Century*. New York: Monthly Review Press.

Callinicos, A. (1983). 'The "new middle class" and socialist politics'. *International Socialism*, second series, 20, 82–119.

Callinicos, A. (1987). 'Looking for alternatives to reformism'. *International Socialism*, second series, 34, 106–117.

Callinicos, A. (1991). 'Drawing the line'. *International Socialism*, second series, 53, 93–102.

Carchedi, G. (1977). *On the Economic Identification of Social Classes*. London: Routledge and Kegan Paul.

Chamberlain, C. (1983). *Class Consciousness in Australia*. Sydney: George Allen and Unwin.

Clarke, J., Hall, S., Jefferson, T. and Roberts, B. (1976). 'Subcultures, cultures and class: a theoretical overview'. In S. Hall and T. Jefferson (eds), *Resistance through Rituals: Youth Sub-cultures in Post-war Britain*. London: Hutchinson/ Centre for Contemporary Cultural Studies.

Clegg, S. and Emmison, M. (1991). 'Classical and contemporary sociological debates'. In J. Baxter, M. Emmison and J. Western (eds), *Class Analysis and Contemporary Australia*. Melbourne: Macmillan.

Cliff, T. (1975). *Lenin*, Vol. 1. London: Pluto Press.

Cohen, G.A. (1978). *Karl Marx's Theory of History: A Defence*. Oxford: Oxford University Press.

Collini, S. (1994). 'Escape from DWEMsville'. *Times Literary Supplement*, 27 May.

Connell, R.W. (1983). 'Logic and politics in theories of class'. In *Which Way Is Up? Essays on Sex, Class and Culture*. London: George Allen and Unwin.

Connell, R.W. and Irving, T.H. (1992). *Class Structure in Australian History*, second edition. Melbourne: Longman Cheshire.

Coser, L.A., Kadushin, C. and Powell, W.W. (1985). *Books: The Culture and Commerce of Publishing*. Chicago: University of Chicago Press.

Dahrendorf, R. (1959). *Class and Class Conflict in Industrial Society*. London: Routledge and Kegan Paul.

Dahrendorf, R. (1964). 'Recent changes in the class structure of the European societies'. *Daedalus*, 93, 225–270.

Dahrendorf, R. (1968). 'On the origin of inequality among men'. In *Essays in the Theory of Society*. London: Routledge and Kegan Paul.

Dahrendorf, R. (1990). *Reflections on the Revolution in Europe: in a letter intended to have been sent to a gentleman in Warsaw*. New York: Times Books.

Davis, K. and Moore, W. (1945). 'Some principles of stratification'. *American Sociological Review*, 10, 242–249.

Debray, R. (1979). *Le Pouvoir intellectuel en France*. Paris: Éditions Ramsay.

Debray, R. (1981). *Teachers, Writers, Celebrities: the Intellectuals of Modern France*. (Translated by D. Macey). London: New Left Books.

Derrida, J. (1994). *Spectres of Marx: The State of the Debt, the Work of Mourning, and the New International*. (Translated by P. Kamuf). London: Routledge.

During, S. (1993). 'Introduction'. In S. During (ed.), *The Cultural Studies Reader*. London: Routledge.

Durkheim, E. (1964). *The Division of Labor in Society*. (Translated by G. Simpson). New York: Free Press.

Eagleton, T. (1976). *Criticism and Ideology*. London: New Left Books.

Eagleton, T. (1990). 'Nationalism: irony and commitment'. In T. Eagleton, F. Jameson and E. Said, *Nationalism, Colonialism and Literature*. Minneapolis: University of Minnesota Press.

Easthope, A. (1988). *British Post-Structuralism since 1968*. London: Routledge.

Eder, K. (1993). *The New Politics of Class: Social Movements and Cultural Dynamics in Advanced Societies*. London: Sage.

Ehrenreich, B. and Ehrenreich, J. (1979). 'The professional-managerial class'. In P. Walker (ed.), *Between Labour and Capital*. Hassocks: Harvester Press.

Emmison, M. (1991). 'Conceptualising class consciousness'. In J. Baxter, M. Emmison and J. Western (eds), *Class Analysis and Contemporary Australia*. Melbourne: Macmillan.

Emmison, M. and Western, J. (1991). 'The structure of social identities'. In J.

Baxter, M. Emmison and J. Western (eds), *Class Analysis and Contemporary Australia*. Melbourne: Macmillan.

Erikson, R. and Goldthorpe, J.H. (1992). *The Constant Flux: A Study of Class Mobility in Industrial Societies*. Oxford: Oxford University Press.

Evans, G. (1996). 'Putting men and women into classes: an assessment of the cross-sex validity of the Goldthorpe class schema'. *Sociology*, 30, 209–234.

Felperin, H. (1985). *Beyond Deconstruction: The Uses and Abuses of Literary Theory*. Oxford: Oxford University Press.

Forbes, J. and Kelly, M. (1995). *French Cultural Studies: An Introduction*. Oxford: Oxford University Press.

Foucault, M. (1980). 'Prison talk'. (Translated by C. Gordon). In *Power/Knowledge: Selected Interviews and Other Writings, 1972–1977*. (Edited by C. Gordon). Brighton: Harvester Press.

Foucault. M. (1991). *The Foucault Effect: Studies in Governmentality, with Two Lectures by and an Interview with Michel Foucault*. (Edited by G. Burchell, C. Gordon and P. Miller). Chicago: University of Chicago Press.

Fowler, B. (1997). *Pierre Bourdieu and Cultural Theory: Critical Investigations*. London: Sage.

Frankel, B. (1997). 'Beyond labourism and socialism: how the Australian Labor Party developed the model of "New Labour" '. *New Left Review*, 221, 3–33.

Frow, J. (1987). 'Accounting for tastes: some problems in Bourdieu's sociology of culture'. *Cultural Studies*, 1, 59–73.

Frow, J. (1995). *Cultural Studies and Cultural Value*. Oxford: Oxford University Press.

Frow, J. and Morris. M. (eds) (1993). *Australian Cultural Studies: A Reader*. Sydney: Allen and Unwin.

Garnham, N. and Williams, R. (1986). 'Pierre Bourdieu and the sociology of culture'. In R. Collins, J. Curran, N. Garnham, P. Scannell, P. Schlesinger and C. Sparks (eds), *Media, Culture and Society: A Critical Reader*. London: Sage.

Gay, P. (1962). *The Dilemma of a Democratic Socialism*. New York: Collier.

Geras, N. (1987). 'Post-marxism?' *New Left Review*, 163, 40–82.

Giddens, A. (1971). *Capitalism and Modern Social Theory: An Analysis of the Writings of Marx, Durkheim and Max Weber*. Cambridge: Cambridge University Press.

Giddens, A. (1981). *The Class Structure of the Advanced Societies*, second edition. London: Hutchinson.

Giddens, A. (1985). *The Nation-State and Violence*. Cambridge: Polity Press.

Giddens, A. (1990). *The Consequences of Modernity*. Cambridge: Polity Press.

Giddens, A. (1991). *Modernity and Self-Identity: Self and Society in the Late Modern Age*. Stanford: Stanford University Press.

Giddens, A. (1994). *Beyond Left and Right: The Future of Radical Politics*. Cambridge: Polity Press.

Giddens, A. (1995). *A Contemporary Critique of Historical Materialism*, second edition. London: Macmillan.

Giddens, A. and Ahmed, M. (1997). 'Changing times'. *LSE Magazine*, 9, 18–19.

Goldmann, L. (1969). *The Human Sciences and Philosophy*. (Translated by H.V. White and R. Anchor). London: Jonathan Cape.

Goldthorpe, J.H. (1980). *Social Mobility and Class Structure in Modern Britain*. (With C. Llewellyn and C. Payne). Oxford: Oxford University Press.

Goldthorpe, J.H. (1982). 'On the service class, its formation and future'. In A. Giddens and G. Mackenzie (eds), *Social Class and the Division of Labour: Essays in Honour of Ilya Neustadt*. Cambridge: Cambridge University Press.

Goldthorpe, J.H. (1983). 'Women and class analysis: in defence of the conventional view'. *Sociology*, 17, 465–488.

Goldthorpe, J.H. (1987). *Social Mobility and Class Structure in Modern Britain*, second edition. (With C. Llewellyn and C. Payne). Oxford: Oxford University Press.

Goldthorpe, J.H. (1990). 'A response'. In J. Clark, C. Modgil and S. Modgil (eds), *John H. Goldthorpe: Consensus and Controversy*. London: Falmer Press.

Goldthorpe, J.H. (1996). 'Class and politics in advanced industrial societies'. In D.J. Lee and B.S. Turner (eds), *Conflicts about Class: Debating Inequality in Late Industrialism*. London: Longman.

Goldthorpe, J.H. and Heath, A. (1992). *Revised Class Schema 1992*. JUSST Working Paper No. 13. Nuffield College and SCPR.

Goldthorpe, J.H. and Hope, K. (1974). *The Social Grading of Occupations: A New Approach and Scale*. Oxford: Oxford University Press.

Goldthorpe, J.H. and Marshall, G. (1992). 'The promising future of class analysis: a response to recent critiques'. *Sociology*, 26, 381–400.

Goldthorpe, J.H., Lockwood, D., Bechhofer, F. and Platt, J. (1968a). *The Affluent Worker: Industrial Attitudes and Behaviour*. Cambridge: Cambridge University Press.

Goldthorpe, J.H., Lockwood, D., Bechhofer, F. and Platt, J. (1968b). *The Affluent Worker: Political Attitudes and Behaviour*. Cambridge: Cambridge University Press.

Goldthorpe, J.H., Lockwood, D., Bechhofer, F. and Platt, J. (1969). *The Affluent Worker in the Class Structure*. Cambridge: Cambridge University Press.

Gouldner, A. (1976). 'Metaphysical pathos and the theory of bureaucracy'. In L.A. Coser and B. Rosenberg (eds), *Sociological Theory: A Book of Readings*. New York: Macmillan.

Gramsci, A. (1957). *The Modern Prince and Other Essays*. (Translated by L. Marks). London: Lawrence and Wishart.

Gramsci, A. (1971). *Selections from Prison Notebooks*. (Translated by Q. Hoare and G. Nowell Smith). London: Lawrence and Wishart.

Gramsci, A. (1977). 'The revolution against *Capital*'. In *Selections from Political Writings 1910–1920*. (Translated by J. Mathews). London: Lawrence and Wishart.

Grossberg, L. (ed.) (1996). 'On postmodernism and articulation: an interview with Stuart Hall'. In D. Morley and K.-H. Chen (eds), *Stuart Hall: Critical Dialogues in Cultural Studies*. London: Routledge.

Grossberg, L., Nelson, C. and Treichler, P. (eds) (1992). *Cultural Studies*. New York: Routledge.

Grosz, E. (1989). *Sexual Subversions: Three French Feminists*. Sydney: Allen and Unwin.

Guha, R. and Spivak, G.C. (eds) (1988). *Selected Subaltern Studies*. Oxford: Oxford University Press.

Habermas, J. (1979). 'Interview with Jürgen Habermas'. (Conducted by D. Horster and W. van Reijen and translated by R. Smith). *New German Critique*, 18, 29–43.

Habermas, J. (1981). 'New social movements'. *Telos*, 49, 33–37.

Hall, S. (1978). 'The hinterland of science: ideology and the "sociology of knowledge"'. In Centre for Contemporary Cultural Studies, *On Ideology*. London: Hutchinson/Centre for Contemporary Cultural Studies.

Hall, S. (1980a). 'Cultural studies: two paradigms'. *Media, Culture and Society*, 2, 57–72.

Hall, S. (1980b). 'Cultural studies and the centre: some problematics and problems'. In S. Hall, D. Hobson, A. Lowe and P. Willis (eds), *Culture, Media, Language*. London: Hutchinson/Centre for Contemporary Cultural Studies.

Hall, S. (1980c). 'Encoding/decoding'. In S. Hall, D. Hobson, A. Lowe and P. Willis (eds), *Culture, Media, Language*. London: Hutchinson/Centre for Contemporary Cultural Studies.

Hall, S. (1983). 'The great moving right show'. In S. Hall and M. Jacques (eds), *The Politics of Thatcherism*. London: Lawrence and Wishart.

Hall, S. (1986). 'Gramsci's relevance for the study of race and ethnicity'. *Journal of Communication Inquiry*, 10, 5–27.

Hall, S. (1988). 'The toad in the garden: Thatcherism among the theorists'. In C. Nelson and L. Grossberg (eds), *Marxism and the Interpretation of Culture*. London: Macmillan.

Hall, S. (1989a). 'Politics and letters'. In T. Eagleton (ed.), *Raymond Williams: Critical Perspectives*. Cambridge: Polity Press.

Hall, S. (1989b). 'The meaning of new times'. In S. Hall and M. Jacques (eds), *New Times: The Changing Face of Politics in the 1990s*. London: Lawrence and Wishart.

Hall, S. (1991). 'Introduction'. In R. Simon, *Gramsci's Political Thought*, second edition. London: Lawrence and Wishart.

Hall, S. (1992). 'Cultural studies and its theoretical legacies'. In L. Grossberg, C. Nelson and P. Treichler (eds), *Cultural Studies*. New York: Routledge.

Hall, S. and Jefferson, T. (eds) (1976). *Resistance through Rituals: Youth Subcultures in Post-war Britain*. London: Hutchinson/Centre for Contemporary Cultural Studies.

Hall, S., Lumley, B. and McLennan, G. (1978). 'Politics and ideology: Gramsci'. In Centre for Contemporary Cultural Studies, *On Ideology*. London: Hutchinson/Centre for Contemporary Cultural Studies.

Harrison, R. (1978). '*Shirley*: relations of reproduction and the ideology of romance'. In Women's Studies Group, *Women Take Issue: Aspects of*

Women's Subordination. London: Hutchinson/Centre for Contemporary Cultural Studies.

Hawthorn, J. (1992). *A Concise Glossary of Contemporary Literary Theory.* London: Edward Arnold.

Heller, A. (1990). 'The end of communism'. *Thesis Eleven*, 27, 5–19

Heller, A. and Fehér, F. (1988). *The Postmodern Political Condition.* Cambridge: Polity Press.

Heller, C.S. (1969). *Structured Social Inequality: A Reader in Comparative Social Stratification*. London: Collier-Macmillan.

Hilton, R. (ed.) (1978). *The Transition from Feudalism to Capitalism*. London: New Left Books.

Hobsbawm, E. (1995). *Age of Extremes: The Short Twentieth Century 1914–1991*. London: Abacus.

Hoggart, R. (1958). *The Uses of Literacy*. Harmondsworth: Penguin.

Hoggart, R. (1995). *The Way We Live Now*. London: Chatto and Windus.

Holton, R.J. and Turner, B.S. (1989). *Max Weber on Economy and Society*. London: Routledge and Kegan Paul.

Holton, R. and Turner, B. (1994). 'Debate and pseudo-debate in class analysis: some unpromising aspects of Goldthorpe and Marshall's defence'. *Sociology*, 28, 799–804.

Horkheimer, M. (1972). 'Traditional and critical theory'. In *Critical Theory: Selected Essays*. (Translated by M.J.O. O'Connell). New York: Seabury Press.

Hunter, I. (1988). *Culture and Government: The Emergence of Literary Education*. London: Macmillan.

Hunter, I. (1992). 'Aesthetics and cultural studies'. In L. Grossberg, C. Nelson and P. Treichler (eds), *Cultural Studies*. New York: Routledge.

Hunter, I. (1993). 'Mind games and body techniques'. *Southern Review*, 26, 172–185.

Hunter, I. (1994). *Rethinking the School: Subjectivity, Bureaucracy, Criticism*. New York: St Martin's Press.

Hyman, H.H. (1966). 'The value systems of different classes: a social psychological contribution to the analysis of stratification'. In R. Bendix and S.M. Lipset (eds), *Class, Status and Power: Social Stratification in Comparative Perspective*. New York: Free Press.

Inglehart, R. (1977). *The Silent Revolution: Changing Values and Political Styles among Western Publics*. Princeton: Princeton University Press.

Inglehart, R. (1990). *Culture Shift in Advanced Industrial Society*. Princeton: Princeton University Press.

Jameson, F. (1971). *Marxism and Form*. Princeton: Princeton University Press.

Jameson, F. (1981). *The Political Unconscious: Narrative as a Socially Symbolic Act*. London: Methuen.

Jameson, F. (1984). 'Postmodernism, or the cultural logic of late capitalism'. *New Left Review*, 146, 53–92.

Jameson, F. (1985). 'Postmodernism and consumer society'. In H. Foster (ed.), *Postmodern Culture*. London: Pluto Press.

Jameson, F. (1988a). 'Introduction'. In *The Ideologies of Theory: Essays 1971–1986; Volume 1: Situations of Theory*. London: Routledge.

Jameson, F. (1988b). 'The politics of theory: ideological positions in the postmodernism debate'. In *The Ideologies of Theory: Essays 1971–1986; Volume 2: The Syntax of History*. London: Routledge.

Jameson, F. (1988c). 'Periodizing the 60s'. In *The Ideologies of Theory: Essays 1971–1986; Volume 2: The Syntax of History*. London: Routledge.

Jameson, F. (1990). *Late Marxism: Adorno, or, The Persistence of the Dialectic*. London: Verso.

Jameson, F. (1991). *Postmodernism, or, The Cultural Logic of Late Capitalism*. London: Verso.

Jameson, F. (1992a). 'Class and allegory in contemporary mass culture: *Dog Day Afternoon* as a political film'. In *Signatures of the Visible*. London: Routledge.

Jameson, F. (1992b). 'Historicism in *The Shining*'. In *Signatures of the Visible*. London: Routledge.

Jameson, F. (1992c). *The Geopolitical Aesthetic: Cinema and Space in the World System*. Bloomington: Indiana University Press.

Jameson, F. (1994). *The Seeds of Time*. New York: Columbia University Press.

Johnson, R. (1979). 'Histories of culture/theories of ideology: notes on an impasse'. In M. Barrett, P. Corrigan, A. Kuhn and J. Wolff (eds), *Ideology and Cultural Production*. London: Croom Helm.

Kaplan, E.A. and Sprinker, M. (eds) (1993). *The Althusserian Legacy*. London: Verso.

Kautsky, K. (1983). 'Terrorism and communism'. In *Karl Kautsky: Selected Political Writings*. (Edited and translated by P. Goode). London: Macmillan.

Kautsky, K. (1996). *The Road to Power: Political Reflections on Growing into the Revolution*. (Translated by R. Meyer and edited by J.H. Kautsky). Atlantic Highlands: Humanities Press.

Laclau, E. (1977). *Politics and Ideology in Marxist Theory: Capitalism, Fascism, Populism*. London: New Left Books.

Laclau, E. and Mouffe, C. (1985). *Hegemony and Socialist Strategy: Towards a Radical Democratic Politics*. (Translated by W. Moore and P. Cammack). London: Verso.

Laclau, E. and Mouffe, C. (1987). 'Post-Marxism without apologies'. *New Left Review*, 166, 79–106.

Lal, V. (1996). *South Asian Cultural Studies*. Delhi: Manohar.

Lash, S. (1990). *Sociology of Postmodernism*. London: Routledge.

Leavis, F.R. (1948). *Education and the University: A Sketch for an 'English School'*. London: Chatto and Windus.

Leavis, F.R. (1962). *Two Cultures?* London: Chatto and Windus.

Leavis, F.R. (1972). *Nor Shall My Sword: Discourses on Pluralism, Compassion and Social Hope*. London: Chatto and Windus.

Leavis, Q.D. (1979). *Fiction and the Reading Public*. Harmondsworth: Penguin.

Lenin, V.I. (1970). *What Is To Be Done?* (Translated by S.V. Utechin and P. Utechin). London: Panther.

Lenin, V.I. (1975a). 'Two tactics of social-democracy in the democratic revolution'. In *Selected Works*, Vol. 1. Moscow: Progress Publishers.

Lenin, V.I. (1975b). ' "Left-wing" communism – an infantile disorder'. In *Selected Works*, Vol. 3. Moscow: Progress Publishers.

Lester, J. (1997). 'Overdosing on nationalism: Gennadii Zyuganov and the Communist Party of the Russian Federation'. *New Left Review*, 221, 34–53.

Lockwood, D. (1966). 'Sources of variation in working class images of society'. *Sociological Review*, 14, 244–267.

Lukács, G. (1971). *History and Class Consciousness*. (Translated by R. Livingstone). London: Merlin Press.

Luxemburg, R. (1986). *The Mass Strike*. London: Bookmarks.

Lyotard, J.-F. (1984). *The Postmodern Condition: A Report on Knowledge*. (Translated by G. Bennington and B. Massumi). Minneapolis: University of Minnesota Press.

Lyotard, J.-F. (1989a). 'Universal history and cultural differences'. (Translated by D. Macey). In A. Benjamin (ed.), *The Lyotard Reader*. Oxford: Basil Blackwell.

Lyotard, J.-F. (1989b). 'Lessons in paganism'. (Translated by D. Macey). In A. Benjamin (ed.), *The Lyotard Reader*. Oxford: Basil Blackwell.

Mallett, S. (1975). *The New Working Class*. (Translated by A. Shephard and B. Shephard). Nottingham: Spokesman Books.

Mann, M. (1970). 'The social cohesion of liberal democracy'. *American Sociological Review*, 35, 423–439.

Mann, M. (1973). *Consciousness and Action among the Western Working Class*. London: Macmillan.

Mann, M. (1986). *The Sources of Social Power. Vol. 1: A History of Power from the Beginning to A.D. 1760*. Cambridge: Cambridge University Press.

Mann, M. (1993). *The Sources of Social Power. Vol 2: The Rise of Classes and Nation-States, 1760–1914*. Cambridge: Cambridge University Press.

Mann, M. (1995). 'Sources of variation in working-class movements in twentieth-century Europe'. *New Left Review*, 212, 14–54.

Marcuse, H. (1971). *Soviet Marxism: A Critical Analysis*. Harmondsworth: Penguin.

Marcuse, H. (1972). *One Dimensional Man*. London: Abacus.

Marshall, G.A., Newby, H., Rose, D. and Vogler, C. (1988). *Social Class in Modern Britain*. London: Hutchinson.

Marx, K. (1970). *Capital: A Critique of Political Economy*, Vol. 1. (Translated by S. Moore and E. Aveling). London: Lawrence and Wishart.

Marx, K. (1973a). 'The eighteenth Brumaire of Louis Bonaparte'. (Translated by B. Fowkes). In *Surveys from Exile*. (Edited by D. Fernbach). Harmondsworth: Penguin.

Marx, K. (1973b). 'Tories and Whigs'. In *Surveys from Exile*. (Edited by D. Fernbach). Harmondsworth: Penguin.

Marx, K. (1974). *Capital: A Critique of Political Economy*, Vol. 3. (Edited by F. Engels). London: Lawrence and Wishart.

Marx, K. (1975a). 'Appendix B. Preface (to a contribution to the critique of political economy)'. In *Early Writings*. (Introduced by L. Colletti). Harmondsworth: Penguin.

Marx, K. (1975b). 'Economic and philosophical manuscripts of 1844'. (Translated by G. Benton). In *Early Writings*. (Introduced by L. Colletti). Harmondsworth: Penguin.

Marx, K. (1975c). 'The holy family or critique of critical criticism: against Bruno Bauer and company'. (Translated by R. Dixon and C. Dutt). In K. Marx and F. Engels, *Collected Works*, Vol. 4. London: Lawrence and Wishart.

Marx, K. (1976). 'The poverty of philosophy. Answer to the *Philosophy of Poverty* by M. Proudhon'. (Translated by H. Quelch). In K. Marx and F. Engels, *Collected Works*, Vol. 6. London: Lawrence and Wishart.

Marx, K. and Engels, F. (1967). *The Communist Manifesto*. (Translated by S. Moore, with an introduction by A.J.P. Taylor). Harmondsworth: Penguin.

Marx, K. and Engels, F. (1970). *The German Ideology*, Part One. (Translated by W. Lough, C. Dutt and C.P. Magill, edited by C.J. Arthur). London: Lawrence and Wishart.

Marxist-feminist Literature Collective (1978). 'Women's writing: *Jane Eyre, Shirley, Villette, Aurora Leigh*'. In F. Barker, J. Coombes, P. Hulme, C. Mercer and D. Musselwhite (eds), *1848: The Sociology of Literature*. Colchester: University of Essex.

McKenzie, R.T. and Silver, A. (1968). *Angels in Marble*. London: Heinemann.

McShane, H. and Smith, J. (1978). *Harry McShane: No Mean Fighter*. London: Pluto Press.

Melucci, A. (1989). *Nomads of the Present: Social Movements and Individual Needs in Contemporary Society*. (Edited by J. Keane and P. Mier). London: Hutchinson Radius.

Merleau-Ponty, M. (1974). *Adventures of the Dialectic*. (Translated by J. Bien). London: Heinemann.

Michels, R. (1959). *Political Parties: A Sociological Study of the Oligarchical Tendencies of Modern Democracy*. (Translated by E. and C. Paul). New York: Dover Publications.

Mills, C.W. (1951). *White Collar: The American Middle Classes*. New York: Oxford University Press.

Mills, C.W. (1970). *The Sociological Imagination*. Harmondsworth: Penguin.

Milner, A. (1993). *Cultural Materialism*. Melbourne: Melbourne University Press.

Milner, A. (1994). *Contemporary Cultural Theory: An Introduction*. London: University College London Press.

Milner, A. (1996). *Literature, Culture and Society*. London: University College London Press.

Moody, K. (1997). 'Towards an international social-movement unionism'. *New Left Review*, 225, 52–72.

Mosca, G. (1939). 'The ruling class'. (Translated by H.D. Kahn). In *The Ruling Class: Elementi di Scienza Politica*. (Edited by A. Livingston). New York: McGraw-Hill.

Nettl, P. (1969). *Rosa Luxemburg*. Oxford: Oxford University Press.

Offe, C. (1985). 'Work: the key sociological category?' In *Disorganised Capitalism: Contemporary Transformations of Work and Politics*. (Edited by J. Keane). Cambridge: Polity Press.

Offe, C. (1987). 'Challenging the boundaries of institutional politics: social movements since the 1960s'. In C.S. Maier (ed.), *Changing Boundaries of the Political: Essays on the Evolving Balance between State and Society, Public and Private in Europe*. Cambridge: Cambridge University Press.

Pahl, R.E. (1989). 'Is the emperor naked? Some comments on the adequacy of sociological theory in urban and regional research'. *International Journal of Urban and Regional Research*, 13, 709–720.

Pareto, V. (1976). 'Treatise on general sociology'. (Translated by D. Mirfin). In *Sociological Writings*. (Edited by S.E. Finer). Oxford: Basil Blackwell.

Parkin, F. (1968). *Middle Class Radicalism: The Social Bases of the British Campaign for Nuclear Disarmament*. Manchester: Manchester University Press.

Parkin, F. (1972). *Class Inequality and Political Order: Social Stratification in Capitalist and Communist Societies*. St Albans: Paladin.

Parkin, F. (1974). 'Strategies of social closure in class formation'. In F. Parkin (ed.), *The Social Analysis of Class Structure*. London: Tavistock.

Parkin, F. (1979). *Marxism and Class Theory: A Bourgeois Critique*. London: Tavistock.

Parsons, T. (1949). *The Structure of Social Action*. New York: Free Press.

Parsons, T. (1954). 'A revised analytical approach to the theory of social stratification'. In *Essays in Sociological Theory*. Glencoe: Free Press.

Pickering, M. (1997). *History, Experience and Cultural Studies*. London: Macmillan.

Poulantzas, N. (1973). 'On social classes'. *New Left Review*, 78, 27–54.

Poulantzas, N. (1975). *Classes in Contemporary Capitalism*. (Translated by D. Fernbach). London: Verso.

Renner, K. (1953). *Wandlungen der modernen Gesellschaft: Zwei Abhandlungen über die Probleme der Nachkriegzeit*. Vienna: Verlag der Wiener Volksbuchhandlung.

Renner, K. (1978). 'The service class'. (Translated by T. Bottomore and P. Goode). In T. Bottomore and P. Goode (eds), *Austro-Marxism*. Oxford: Oxford University Press.

Roemer, J. (ed.) (1986). *Analytical Marxism*. Cambridge: Cambridge University Press.

Runciman, W.G. (1972). *Relative Deprivation and Social Justice: A Study of*

Attitudes to Social Inequality in Twentieth-century England. Harmondsworth: Penguin.

Runciman, W.G. (1974). 'Towards a theory of social stratification'. In F. Parkin (ed.), *The Social Analysis of Class Structure.* London: Tavistock.

Said, E.W. (1984). *The World, the Text, and the Critic.* London: Faber and Faber.

Salvadori, M. (1979). *Karl Kautsky and the Socialist Revolution 1880–1938.* (Translated by J. Rothschild). London: New Left Books.

Samuel, R. (1982). 'The SDP and the new political class'. *New Society,* 22 April.

Sardar, Z. and Van Loon, B. (1997). *Cultural Studies for Beginners.* Cambridge: Icon Books.

Sartre, J.-P. (1960). *Critique de la raison dialectique. Tome I: Théorie des ensembles pratiques.* Paris: Librairie Gallimard.

Sartre, J.-P. (1976). *Critique of Dialectical Reason. Vol. I: Theory of Practical Ensembles.* (Translated by A. Sheridan-Smith, edited by J. Rée). London: New Left Books.

Scott, J. (1994). 'Class analysis: back to the future'. *Sociology,* 28, 933–942.

Scruton, R. (1985). *Thinkers of the New Left.* Harlow: Longman.

Serge, V. (1967). *Memoirs of a Revolutionary 1901–1941.* (Translated by P. Sedgwick). Oxford: Oxford University Press.

Smart, B. (1992). *Modern Conditions, Postmodern Controversies.* London: Routledge.

Sokal, A. (1996). 'Transgressing the boundaries: towards a transformative hermeneutics of quantum gravity'. *Social Text,* 14, 217–252.

Sokal, A. and Bricmont, J. (1998). *Intellectual Impostures: Postmodern Philosophers' Abuse of Science.* London: Profile Books.

Sparks, C. (1996). 'Stuart Hall, cultural studies and marxism'. In D. Morley and K.-H. Chen (eds), *Stuart Hall: Critical Dialogues in Cultural Studies.* London: Routledge.

Spriano, P. (1975). *The Occupation of the Factories: Italy 1920.* (Translated by G.A. Williams). London: Pluto Press.

Stratton, J. and Ang, I. (1996). 'On the impossibility of a global cultural studies: "British" cultural studies in an "international" frame'. In D. Morley and K.-H. Chen (eds), *Stuart Hall: Critical Dialogues in Cultural Studies.* London: Routledge.

Tatchell, P. (1996). 'Cashing in, coming out'. *The Guardian,* supplement, 29 August.

Thompson, E.P. (1963). *The Making of the English Working Class.* London: Victor Gollancz.

Thompson, E.P. (1978a). 'Eighteenth-century English society: class struggle without class?' *Social History,* 3, 133–165.

Thompson, E.P. (1978b). *The Poverty of Theory and Other Essays.* London: Merlin Press.

Thompson, E.P. (1993). *The Mark of the Beast: William Blake and the Moral Law*. Cambridge: Cambridge University Press.

Touraine, A. (1966). *La Conscience ouvrière*. Paris: Éditions du Seuil.

Touraine, A. (1971) *The Post-Industrial Society. Tomorrow's Social History: Classes, Conflicts and Culture in the Programmed Society*. (Translated by L.F.X. Mayhew). New York: Random House.

Touraine, A. (1981). *The Voice and the Eye: An Analysis of Social Movements*. (Translated by A. Duff). Cambridge: Cambridge University Press.

Turner, B.S. (1996). *For Weber: Essays on the Sociology of Fate*. London: Sage.

Walby, S. (1986). *Patriarchy at Work: Patriarchal and Capitalist Relations in Employment*. Cambridge: Polity Press.

Walby, S. (1990). *Theorizing Patriarchy*. Oxford: Basil Blackwell.

Walker, M. (1997). 'Progressives make their presence felt'. *The Guardian Weekly*, 19 January.

Weber, M. (1930). *The Protestant Ethic and the Spirit of Capitalism*. (Edited and translated by T. Parsons). London: Unwin.

Weber, M. (1948a). 'The social psychology of the world religions'. In *From Max Weber: Essays in Sociology*. (Edited and translated by H.H. Gerth and C.W. Mills). London: Routledge and Kegan Paul.

Weber, M. (1948b). 'Class, status, party'. In *From Max Weber: Essays in Sociology*. (Edited and translated by H.H. Gerth and C.W. Mills). London: Routledge and Kegan Paul.

Weber, M. (1948c). 'National character and the Junkers'. In *From Max Weber: Essays in Sociology*. (Edited and translated by H.H. Gerth and C.W. Mills). London: Routledge and Kegan Paul.

Weber, M. (1948d). 'Bureaucracy'. In *From Max Weber: Essays in Sociology*. (Edited and translated by H.H. Gerth and C.W. Mills). London: Routledge and Kegan Paul.

Weber, M. (1949). *The Methodology of the Social Sciences*. (Translated by E.A. Shils and H.A. Finch). New York: Free Press.

Weber, M. (1958). *The Rational and Social Foundations of Music*. (Translated by D. Martindale, J. Riedel and G. Neuwirth). Carbondale: Southern Illinois University Press.

Weber, M. (1964). *The Theory of Social and Economic Organization*. (Translated by A.M. Henderson and T. Parsons). New York: Free Press.

Weber, M. (1968). *Economy and Society: An Outline of Interpretive Sociology*, Vol. 1. (Edited by G. Roth and C. Wittich, translated by E. Fischoff et al.). New York: Bedminster Press.

Westergaard, J.H. (1970). 'The rediscovery of the cash nexus'. In R. Miliband and J. Saville (eds), *The Socialist Register 1970*. London: Merlin.

Westergaard, J.H. (1977). 'Class, inequality and "corporatism" '. In A. Hunt (ed.), *Class and Class Structure*. London: Lawrence and Wishart.

Westergaard, J.H. (1990). 'Social mobility in Britain'. In J. Clark, C. Modgil and S. Modgil (eds), *John H. Goldthorpe: Consensus and Controversy*. London: Falmer Press.

Westergaard, J.H. (1995). *Who Gets What?: The Hardening of Class Inequality in the Late Twentieth Century*. Cambridge: Polity Press.

Westergaard, J.H. (1996). 'Class in Britain since 1979: facts, theories and ideologies'. In D.J. Lee and B.S. Turner (eds), *Conflicts about Class: Debating Inequality in Late Industrialism*. London: Longman.

Westergaard, J.H. and Resler, H. (1975). *Class in a Capitalist Society: A Study of Contemporary Britain*. London: Heinemann.

Western, J., Western, M., Emmison, M. and Baxter, J. (1991). 'Class analysis and politics'. In J. Baxter, M. Emmison and J. Western (eds), *Class Analysis and Contemporary Australia*. Melbourne: Macmillan.

Williams, G.A. (1975). *Proletarian Order: Antonio Gramsci, Factory Councils and the Origins of Communism in Italy 1911–1921*. London: Pluto Press.

Williams, R. (1963). *Culture and Society 1780–1950*. Harmondsworth: Penguin.

Williams, R. (1965). *The Long Revolution*. Harmondsworth: Penguin.

Williams, R. (1976). *Keywords: A Vocabulary of Culture and Society*. Glasgow: Fontana.

Williams, R. (1977). *Marxism and Literature*. Oxford: Oxford University Press.

Williams, R. (1980). 'Base and superstructure in Marxist cultural theory'. In *Problems in Materialism and Culture: Selected Essays*. London: New Left Books.

Williams, R. (1981). *Culture*. Glasgow: Fontana.

Williams, R. (1983). *Towards 2000*. London: Chatto and Windus.

Williams, R. (1986). 'The uses of cultural theory'. *New Left Review*, 158, 19–31.

Williams, R. (1989a). *The Politics of Modernism: Against the New Conformists*. (Edited by T. Pinkney). London: Verso.

Williams, R. (1989b). *Resources of Hope: Culture, Democracy, Socialism*. (Edited by R. Gable). London: Verso.

Williamson, J. (1986). 'Woman is an island'. In T. Modleskli (ed.), *Studies in Entertainment*. Bloomington: Indiana University Press.

Women's Studies Group (1978). *Women Take Issue: Aspects of Women's Subordination*. London: Hutchinson/Centre for Contemporary Cultural Studies.

Wood, E.M. (1986). *The Retreat from Class: A New 'True' Socialism*. London: Verso.

Wright, E.O. (1976). 'Class boundaries in advanced capitalist societies'. *New Left Review*, 98, 3–41.

Wright, E.O. (1979). *Class, Crisis, and the State*. London: Verso.

Wright, E.O. (1985). *Classes*. London: Verso.

Wright, E.O. (1989a). 'The comparative project on class structure and class consciousness: an overview'. *Acta Sociologica*, 32, 3–22.

Wright, E.O. (1989b). 'A general framework for the analysis of class structure'. In E.O. Wright (ed.), *The Debate on Classes*. London: Verso.

Wright, E.O. (1989c). 'Rethinking, once again, the concept of class structure'. In E.O. Wright (ed.), *The Debate on Classes*. London: Verso.

Wright, E.O. (1994). *Interrogating Inequality: Essays on Class Analysis, Socialism and Marxism*. London: Verso.

Wright, E.O. (1997). *Class Counts: Comparative Studies in Class Analysis.* Cambridge: Cambridge University Press.

Young, M. and Willmott, P. (1956). 'Social grading by manual workers'. *British Journal of Sociology,* 7, 337–345.

Zweig, F. (1961). *The Worker in an Affluent Society: Family Life and Industry.* London: Heinemann.

Index